IN ASSOCIATION WITH
IMPERIAL WAR MUSEUMS

1914–1918
THE WESTERN FRONT

GARY SHEFFIELD

CARLTON
BOOKS

CONTENTS

THIS IS A CARLTON BOOK

This edition published in 2014 by Carlton Books Limited.

A division of the Carlton Publishing Group
20 Mortimer Street
London W1T 3JW

A CIP catalogue for this book is available from the British Library

Printed in Dubai

ISBN: 978 1 78097 525 2

Removable memorabilia

The National Archives of the UK (P.R.O), Kew: Item 1 (WO 32/5590); Item 2 (WO 142/241); Item 3 (339/53917).
The British Library: Item 4 (Add.45416.f1).
Imperial War Museums (text in brackets indicates accession numbers and departments): Item 5 (Printed Books)

INTRODUCTION

The Western Front continues to appal and fascinate in equal measures. The killing fields of the First World War retain their grip on our imagination. Names such as Ypres, the Somme, Verdun, Chemin des Dames and many others continue to resonate. The incongruous sight of a small Commonwealth War Graves cemetery next to a busy road, or a monument to a long gone division or regiment might be the only indication that a great battle was once fought there. But in our minds we can picture fields and roads, barns and town squares, with the Poilu, Tommy and Landser of years gone by.

The trenches continue to live in our minds. The Western Front remains a fertile source of inspiration for writers, television and filmmakers, artists and poets. In Britain, opinion is sharply polarized between those who see the war as a monstrous tragedy which should never have happened, and those who agree it was a tragedy but say that it was not of Britain's making and Britain had no choice but to get involved. From a French or German perspective it can be seen as the third round in a Franco-German war that began in 1870 and only ended in 1945. The generals of the Western Front still excite passionate debates, with individuals lined up for and against. Haig and Pétain remain controversial figures, although for very different reasons; and historians still debate the merits of Foch, French, Pershing, Joffre, Currie and Monash as commanders. But increasingly the ordinary soldier has taken centre stage.

This book enables us explore the First World War on the Western Front through text, pictures and memorabilia. I hope that it gives readers some idea of the issues at stake, the strategies, tactics and battles, and the lives of the men who were there.

Gary Sheffield

MAP INDEX

MAP KEY

Common symbols used on maps in this book:

NATIONAL COLOURS

British, Dominion & Empire

French

Belgian

German

American

SIZE OF MILITARY UNITS

XXXX Army

XXX Corps

XX Division

X Brigade

III Regiment

II Battalion

MILITARY TYPES

Infantry

Tanks

Cavalry

MILITARY SYMBOLS

XXXXX Army group boundary line

XXXX Army boundary line

XXX Corps boundary line

XX Division boundary line

Troops attacking

Unsuccessful attack

Planned withdrawal

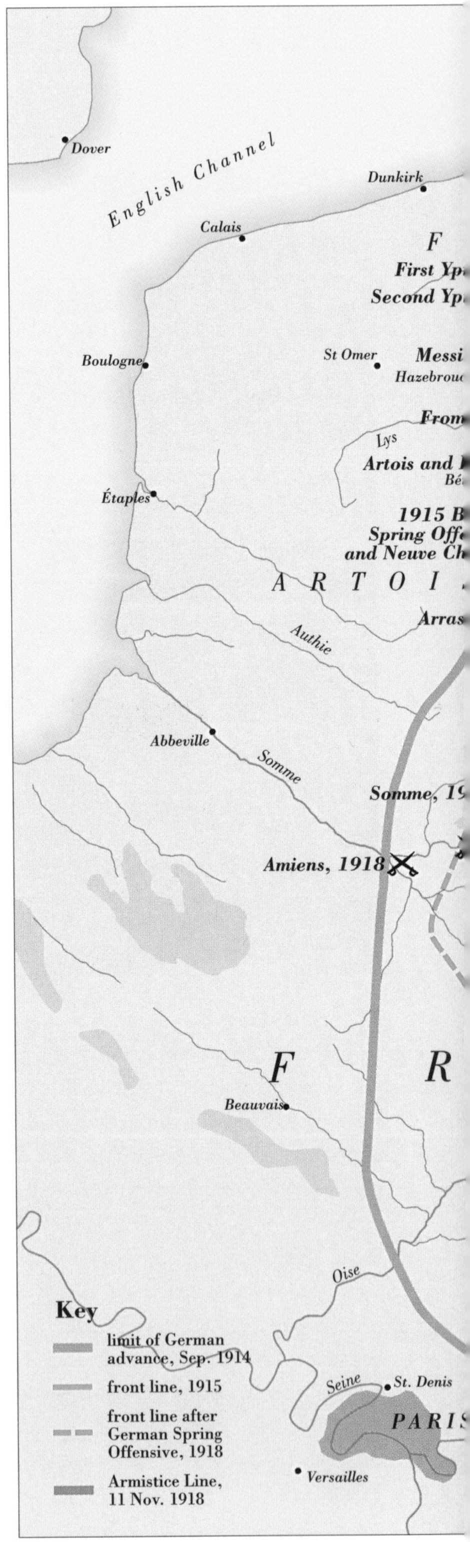

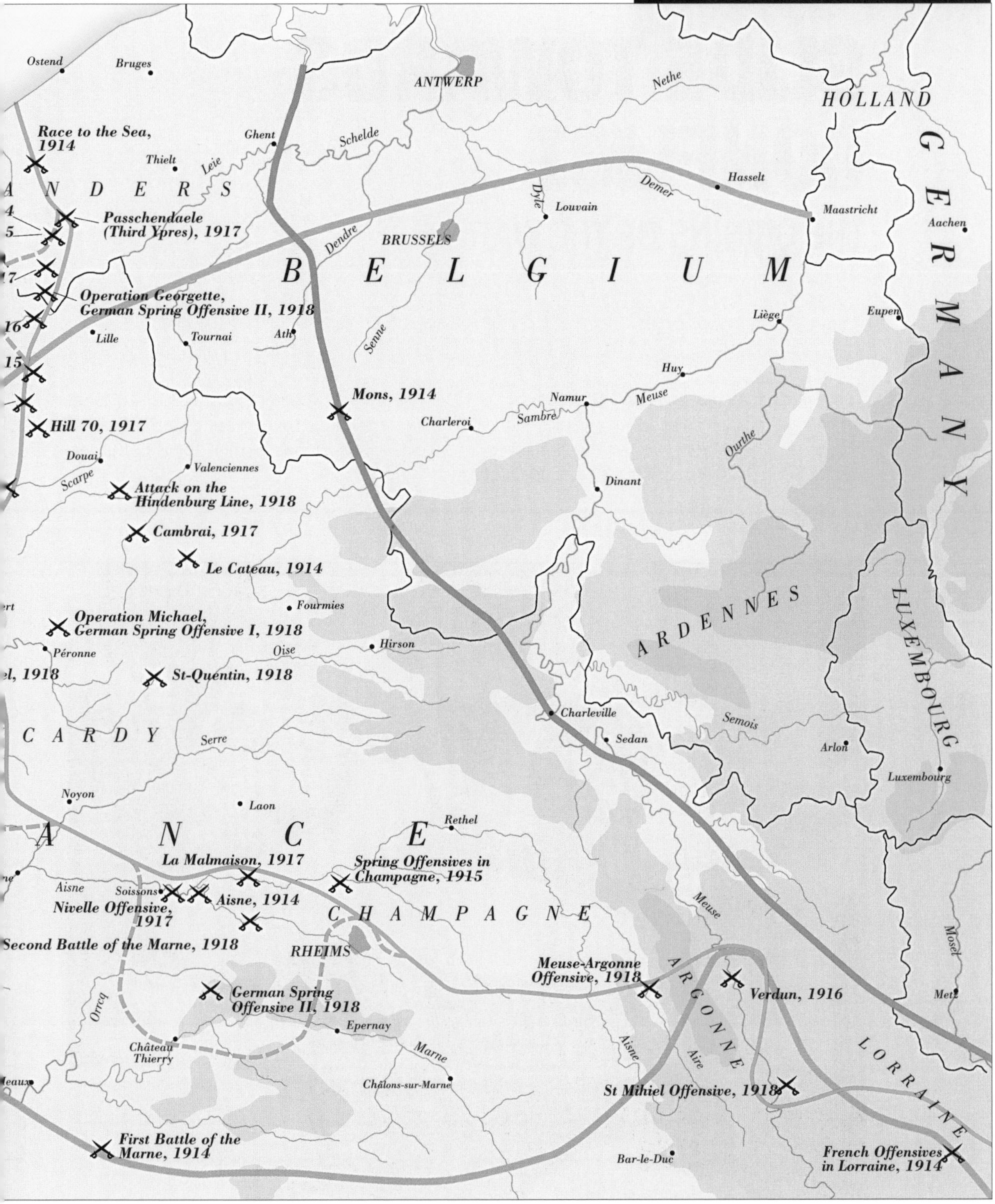
Ostend
Bruges
ANTWERP
Nethe
HOLLAND
GERMANY
Race to the Sea, 1914
Ghent
Schelde
Thielt
Leie
Hasselt
Demer
Dyle
Louvain
Maastricht
Aachen
Passchendaele (Third Ypres), 1917
Dendre
BRUSSELS
BELGIUM
Operation Georgette, German Spring Offensive II, 1918
Liège
Eupen
Lille
Tournai
Ath
Senne
Huy
Mons, 1914
Namur
Meuse
Charleroi
Sambre
Hill 70, 1917
Ourthe
Douai
Valenciennes
Scarpe
Dinant
Attack on the Hindenburg Line, 1918
Cambrai, 1917
Le Cateau, 1914
ARDENNES
LUXEMBOURG
Fourmies
Operation Michael, German Spring Offensive I, 1918
Péronne
Hirson
Oise
St-Quentin, 1918
Charleville
Semois
Sedan
Arlon
Serre
Luxembourg
Noyon
Laon
Rethel
La Malmaison, 1917
Spring Offensives in Champagne, 1915
Aisne
Soissons
Nivelle Offensive, 1917
Aisne, 1914
CHAMPAGNE
Meuse
Second Battle of the Marne, 1918
RHEIMS
Mosel
Meuse-Argonne Offensive, 1918
ARGONNE
Verdun, 1916
Metz
German Spring Offensive II, 1918
Orrcq
Epernay
Château Thierry
Marne
Aisne
Aire
LORRAINE
Châlons-sur-Marne
St Mihiel Offensive, 1918
First Battle of the Marne, 1914
Bar-le-Duc
French Offensives in Lorraine, 1914

28 JUNE–4 AUGUST 1914

SLIDE TOWARDS CONFLICT

THE ORIGINS OF THE WAR

The events that plunged Europe into war in 1914 moved with dizzying speed. On 28 June, Archduke Franz Ferdinand of Austria-Hungary was assassinated by a young Serb, Gavrilo Princip. A month later, Austria declared war on Serbia, which Vienna blamed for the murder, and by 5 August the major states of Europe were at war.

OPPOSITE: Franz Ferdinand and his wife Sophie are photographed getting into a car just minutes before their murder by Gavrilo Princip (inset left).

LEFT: HMS *Dreadnought* was the first of the "all big gun" battleships, brought into service by Fisher.

The immediate trigger for the First World War was thus rivalry between states in the Balkans. Russia backed Serbia, the latter state posing as the protector of the Serbs in the polyglot Habsburg Empire. Austria risked war with Russia to preserve its influence in the Balkans, having received on 5 July a firm promise of support from its ally Germany. Russia, alarmed by the threat to its security and prestige, mobilized its forces, followed by Germany and then France, Russia's ally since 1892. The German attack on Belgium on 4 August then brought Britain into the war. In retrospect, the war seemed to many to be almost accidental, with states slipping into an unwanted conflict.

However, there were wider issues at play. The German defeat of Napoleon III's France in 1870–71 had destroyed the existing international balance of power. But Germany, despite its ever increasing economic power, chose, under the leadership of the "Iron Chancellor", Otto von Bismarck, to live within the new situation it had created, and to avoid threatening its neighbours, while keeping France isolated. All this changed when the young and mentally unbalanced Kaiser Wilhelm II came to the throne in 1888. In 1890 Wilhelm dismissed Bismarck, and the system of treaties that the Chancellor had carefully constructed to protect Germany began to unravel. Wilhelm's bellicose *Weltpolitik* (world policy) led to diplomatic encirclement, having thoroughly frightened Britain, France and Russia. The British government abandoned its policy of non-alignment and established an Entente – although not a formal alliance – with France and Russia in 1904.

By 1914, Germany had backed itself into a corner. Many historians agree that Germany took advantage of the situation in the Balkans to attempt to break up the Entente, even at the risk of a major war. Others argue that Germany actually desired and planned for war. Russia, defeated by the Japanese in 1904–05, was rapidly rebuilding its military strength, and some of the German élite favoured a war to prevent it from re-emerging as a rival. At the very least, the ambitious programme of annexations and the creation of de facto economic colonies across Europe that was drawn up by Germany shortly after the Russo-Japanese War began indicates that it was willing to take advantage of the opportunity to undertake aggressive expansionism. Likewise, there was nothing accidental about Austria-Hungary's decision to crush Serbia, regardless of the risks of wider war. The Austrians, excluded over the previous century from spheres of influence in Germany and Italy, believed that they could not afford to be marginalized in the Balkans. Striking a blow against nationalism, a force that threatened to rot the multi-national Habsburg Empire from within, was also highly attractive.

There, were of course, other factors in the outbreak of the First World, War. Although arms races do not in themselves cause wars, military competition before 1914 added to the sense of impending crisis. The Anglo-German naval rivalry was particularly dangerous. Britain's primary defence force was the Royal Navy, and the German fleet-building programme initiated under Admiral Tirpitz posed a direct threat to the security of the British homeland and the British Empire. In response, the British drew closer to France and Russia and, in 1906 launched HMS *Dreadnought*. This revolutionary new battleship, the brainchild of Admiral Sir John "Jacky" Fisher, was superior to anything else afloat. It forced the Germans to respond, ratcheting the naval race to a more dangerous level.

Domestic politics were also significant. Sir Edward Grey, British Foreign Secretary, has been accused of failing to deter Germany by not sending strong enough signals concerning British intentions; yet his hand was weakened by the unwillingness of many of his Liberal colleagues in the Cabinet to contemplate war. In France, Germany's decision to seize the province of Alsace and Lorraine in 1871 caused lasting resentment. In Germany, the rise of the Social Democrats alarmed the Imperial government and may have contributed to a desire for a popular war. Above all, a pan-European current of militarism, and a general belief in Social Darwinism – the idea that the survival of the fittest applied to nations and peoples – led to a febrile atmosphere in which resorting to war to settle disputes came to be seen as natural and acceptable. For all that, when article 231 of the 1919 Treaty of Versailles (that ended the war in the West) blamed Germany and its allies for the outbreak of the war, it encapsulated an essential truth.

25 JULY–28 JULY 1914

MOBILIZATION

THE OUTBREAK OF WAR

For years before 1914, general staffs in Europe had prepared elaborate plans for mobilization in the event of war. During the nineteenth century, most states had adopted a system of conscripting men into the army for a set, often fairly short, period of time, then sending them back to civilian life. These reservists were then recalled to the colours in time of emergency.

This arrangement allowed armies to put vast numbers of men into the field. Germany's field army of 82 infantry divisions included 31 reserve formations; the French had 73 divisions, 25 of which were composed of reservists. The major exception was Britain, which relied on a long-service regular army backed up by a volunteer part-time Territorial Force, rather than on conscription. Shortly after the war began, the new Secretary of State for War, Field Marshal Lord Kitchener called for volunteers for a new, mass army. This ensured that by 1916 Britain had an army comparable in size to its allies and enemies. But in August 1914, Britain could only put a mere six infantry divisions in the field – in addition, of course, to the might of the Royal Navy.

The war plans of the Great Powers dictated that no time could be wasted between mobilizing and fighting. The German pre-war plan, developed under General Alfred von Schlieffen, was designed to compensate for the fact that Germany would face a war on two fronts. Hurling the bulk of its forces westwards, and invading neutral Belgium to outflank the French frontier defences, Germany would defeat France in a matter of weeks. Its forces would then redeploy via the strategic railway system to face the Russian Army, which the Germans calculated would be slow to move. That infringement of Belgian territory was likely to bring the British into the war was discounted. The operational concept was based on the idea of encirclement, a favourite German military gambit that served them well in the Franco-Prussian War of 1870–71 (and was to be repeated on numerous occasions in the Second World War). If the French advanced into Lorraine, so much the better; the German trap would close behind them. The Schlieffen Plan, hotly debated by historians in recent years, stands as an example of a gamble of breathtaking proportions. If it failed, Germany would be in deep trouble.

The French army pinned its hopes on Plan XVII, a strategy developed by the French general staff under the leadership of General Joseph Joffre. Plan XVII was founded on the concept of the all-out offensive, an aggressive military doctrine associated with Lieutenant General (later

ENTENTE CORDIALE

In 1898, the Fashoda Incident, a confrontation between British and French troops in southern Sudan, brought the two countries close to war. A desire to settle colonial disputes and increasing fear of Germany brought the British and French together. An agreement (the "Entente Cordiale") was signed in 1904, and by 1914 their military plans were being co-ordinated. The French navy deployed in the Mediterranean, leaving the Royal Navy to protect the Channel coast. The arrival in August 1914 of the BEF to fight alongside the French Army was the logical outcome of this rapprochement.

OPPOSITE: German troops on a pre-war training exercise. They are wearing the spiked helmet replaced during the war by the "coal-scuttle".

LEFT: British recruitment poster featuring Field Marshal Earl Kitchener of Khartoum, Secretary of State for War and a British national icon.

ABOVE: King Edward VII reviews French regimental flags at Vincennes, 1903. Edward played a significant role in bringing France and Britain together.

ABOVE: Alfred von Schlieffen died before he saw the disaster that his plan inflicted upon his country and Europe.

ABOVE: A large proportion of the British battalions that went to war in 1914 were composed of reservists, like these men.

BELOW: A German poster of Allied uniforms from 1914. The drab khaki clothing of the British contrasts with the colourful French and Belgian uniforms.

THE FRENCH ARMY IN 1914

French soldiers went to war in 1914 wearing antiquated uniforms of blue coats, and bright red trousers that symbolized the élan of the army. By contrast, the Germans had dull, grey uniforms that made their soldiers less conspicuous. The British took this trend the furthest, wearing practical khaki ("dust-coloured") clothing. During the course of the war, the French switched to a more sensible "horizon blue" uniform, and the Germans similarly modified their dress,swapping the spiked pickelhaube for the "coal scuttle" steel helmet.

Marshal) Ferdinand Foch. Both Joffre and Foch were to go on to play extremely prominent roles during the First World War. On the outbreak of war, major French forces would surge into Lorraine to recapture the provinces lost to Germany after the Franco-Prussian War, while others would advance farther to the north. Everywhere, the French would carry the war to the enemy. As the consequence of secret talks between the British and French staffs, it was decided that the British Expeditionary Force (BEF), too small to carry out an independent strategy, would take its place on the left of the French Army, a decision reluctantly confirmed by an ad hoc war council of politicians and generals convened on the outbreak of war. The Belgian Army, less than 120,000 strong in 1914, could do little but resist the Germans as best they could until joined by Franco-British forces.

The French, British and German armies were armed with broadly similar weapons – bolt-action, magazine rifles capable of rapid fire; modern, quick-firing artillery; and a limited number of machine guns. All retained considerable numbers of cavalry, armed with both firearms and swords, for reconnaissance and the charge. Every army also had a small number of primitive airplanes. General staffs had studied the most recent military campaigns, in South Africa (1899–1902) and Manchuria (1904–05), and had incorporated the perceived lessons into their thinking. None were unaware of the devastating power of modern weapons, or the difficulty in overcoming fixed fortifications. To strike first and win quickly, before the front could congeal into trench warfare, seemed a logical extrapolation from recent wars; and the Russo-Japanese War apparently demonstrated that determined troops with high morale could overcome entrenched defenders, albeit at a heavy cost in casualties. The French were the most extreme exponents of the cult of the offensive and the "moral battlefield", in which heavy emphasis was placed on morale (the words being used interchangeably at this time), but these concepts also influenced the British and Germans. These pre-war doctrines were not entirely wrong, but undoubtedly contributed to the huge "butcher's bill" in the early months of the war.

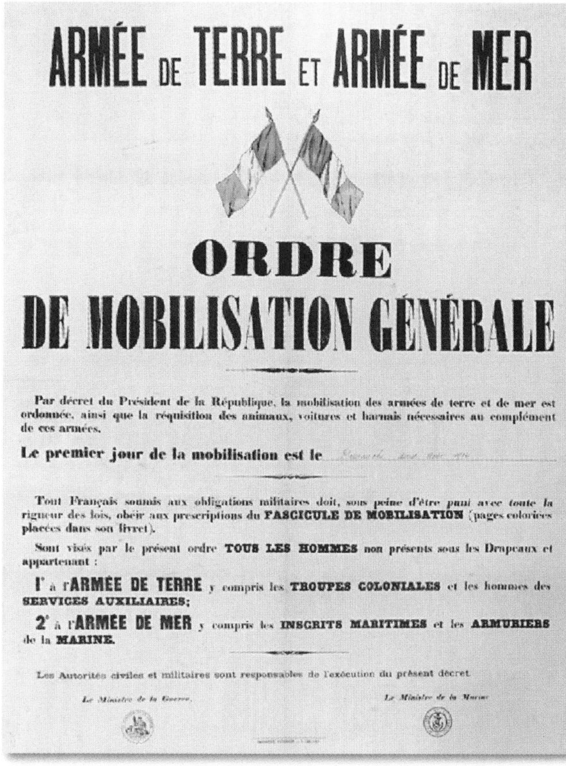

ABOVE This French poster of 1914 announces general mobilization, which includes requisitioning of animals and vehicles for service with the military.

RIGHT: Among this crowd in Munich in August 1914 was the young Adolf Hitler, captured, by a remarkable coincidence, in this photograph.

29 JULY–22 AUGUST 1914

BATTLE OF THE FRONTIERS

LORRAINE AND THE SCHLIEFFEN PLAN

The first shots of the war were fired by the Austrians against the Serbs on 29 July, but the outbreak of fighting in Western Europe was not long delayed. The first major clash came on 5 August with the German attack on the Belgian fortress of Liège, which held out until 13 August.

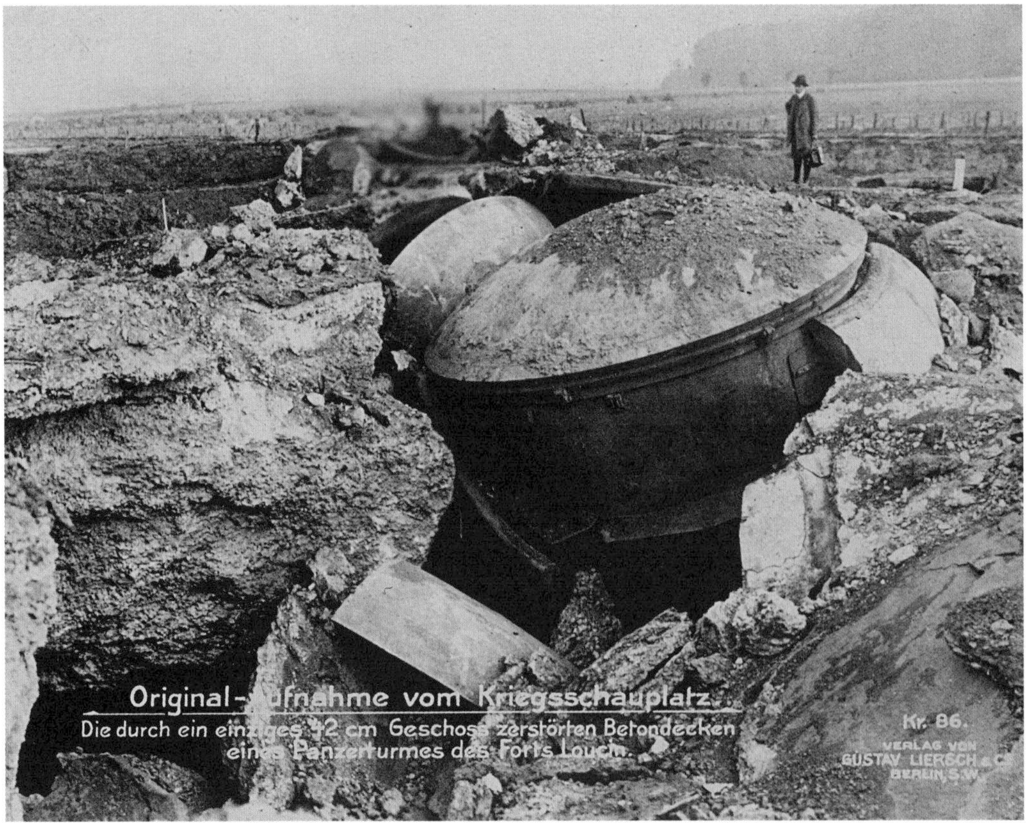

Original-Aufnahme vom Kriegsschauplatz.
Die durch ein einziges 42 cm Geschoss zerstörten Betondecken eines Panzerturmes des Forts Louch.
Kr. 86.
VERLAG VON GUSTAV LIERSCH & Co BERLIN, S.W.

MAP KEY

Schlieffen Plan
French plan XVII

GERMAN & FRENCH WAR PLANS: 1914

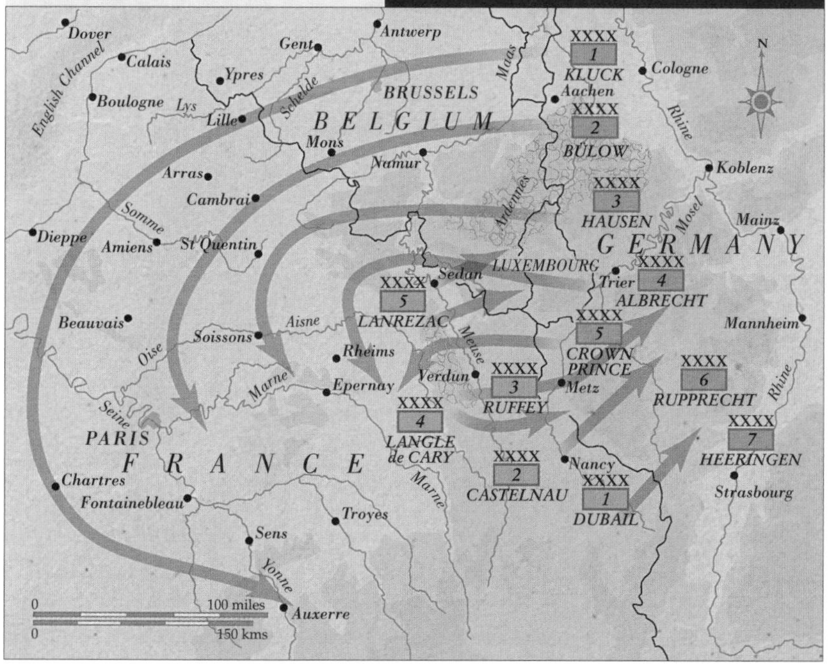

OPPOSITE: The concrete roof of a gun emplacement on one of the Liège fortresses, destroyed by a German 420mm shell.

This was highly significant, because the longer the Belgians could impede the German advance, the further behind schedule the Schlieffen Plan would fall. The Belgian Army held the line of the River Gette before retreating into the fortress of Antwerp on 20 August, and the Belgian capital, Brussels, was lost the same day. The Germans continued to advance, capturing the fortress of Huy (on the River Meuse) and beginning a short siege of Namur, which fell on 23 August.

Moltke, who had succeeded Schlieffen as Chief of the Great General Staff in 1906, was forced to deploy a sizeable force to mask Antwerp, and to protect the flank of the main German advance from a Belgian sortie. On 5 October, the port was reinforced by a British force, in a demonstration of British sea power. This further weakened and slowed the German main effort. Partly out of frustration, partly to discourage guerrilla activity, the Germans carried out *Schrecklichkeit*, a policy of terror that included sacking the medieval city of Louvain and killing civilians. The oft-mocked Allied propaganda about German atrocities, although frequently exaggerated, did have foundations in truth.

Plan XVII was initiated on 6 August with the movement of a French corps into Alsace, only for it to be repulsed by the defenders. A follow-up attack under General Paul Pau resulted in the capture of Mulhouse on 8 August. The French troops were greeted by cheering crowds, glad to welcome their liberators. However, shortly afterwards the victorious French

JOSEPH JACQUES CÉSAIRE JOFFRE (1852–1931)

Joffre, Chief of the French General Staff 1911–14 and Commander-in-Chief 1914–16, oversaw the development and implementation of Plan XVII, but then was able to rescue the French army from the consequences of that plan. His legendary calmness reflected ability of a very high order to cope with the shocks of war. Joffre, the ruthless sacker of subor-dinates, was himself removed from command at the end of 1916, having failed to break the deadlocked Western Front over the previous two years.

LEFT: Belgian carabineers retreating to Antwerp on 20 August 1914. Note the antiquated uniforms and machine guns drawn by dogs.

BELOW LEFT: A German 77mm field gun and its shell-transport baskets. With a range of 8.5 km (5.3 miles), the 77mm was one of the standard German artillery pieces of the First World War.

were ordered to abandon their gains so that troops could be switched to meet the growing crisis to the north. The major French offensive into Lorraine commenced on 14 August with two Armies (First and Second). This was a complex undertaking, as the further the French advanced, the wider their frontage of attack became. In spite of the fact that, according to the Schlieffen Plan, the German forces should have kept to the defensive, they went onto the attack and on 20 August defeated the French in the twin battles of Morhange and Sarrebourg, and then pushed on to the French frontier. Some French formations fought well. General Foch's XX ("Iron") Corps held its ground stubbornly at Morhange, and was preparing to counter-attack, when to Foch's astonishment it received orders to pull back. "You don't know what is happening to the neighbouring corps", his Chief of Staff, General Denis Duchêne, sourly commented. XX Corps, weary but in good order covered the retreat of Second Army. A few days later, Foch's son, a junior officer with 131st Infantry Regiment, was killed in battle just a short distance away.

The French stabilized the situation, just as a new German offensive was getting underway. Joffre, the Commander-in-Chief (C-in-C) had ordered two armies to attack into the hilly, wooded terrain of the Ardennes in the belief that the German forces in this sector were weak. This misapprehension was based on an intelligence failure: the French had not realized the extent to which the Germans would use reserve troops to create new divisions. In encounter battles (unplanned meeting engagements) at Neufchâteau and Virton on 21–22 August, the attackers suffered further heavy losses and were pulled back behind the River Meuse.

Plan XVII was proving a bloody failure. Around 300,000 French soldiers became casualties in the Battle of the Frontiers. A report from Second Army in Lorraine stated: "The troops, infantry and artillery have been sorely tested. Our artillery is held at a distance by the long-range artillery of our enemy; it cannot get close enough for counterbattery fire. Our infantry has attacked with élan, but have been halted primarily by enemy artillery fire and by unseen enemy infantry hidden in trenches." In spite of the setbacks, "Papa" Joffre remained imperturbably calm, although he energetically sacked incompetent, or perhaps merely unlucky, commanders. In little more than a month, he removed 50 generals, including no less than 38 divisional commanders, and promoted talented, and by now battle-hardened leaders from further down the military hierarchy. One such officer was Ferdinand Foch, promoted to command Ninth Army.

By mid-August, both Joffre and Moltke were less focused on Alsace-Lorraine. Now they looked towards Belgium. For it was there, as the Germans advanced, that a major crisis was brewing.

ABOVE: Soldiers of German 47th Infantry Regiment (10th Division), August 1914. Infantry losses were heavy in the opening months of the war.

BELOW: Ruins of the Hotel de Ville in Louvain, September 1914. The German sack of the Belgian city caused international outrage.

HELMUTH VON MOLTKE "THE YOUNGER" (1848–1916)

Von Moltke was the nephew of Helmut von Moltke "the elder", the German victor of the 1870–71 Franco-Prussian War. Although a belligerent advocate of war in the summer of 1914, he lacked his uncle's qualities of self-belief and ruthlessness. On campaign, finding it increasingly difficult to control the vast German armies, he collapsed with a nervous breakdown after the Battle of the Marne. He was blamed by contemporaries and some historians for meddling with Schlieffen's original plan. This is unfair as the plan was likely to fail on logistic grounds alone.

21 AUGUST–26 AUGUST 1914

MONS AND LE CATEAU

FIRST ACTIONS OF THE BEF

The Kaiser, in an order of 19 August, referred to "General French's insignificant little army". The word "insignificant" was translated into English as "contemptible". Revelling in the insult, the BEF of 1914 acquired its nickname: the "Old Contemptibles".

OPPOSITE: British soldiers and French cavalrymen fraternize outside a café, 1914. The Mons campaign of August strained inter-Allied relations.

LEFT: The 4th Royal Fusiliers resting in Mons, Saturday 22 August, 1914. On the next day the battalion saw heavy fighting.

Wilhelm II's order illustrated how casually the German High Command regarded the British Army's presence on the Continent. In fact, Moltke welcomed the opportunity to defeat the BEF as well as the French Army. Given the disarray of the Allies, it seemed that this was a distinct possibility. Lanrezac's French Fifth Army pushed into Belgium with Sir John French's BEF on its left. But as French Third and Fourth Armies fell back, the flank of Lanrezac's Fifth Army was uncovered, and it found itself threatened by three German armies: from the east by Third Army (von Hausen); to the front by von Bülow's Second Army; and von Kluck's First Army to the west. In the Battle of the Sambre (21–23 August), the French met defeat. However, the manoeuvres of the three German armies were poorly synchronized and they were unable to profit fully from their successes.

On Lanrezac's left, on 23 August the British fought their first battle in Western Europe since Waterloo, 99 years before. The problems encountered by Sir John French and Lanrezac – neither of whom was fluent in the other's language – in attempting to co-ordinate their operations reveals much about the challenges posed by fighting alongside allies, and the British and French in effect fought two separate but adjacent battles. Mons was a classic encounter battle. Led by the 9th Lancers, the British II Corps under General Sir Horace Smith-Dorrien reached Mons

SIR JOHN DENTON PINKSTONE FRENCH (1852–1925)

Field Marshal French took the BEF to France in 1914 as its Commander-in-Chief. An Irish cavalryman, he established his reputation as an able commander of mounted troops during the South African (or Second Boer) War (1899–1902), when he forged an effective partnership with his chief of staff, Douglas Haig. He did not cope well with the demands of commanding the BEF and was replaced in December 1915 by Haig after the failure of the battle of Loos. F rench never forgave his former protégé.

on 21–22 August. Mons was a mining area of slag heaps and chimneys – not an ideal place to fight a battle. By the following day, 3rd and 5th Divisions had taken up positions along the banks of the Mons-Condé canal, in Mons itself and in outlying villages. The Cavalry Division was held in reserve. When German First Army appeared on the scene, they were taken by surprise, as Kluck believed the BEF was at Tournai. Mounting clumsy frontal assaults, the attackers were bloodily repulsed in most places. The sheer pressure of German forces and heavy artillery fire meant that the outnumbered BEF could not hold on indefinitely. Mons was not an affair in which generals calmly manoeuvred troops as if on a giant chessboard. Rather, individual units and sub-units fought a series of almost private battles. The machine gun section of the 4th Royal Fusiliers conducted a rearguard action at a bridge that resulted in the award of two Victoria Crosses, one posthumous.

Late on 23 August, II Corps began to fall back a new position. Lanrezac's Fifth Army was in full retreat. When French discovered this, the BEF too disengaged and slipped away from the Mons battlefield. Mons was a tactical victory for the British at the cost of 1,600 casualties (which was very light by later standards), but strategically the Germans had the upper hand and continued to drive forward. Command and control was fragile. British I Corps, under General Sir Douglas Haig, remained in touch with Lanrezac's French Fifth Army, but Haig lost contact with Smith-Dorrien; and Sir

ABOVE: Badge of 9th (Queen's Royal) Lancers. British cavalry proved superior to their German counterparts on the retreat from Mons, successfully screening the retreating infantry.

MAURICE JAMES DEASE VC

Lieutenant Dease, 4th Royal Fusiliers, was posthumously awarded the first Victoria Cross (VC) of the war for his actions at Mons.

SIDNEY FRANK GODLEY VC

After Dease was wounded, Private Godley took over a machine gun and held off the Germans. Awarded the VC, he lived until 1957.

SIR HORACE LOCKWOOD SMITH-DORRIEN (1858–1930)

General Smith-Dorrien first saw action during the Zulu War of 1879, where he escaped from the Battle of Isandhlwana. His brilliant handling of II Corps in August 1914 played a major role in ensuring the survival of the BEF, but he was unfairly sacked by Sir John French during the Second Battle of Ypres that began on 22 April 1915. The two had fallen out before the war, and French was a vindictive man. Smith-Dorrien's reputation has endured rather better than French's.

John French at General Headquaters (GHQ) was able to exercise little control over the BEF's two corps. On 26 August, a German advance briefly threatened I Corps headquarters at Landrecies, causing some short-lived panic.

For the BEF, the retreat from Mons was a gruelling experience. Apart from the hard march under a hot sun, retreating from an enemy they believed they had defeated was demoralizing for many British soldiers. Spirits rose when, on 26 August, the order was given to halt and deploy for battle. With the Germans in pursuit, Smith-Dorrien was forced to turn and fight at Le Cateau, 50km (30 miles) south of Mons. Once again, II Corps inflicted a sharp tactical defeat on the Germans, who were as tired as the British. But this time British losses were much heavier – some 7,800. 1st Gordon Highlanders were accidentally left behind when the rest of the Corps retreated and were forced to surrender. The Germans, too, suffered badly and Smith-Dorrien was able to resume the retreat. The BEF was battered but intact and had fulfilled a vital role on the flank of French Fifth Army. French, however, temporarily lost his nerve and wanted to pull out of the line to refit. Kitchener had to cross over from England to forbid it. The end of August neared with the campaign still in the balance.

BELOW: Men of British 5th Cavalry Brigade on the retreat from Mons. British cavalry alternated between walking and riding to spare their horses.

29 AUGUST–15 OCTOBER 1914

THE MARNE AND THE AISNE

PUSHING BACK THE GERMAN OFFENSIVE

By the end of August, Joffre had decided his force should go onto the defensive, and formed a new Army (the Sixth, under General Maunoury) to plug the gap on the left of the BEF.

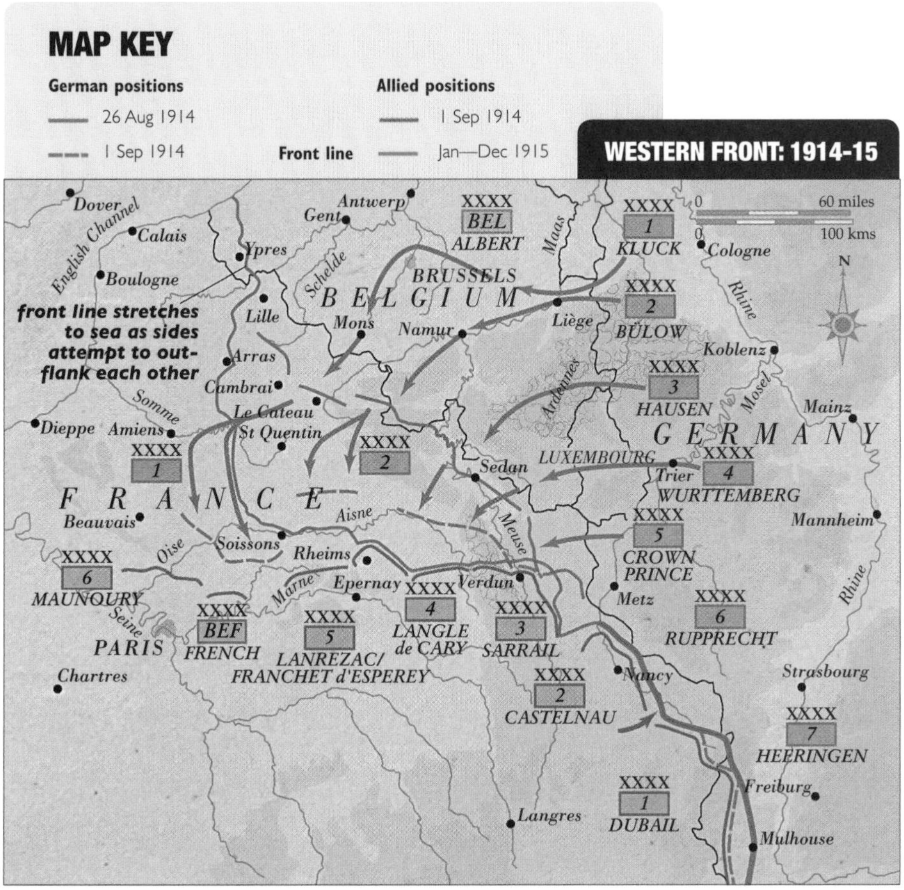

OPPOSITE TOP: A long column of German troops on the march, passing ambulances (note the red crosses on the flags) moving to the rear.

OPPOSITE BOTTOM: The "taxis of the Marne", used to transport troops during the fighting, have become an enduring symbol of the battle.

However, local offensives continued. At Guise on 29 August, French Fifth Army mauled the flank of German Second Army, which caused Bülow to halt his advance for two days. Lanrezac, shortly to be replaced by Franchet d'Esperey, had pulled back after the battle. Kluck, believing that Fifth Army was vulnerable and that the BEF no longer posed a threat, decided to wheel his army in front of Paris, rather than adhering to the letter of the Schlieffen plan and encircling the French capital. On 3 September, Allied aircraft spotted that the direction of Kluck's advance had changed. The French now had a golden opportunity to seize the strategic initiative by striking the German flank.

In Lorraine, too, the French were on the defensive. Crown Prince Rupprecht's forces advanced towards the 65-km (40-mile) gap between the fortresses of Épinal and Toul. Hampered by a stream of contradictory orders from Moltke's headquarters, Rupprecht's advance was slowed by a tough fight near Nancy. In late August, at Verdun, the German Crown Prince, Friedrich Wilhelm's Fifth Army forces were battered by the French Third Army under General Sarrail. On 9 September, the Germans gave up and fell back to their starting positions of 17 August.

In the northern sector, it did not prove easy to reverse the Allied retreat. Some troops, including the BEF, continued southwards after the order to turn around had been issued. Fortunately, the military governor of Paris, General Gallieni, moved up Sixth Army on 4 September, two days ahead of Joffre's order for a general offensive. The Germans were poorly placed to respond to the Allied attack. Kluck, after prodding from Moltke, was slowly deploying to protect the flanks of Second and Third Armies when advanced elements of Maunoury's forces attacked on 5 September. The rest of Sixth Army, plus Fifth Army and the BEF joined the battle on the following day. What became known as the First Battle of the Marne

RIGHT: French soldiers went to war in 1914 wearing the characteristic soft "kepi" as headgear. This example belonged to a sergeant of 132 Infantry Regiment.

was a hard struggle. At one stage the French were reinforced by "the taxis of the Marne", which ferried a brigade of troops from Paris. The battle was ultimately decided not on the ground, but in the minds of the German High Command. Moltke was startled by the reappearance of the BEF, which he had thought destroyed, advancing alongside French Fifth Army into the lightly defended gap between Bülow's and Kluck's forces. As the result of the visit of one of Moltke's staff officers, Colonel Hentsch, it was decided that German Second Army would retreat if the Allies crossed the Marne. On 9 September, the BEF did just that. Bülow fell back, with Kluck conforming to the retreat. The Germans had been stopped at the Marne. It was a great strategic victory. Some called it a miracle.

The Allies followed the retreating Germans and briefly victory seemed in sight. On reaching the heights above the River Aisne on 12–13 September, however, the Germans were discovered to be occupying primitive trenches. Joffre on 15 September realized that it was "no longer a question of pursuit, but of methodical attack". The Aisne was another strategic victory, this time for the Germans. Had they been unable to hold the line there, they would have retreated some 65 km (40 miles). As a by-product of the Aisne, trench warfare was begun – it was to endure for another four years.

Moltke was sacked on 14 September, and his successor, Erich von Falkenhayn, went on to the offensive by attempting to outflank the Allied left. Joffre replied in kind, and there followed a series of attempts to turn the enemy's flank as the centre of the struggle moved steadily to the north. This is erroneously known as the "Race to the Sea"; the generals were not seeking to reach the coast, but to get round their opponent's flank. One such action took place at Dixmude in Belgium in mid October. Here, the defenders included French marines and Tirailleurs Sénégalais (Senegalese light infantry). Between 2 and 15 October, the BEF was transferred to Flanders, and from 10 October onwards its corps came into battle in places whose names were to become dreadfully familiar over the next four years – La Bassée, Messines, Armentières. The fall of Antwerp on 10 October released German troops for use in Flanders. These, together with some newly raised divisions, allowed the Germans to make one last attempt to smash through the congealing trench lines.

ABOVE: A French 75mm gun in action, October 1914. This photograph shows the moment of firing – the barrel is at full recoil.

LEFT: Erich von Falkenhayn (on the left) succeeded Moltke the Elder after the failure of the Schlieffen plan.

RIGHT: A German gravemarker. This identified the resting place of Peter Kollwitz (207th Reserve Infantry Regiment) killed on 23 October 1914 at Dixmude. His artist mother, Kathe, created the famous Mourning Parents sculpture.

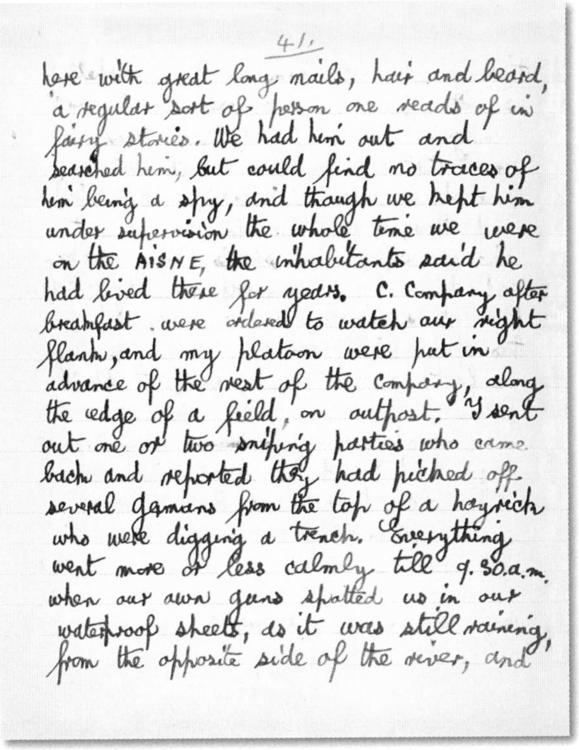
41.

here with great long nails, hair and beard, a regular sort of person one reads of in fairy stories. We had him out and searched him, but could find no traces of him being a spy, and though we kept him under supervision the whole time we were on the AISNE, the inhabitants said he had lived there for years. C. Company after breakfast were ordered to watch our right flank, and my platoon were put in advance of the rest of the Company, along the edge of a field, on outpost. I sent out one or two sniping parties who came back and reported they had picked off several Germans from the top of a hayrick who were digging a trench. Everything went more or less calmly till 9.30 a.m. when our own guns spotted us in our waterproof sheets, as it was still raining, from the opposite side of the river, and

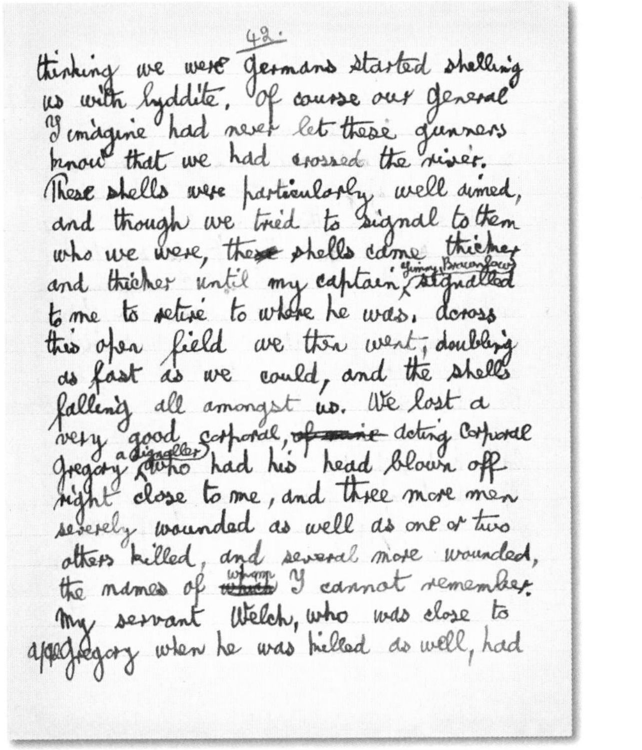
42.

thinking we were Germans started shelling us with lyddite. Of course our General I imagine had never let these gunners know that we had crossed the river. These shells were particularly well aimed, and though we tried to signal to them who we were, these shells came thicker and thicker until my captain, Jimmy Brownlow, signalled to me to retire to where he was. Across this open field we then went, doubling as fast as we could, and the shells falling all amongst us. We lost a very good corporal, ~~of mine~~ Acting Corporal Gregory, a signaller, who had his head blown off right close to me, and three more men severely wounded as well as one or two others killed, and several more wounded, the names of ~~which~~ whom I cannot remember. My servant Welch, who was close to ~~app~~ Gregory when he was killed as well, had

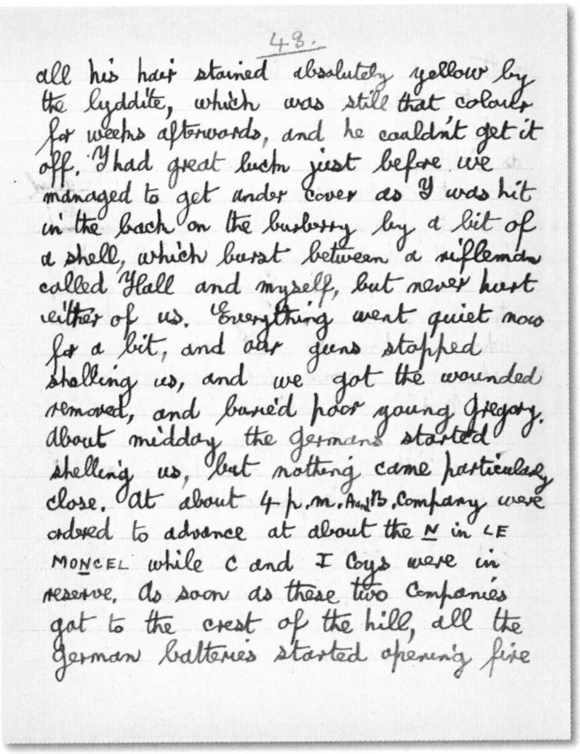
43.

all his hair stained absolutely yellow by the lyddite, which was still that colour for weeks afterwards, and he couldn't get it off. I had great luck just before we managed to get under cover as I was hit in the back on the busby by a bit of a shell, which burst between a rifleman called Hall and myself, but never hurt either of us. Everything went quiet now for a bit, and our guns stopped shelling us, and we got the wounded removed, and buried poor young Gregory. About midday the Germans started shelling us, but nothing came particularly close. At about 4 p.m. A and B Company were ordered to advance at about the N in LE MONCEL while C and I Coys were in reserve. As soon as these two Companies got to the crest of the hill, all the German batteries started opening fire

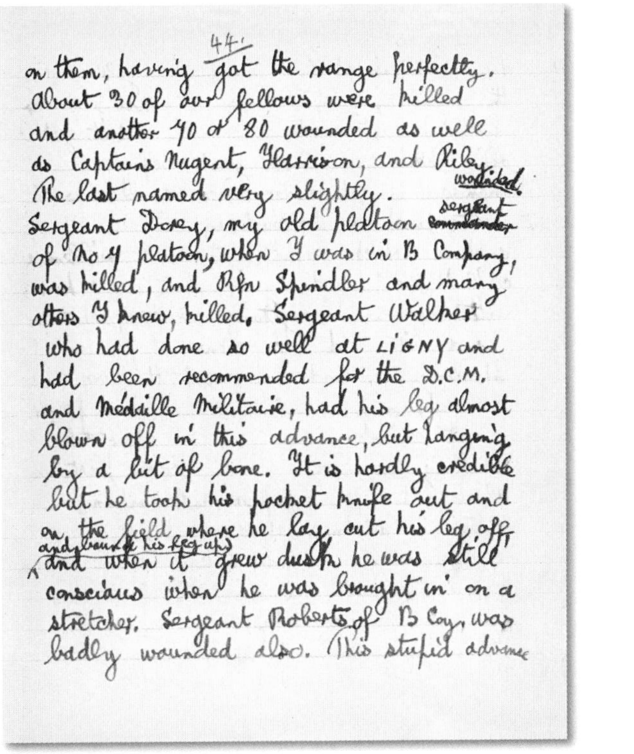
44.

on them, having got the range perfectly. About 30 of our fellows were killed and another 70 or 80 wounded as well as Captains Nugent, Harrison, and Riley. The last named very slightly wounded. Sergeant Dovey, my old platoon sergeant ~~commander~~ of No 4 platoon, when I was in B Company, was killed, and Rfn Spindler and many others I knew, killed. Sergeant Walker who had done so well at LIGNY and had been recommended for the D.C.M. and Médaille Militaire, had his leg almost blown off in this advance, but hanging by a bit of bone. It is hardly credible but he took his pocket knife out and on the field where he lay cut his leg off, and bound his leg up and when it grew dusk he was still conscious when he was brought in on a stretcher. Sergeant Roberts of B Coy, was badly wounded also. This stupid advance

ABOVE: Excerpts from the diary of 2nd Lieutenant Lionel (later Lord) Tennyson, 1st Rifle Brigade, covering the battles of the Marne and Aisne.

20 OCTOBER–22 NOVEMBER 1914

THE FIRST BATTLE OF YPRES

BLOODY STALEMATE

The German attack of 20 October 1914 initiated a series of engagements that have become known to history as the First Battle of Ypres. It was an offensive on a large scale, from the Béthune area to the coast. Rupprecht's Sixth Army, recently transferred from Lorraine, attacked towards the northeast from the direction of Lille.

OPPOSITE: French soldiers in Ypres, October 1914. First Ypres was a genuinely Allied battle, involving the French, British and Belgian armies.

LEFT: Civilian buses, complete with incongruous advertisements for soap and whisky, pressed into service to transport troops on the Western Front.

ABOVE: Cap badge of the 14th Battalion the London Regiment, or London Scottish. The 1/14th was the first Territorial infantry battalion to go into action, at Messines, on Halloween 1914.

The newly created Fourth Army moved west on a front between Ypres and Nieuport. In an extremely fortuitous piece of timing, Haig's I Corps arrived at Ypres from the Aisne on 20 October and helped stabilize the situation there. In the La Bassée-Messines sector, II and III Corps also repulsed German attacks. The heavy losses among young and inexperienced German volunteers caused the fighting to be dubbed the Kindermord ("massacre of the innocents"). The attackers had far more success against the Belgians on the River Yser: Nieuport and Dixmude were held (the former by French 42nd Division, the latter by the French marines); but elsewhere the Belgians were forced back to hold the line of the Dixmude-Nieuport railway. This terrain is extremely low-lying, and in desperation, in late October, the sea defences were deliberately breached and the sea allowed to flood the land. This created a highly effective barrier to a further German advance; so much so, that for the rest of the war this was a relatively quiet sector of the Western Front.

On 31 October, the Germans tried again. This time they concentrated on Ypres, using seven divisions commanded by General von Fabeck to assault the front between Messines and Gheluvelt. Under the cover of a heavy bombardment, the Germans made good progress. Haig's I Corps and Allenby's cavalry were in the path of the attack and, exhausted, began to give way. The Germans seized and held Messines Ridge, a battle in which the London Scottish became the first battalion of the Territorial Force, a reserve army of part-time soldiers originally raised for home defence, to go into battle. Further north, a chance shell fatally wounded the commander of British 1st Division and stunned his 2nd Division counterpart. Haig, receiving information that his line had been broken, mounted his horse and rode forward to the front. Briefly, Ypres was within the reach of the Germans, but they failed to grasp the opportunity.

Delays in bringing forward troops and the general chaos of battle allowed the 2nd Worcesters to counter-attack at Gheluvelt and

FAR LEFT: An officer of the 2nd Argyll and Sutherland Highlanders, Captain Moorhouse, firing his Short Magazine Lee-Enfield rifle, Bois Grenier sector, near Ypres, November 1914.

LEFT: A Highland "Balmoral", named after the Royal residence in Scotland, the bonnet of the Black Watch (The Royal Highlanders).

BELOW: Troops beside the medieval Cloth Hall in Ypres. Already damaged, this building was to be reduced to ruins later in the war.

SIR DOUGLAS HAIG (1861–1928)

General (later Field Marshal) Haig made his name as a corps commander at First Ypres. He became Commander-in-Chief of the BEF in late 1915. The most controversial general in British history, Haig has been condemned for the attritional battles of Passchendaele and the Somme, but rarely given the credit for the victory in 1918. He claimed that without the wearing down of the German army in 1916–17, the final victory would have been impossible, an argument that has never been satisfactorily refuted by historians.

THE CHRISTMAS TRUCE

Over Christmas 1914, a number of British and German – and to a lesser extent, French – units observed strictly unofficial truces. The Christmas Truce has been much mythologized. It was by no means universal; 2nd Grenadier Guards were involved in some tough fighting on Christmas Day. But it is clear that in some places fighting ceased, soldiers fraternized in No Man's Land, and, according to a persistent story, German and British soldiers played football. Although a truce on such a scale never reoccurred, low-level fraternization took place throughout the war.

restore the situation. Foch, appointed by Joffre as commander of the French left wing, fed in reserves, including French XVI and IX Corps, and put General D'Urbal in command of all French troops in the Ypres sector. The Allies had survived the crisis – for the moment.

While the fighting did not die away entirely, both sides spent the next few days regrouping, a breathing space for which the Allies were profoundly grateful. On 1 November, the new commander of 1st Division reported to Haig that his men could not resist an "organized attack". Over the next few days, more Allied troops reached Ypres, but the Germans, too, brought up another corps, which attacked on 11 November. South of the Menin Road, the British fought off the attacks, but north of it a fresh crisis developed. Once again, Haig's I Corps was brought to the point of defeat as the Prussian Guards smashed through the weakened defenders. In the process, the attackers were themselves weakened and the impetus of the assault diminished. The artillery of 2nd Division, its covering screen of infantry having vanished, continued to pound away at the attackers. A force of batmen, cooks, headquarters staff and other "odds and ends" mounted a desperate counter-attack that did just enough, just in time, and then the 2nd Oxfordshire and Buckinghamshire Light Infantry made a decisive intervention. The battle dragged on until 22 November, but the Allied line had been stabilized and Ypres, one of the few Belgian cities still in Allied hands, had been held. The French and British held an awkward salient around the city, surrounded on three sides by the Germans.

The campaigns in the West since August 1914 had been shockingly costly: perhaps 300,000 Frenchmen had been killed; the BEF had lost 86,000 men killed, wounded and missing; the Germans lost at least 134,000 (19,600 of them dead) at First Ypres alone. The attempt to win a rapid war of movement had ended in trench deadlock. A French offensive that began on 14 December (the First Battle of Artois) did nothing to break it. But there was a common belief that this was only a temporary phase. As British, French and German soldiers held their trenches, their generals planned for a resumption of mobile warfare in the New Year.

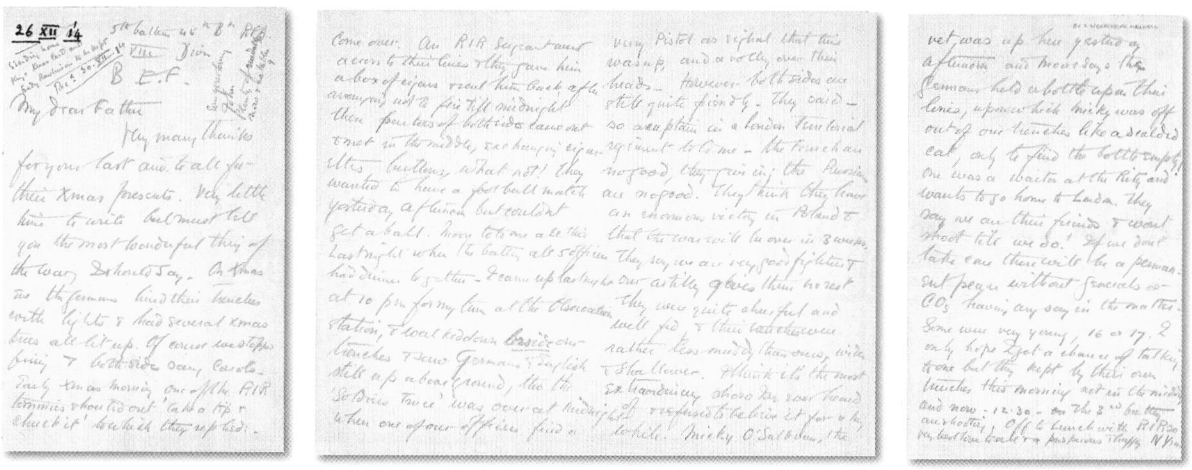

26 XII 14 5th Batt. 45th "B" RFA
VIII Div
B.E.F.

My dear Father

Very many thanks for your last and to all for their Xmas presents. Very little time to write but must tell you the most wonderful thing of the war I should say. On Xmas Eve the Germans lined their trenches with lights & had several Xmas trees all lit up. Of course we stopped firing & both sides sang carols. Early Xmas morning one of the RIR Tommies shouted out 'take a tip & chuck it' to which they replied: 'Come over'. An RIR Sergeant went across to their lines & they gave him a box of cigars & sent him back after arranging not to fire till midnight. Then parties of both sides came out & met in the middle, exchanging cigarettes, buttons, what not! They wanted to have a football match yesterday afternoon but couldn't get a ball. [illegible] all this last night when the battery all 5 officers had dinner together – I came up last night at 10 pm for my turn at the Observation Station, & looked down beside our trenches & saw Germans & English still up above ground, tho the 'Soldiers Truce' was over at midnight when one of our officers fired a Very Pistol as signal that time was up, and a volley over their heads. However both sides are still quite friendly. They said – so a captain in a London Territorial regiment told me – the French are no good, they [illegible] the Russians are no good. They think they have an enormous victory in Poland & that the war will be over in 3 weeks. They say we are very good fighters & our artillery gives them no rest. They were quite cheerful and well fed, & their trenches were rather less muddy than ours, wider & shallower. I think it's the most extraordinary show [illegible] refused to believe it for a while. Micky O'Sullivan, the vet, was up here yesterday afternoon and [illegible] the Germans held a bottle up on their lines, upon which Micky was off out of our trenches like a scalded cat, only to find the bottle empty!! One was a waiter at the Ritz and wants to go home to London. They say we are their friends & won't shoot till we do. If we don't take care there will be a permanent peace without generals or CO's having any say in the matter. Some were very young, 16 or 17. I only hope I get a chance of talking to one but they kept by their own trenches this morning not in the middle and now – 12.30 – [illegible] the 3rd battery are shooting. Off to lunch with RIR [illegible]

ABOVE: A letter from 2nd Lieutenant John Wedderburn-Maxwell, 5th Battery, XLV Brigade, Royal Field Artillery, describing the 1914 Christmas Truce.

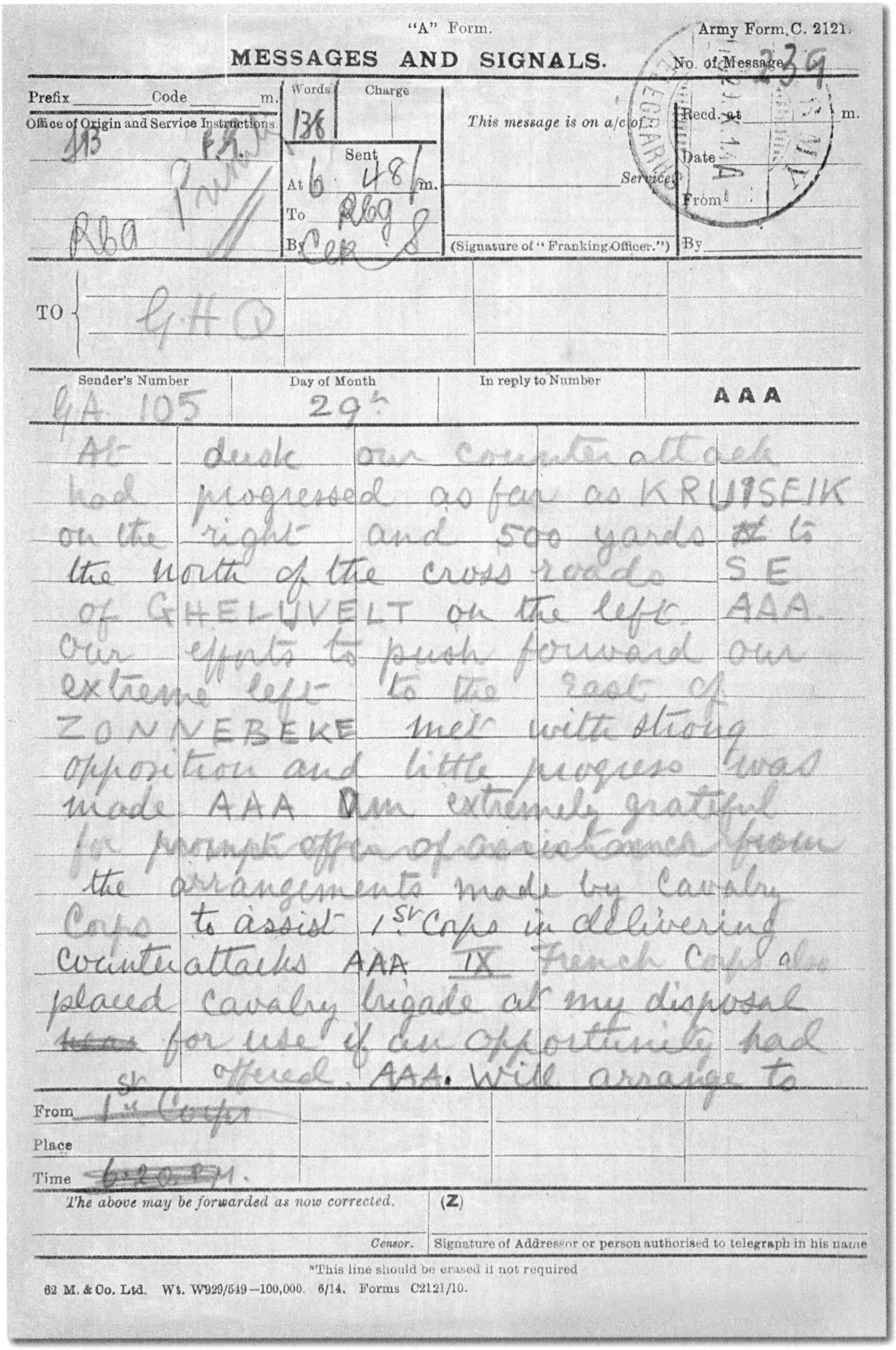

"A" Form. Army Form C. 2121.

MESSAGES AND SIGNALS. No. of Message 239

Prefix ____ Code ____ m. | Words 138 | Charge

Office of Origin and Service Instructions: RBa

Sent At 6 48 p m. To RBG By Cer S

This message is on a/c of: ____ Service.

(Signature of "Franking Officer.")

Recd. at ____ m. Date ____ From ____ By ____

TO { G.H.Q.

Sender's Number	Day of Month	In reply to Number	AAA
GA 105	29th		

At dusk our counter attack had progressed as far as KRUISEIK on the right and 500 yards ~~at~~ to the north of the cross roads S E of GHELUVELT on the left. AAA Our efforts to push forward our extreme left to the east of ZONNEBEKE met with strong opposition and little progress was made AAA Am extremely grateful for prompt offer of assistance from the arrangements made by Cavalry Corps to assist 1st Corps in delivering counter attacks AAA IX French Corps also placed cavalry brigade at my disposal ~~....~~ for use if an opportunity had offered. AAA. Will arrange to

From 1st Corps
Place
Time ~~6.20 P~~M.

The above may be forwarded as now corrected. (Z)

Censor. Signature of Addressor or person authorised to telegraph in his name

*This line should be erased if not required

62 M. & Co. Ltd. Wt. W929/549—100,000. 6/14. Forms C2121/10.

ABOVE AND OPPOSITE RIGHT: Communications between headquarters were difficult in 1914. These are messages sent between British GHQ and I Corps during the First Battle of Ypres.

"A" Form. Army Form C. 2121.

MESSAGES AND SIGNALS. No. of Message

Prefix Code m. | Words | Charge | This message is on a/c of: | Recd. at m.

Office of Origin and Service Instructions.

Sent At 6·48 p.m. To RB9 By CER S

Service.

(Signature of "Franking Officer.")

Date

From

By

TO

Sender's Number	Day of Month	In reply to Number	AAA
*			

return London Scottish tomorrow AAA. Prisoners taken stated they belonged 16th reserve regiment and thought their Corps was the twenty fourth which had just arrived from LILLE AAA Further stated that this is their first engagement.

From 1st Corps

Place

Time 6·30 pm

The above may be forwarded as now corrected. (Z) JE Gough BG

Censor. Signature of Addressor or person authorised to telegraph in his name

*This line should be erased if not required

62 M. & Co. Ltd. Wt. W929/549—100,000. 6/14. Forms C2121/10.

27 SEPTEMBER 1914–16 MAY 1915

1915 SPRING OFFENSIVES

ARTOIS AND CHAMPAGNE

The end of mobile warfare in 1914 left the Germans in control of most of Belgium and of some of the most important industrial areas of France. The opposing lines stretched from the Channel coast near Nieuport all the way to the Swiss frontier. At the beginning of 1915, the trench system was still fairly rudimentary – sometimes little more than holes in the ground hastily joined together.

In some places the terrain was unsuitable for the digging of trenches. In the Vosges mountains they sometimes had to be cut into rock with explosives. At this stage the French provided by far the largest Allied army, although the BEF grew as new formations arrived.

French offensives continued over the winter. Joffre's strategy was one of constant offensives, "nibbling" (as he called it) the enemy. He aimed to pinch out the great bulge in the German line – the Noyon Salient – by attacking in Artois and Champagne. But the First Battle of Artois (27 September–10 October 1914), an ambitious attempt to capture key objectives, including the dominating heights of Vimy Ridge that overlooked the German-held Douai plain, made little headway and was ended in early January. Another offensive was begun in Champagne on 20 December 1914, which continued in stages until the end of March. Again, despite fierce fighting, the French had little to show for this effort except 240,000 casualties. The Germans captured the high ground of the Chemin des Dames ("Ladies's Road", named after Louis XV's daughters) running east and west in the département of the Aisne in November 1914, and in January 1915 a German attack seized the last French position on the plateau, Creute farm (later known as the Dragon's Cave). In the Vosges, a bitter struggle for the Hartmannsweilerkopf peak resulted in 20,000 French losses over four months before they secured the heights in April.

The early fighting in 1915 demonstrated how important heavy and accurate artillery fire was to battlefield success, particularly now the armies were faced with siege warfare. The British offensive at Neuve Chapelle on 10 March gave further evidence confirming this reality. The battle was well planned by Haig's First Army staff: the initial bombardment, which was heavy by contemporary standards and lasted only 35 minutes, mostly overwhelmed the German infantry and allowed the British to take the front-line trenches. But resistance on the flanks, the difficulty of following up the initial success and the arrival of German reserves meant the battle soon bogged down. A mere 1,100 m (1,200 yds) was gained for 13,000 British and 12,000 German casualties.

With the exception of the the German attack at Ypres in April (see pages 34–35), it was the Allies who remained on the offensive

OPPOSITE: No Man's Land, Bois Grenier sector, June 1915. British positions are marked with an "O" and German lines with an "X".

LEFT: A binocular periscope. Since it could be lethal to look over the parapet, trench periscopes were very common. Many of the early ones were improvised from whatever materials were available.

BELOW: The Liverpool Scottish attack Bellewaerde on 16 June 1915.

THE LIVERPOOL SCOTTISH AT HOOGE

One of the myriad of minor actions fought in the first half of 1915 was at Hooge, near Ypres, in June 1915. One of the units involved was the Liverpool Scottish, a Territorial unit. The Medical Officer of the Liverpool Scottish, Captain Noel Chavasse, was given the Military Cross for his exploits at Hooge, and subsequently was awarded the Victoria Cross twice; sadly, the second award was posthumous. Chavasse was one of only three men in the history of the decoration to have been honoured in this way.

in Spring 1915. French First and Third Armies fought a bloody and unsuccessful battle to reduce the St-Mihiel salient (5–18 April), and Joffre launched another hammer blow in Artois in May. Bad news from the Eastern Front – the Central Powers inflicted a major defeat on the Russians at Gorlice-Tarnow in early May – lent particular urgency to this offensive. It also offered an opportunity to strike in the West while the Germans were heavily committed in the East. Joffre ordered D'Urbal's Tenth Army to smash through the German defences in Artois and re-open mobile warfare. On 9 May, Tenth Army, with 1,075 guns (including 293 heavies), attacked Vimy Ridge and positions flanking it. The main attack in the centre was assigned to Philippe Pétain's XXXIII Corps. The defenders wilted under the weight of the bombardment, and within 90 minutes, the 77th and Moroccan Divisions had pressed forward onto the crest of Vimy Ridge. Then, the problems of trench warfare reasserted themselves. Lacking modern radio communictions, reserves could not be summoned forward to exploit the gains. When they did

ABOVE: A French staff officer in the trenches, near Souchez, 15 May 1915. This area was heavily fought over in 1915.

arrive, it was too late as German reserves first shored up the front and then drove the attackers back.

On 9 May the BEF again attacked over the Neuve Chapelle battlefield after another brief bombardment. In a day's fighting Haig's First Army achieved nothing apart from casualties of 11,000 in what became known as the battle of Aubers Ridge. Sir John French was pressed by the French to continue offensive operations, and, after reverting to a bombardment that lasted four days, on 15–16 May, First Army attacked at Festubert with the aim of inflicting heavy casualties on the Germans and pinning their forces to this front. This brought some modest gains, but again at the price of heavy losses. Festubert was the first time the British fought a deliberately attritional battle, and the limited success helped to create the idea that "artillery conquers, infantry occupies" that was to have terrible repercussions in July 1916.

THE BATTLE OF NEUVE CHAPELLE, 10 MARCH 1915

The Battle of Neuve Chapelle was the first major British offensive of 1915. Before the action, the Royal Flying Corps carried out photo-reconnaissance missions over the German trenches to produce maps that improved the accuracy of the British bombardment. The principles of traffic control, a mundane but essential facet of modern warfare, began to emerge as a result of the battle. The attack was carried out by IV Corps and Indian Corps, the latter consisting of Indian, British and Gurkha troops under Lieutenant-General Sir James Willcocks.

"Je les grignote"
("I keep nibbling them")
Joffre

ABOVE: Two typical *fantassins* – French infantrymen – loaded with kit. Such men were the backbone of the French army in the war.

LEFT: German trench artillery, 1915: the Granatenwerfer (grenade thrower) and its Wurfgranaten missile, which weighed 1.8 kg (4 lb).

22 APRIL–25 MAY 1915

THE SECOND BATTLE OF YPRES

THE FIRST USE OF POISON GAS

In their search for a way to break the deadlock on the Western Front, the belligerents made ample use of new technologies. Gas had first been tried on the Eastern Front at Bolimov in January 1915 and gas canisters had been used in shrapnel at Neuve Chapelle.

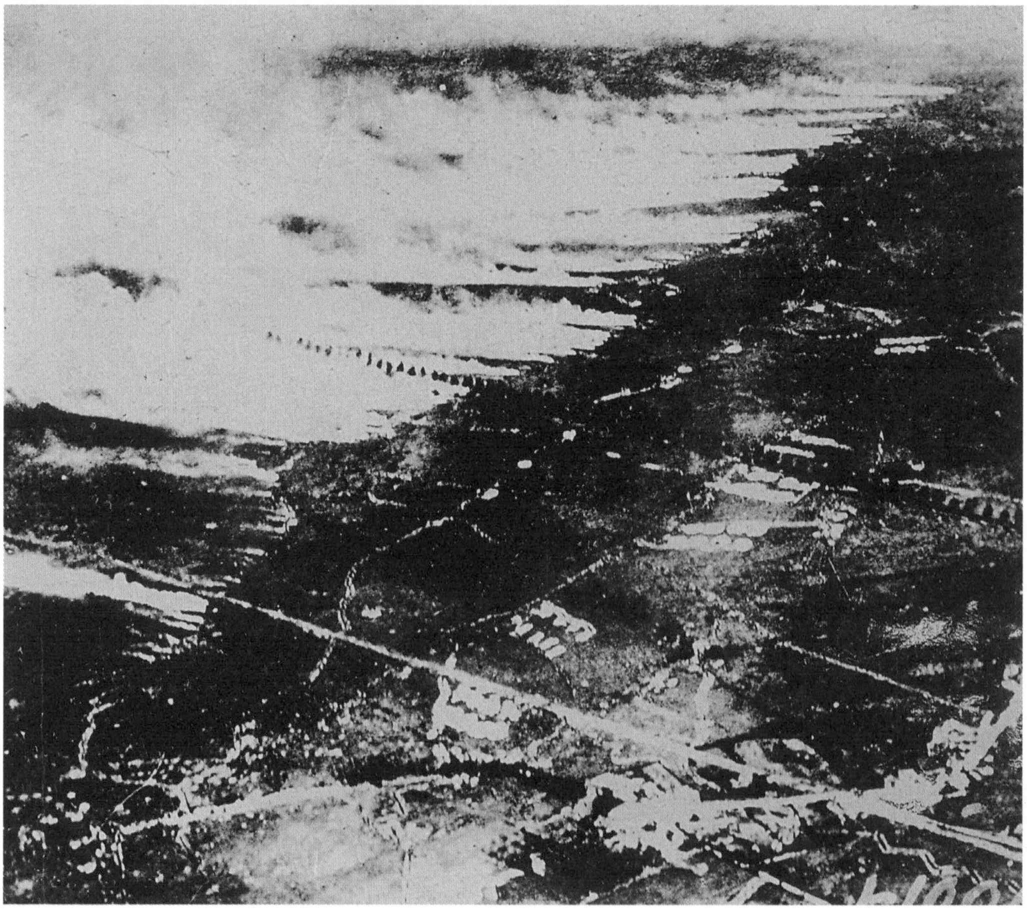

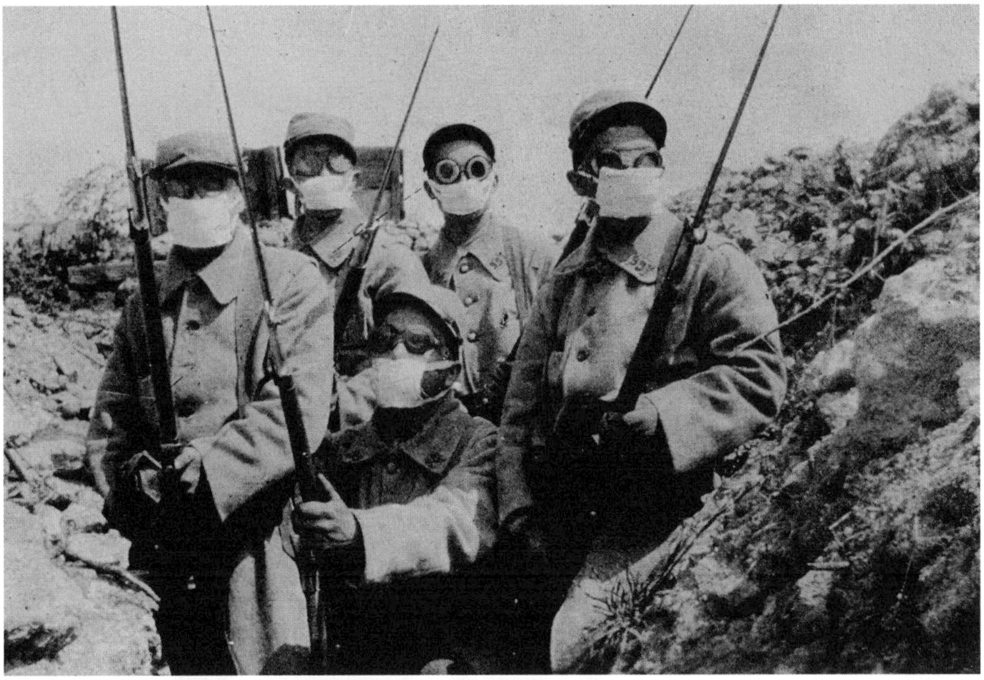

OPPOSITE: A cloud of gas moves across the battlefield during the Second Battle of Ypres, 1915.

LEFT: A posed photograph of French troops during the Second Battle of Ypres. They are wearing a primitive form of gas mask.

BELOW: German troops discharging poison gas from canisters.

The French had also previously used tear gas canisters but at the Second Battle of Ypres this search saw the first use of poison gas on a large scale. The fighting of October–November 1914 had left the Allies holding a vulnerable salient jutting out 8 km (6 miles) into German-held territory. Falkenhayn ordered a limited offensive at Ypres in April 1915 that would test a recently developed weapon, chlorine gas, and – it was hoped – would divert attention from the Eastern Front, where the main German effort was taking place. Fourth Army had 11 divisions in the area, but as this was not intended as a major attack, no further reserves were provided. The attackers faced two French, four British and the 1st Canadian Division, the latter having arrived on the Western Front in February 1915.

The German attack achieved almost complete surprise, no less than 5,830 metal cylinders containing the gas having been installed on the front lines without attracting attention. This represented a substantial intelligence failure on the part of the Allies. A German deserter had warned the French several weeks earlier of a plan to use gas, and similar reports arrived from other sources. Suspecting a deception operation, and rather naïvely believing that the Germans would abide by the international law that forbade the use of such weapons, the French High Command ignored the warnings. The Germans relied on the wind blowing in the right direction for the gas to be effective, and in the late afternoon the atmospheric conditions were judged to be right. At 17:00 the defenders came under intense artillery fire, and the 45th (Algerian)

POISON GAS

Following the first major use of gas at Second Ypres, both sides used chemical weapons freely. The original clumsy use of wind-borne agents was superseded later in the war by projectiles such as those fired by the British Livens Projector. Chlorine gas was superseded by phosgene, and later by mustard gas. Gas never became a decisive weapon, in part because anti-gas protection steadily improved. The soldiers of early 1915 had crude mouth and nose pads; by the end of the war soldiers were issued with more sophisticated respirators.

and French 87th Divisions – the latter consisting of overage territorials – holding the northern part of the Ypres salient saw mist – described by some as bluish-white, by others as yellow-green – drift over from the German trenches. Utterly unprepared for a chemical attack, the French troops gave way and fled in rout. Faced with a 3.25-km (2-mile) gap in their line, the Allies seemed on the verge of a major defeat.

However, the Germans followed up their success with some hesitation, cautiously advancing about 3.25 km (2 miles) and then, on reaching the gas cloud, digging in. This uncharacteristic lack of drive was probably related to the rudimentary anti-gas protection with which the German troops were provided. This German failure to exploit the Allied crisis bought valuable time for British and French reinforcements to reach the battlefield. The inexperienced Canadians, suddenly finding that their flank was open, were particularly vulnerable to a renewed German advance. Improvising gas masks out of cloth soaked in water or urine, ten British and Canadian battalions plugged the gap. On 23 April, the French and Canadians were able to link hands across the salient. The following day saw the Canadians again engulfed by a gas cloud, but they held their ground, their staunch behaviour proving that any fears that British regulars might have had about the reliability of this largely citizen force were groundless. The defensive actions of the French, Canadians and British helped hold the Allied position together. French reinforcements arrived, but nonetheless the situation was growing serious as the salient became steadily compressed. On 27 April, Smith-Dorrien, the local army commander, sensibly told Sir John French that he wanted to fall back to a more defensible position 4 km (2.5 miles) in the rear. French, who hated Smith-Dorrien, used this as an excuse to remove him from his command. Smith-Dorrien's replacement, V Corps commander Sir Herbert Plumer, recommended the same course of action, although more tactfully, and this time the French agreed to a retirement. Plumer, described by one historian as "almost an ideal general for siege warfare", was to command in the Ypres Salient for most of the next three years.

Although any chance of the Germans achieving a clean breakthrough had vanished, the Second Battle of Ypres had not yet finished. A French attack on 30 April gained about 180 m (200 yds), while on 8 May the Germans mounted a major assault on Frenzenberg Ridge. British 27th and 28th Divisions took the main force of the attack, and had to be reinforced by dismounted cavalry. In a week of intense fighting, the defenders were gradually forced back about 1,100 m (1,200 yds). One last spasm of fighting erupted around Bellewaarde on 24–25 May, and then the battle burned out. The Germans had forced the Allies back towards Ypres, but had failed to capitalize on the surprise gained by the initial gas attack. It was a great opportunity missed.

ABOVE: British soldiers of King's Liverpool Regiment in shallow "scrapes" during the Second Battle of Ypres.

BELOW: Later in the war, the German army was much better prepared for chemical warfare. Here, driver and horses are wearing respirators.

RIGHT ABOVE: French victims of German gas at Second Ypres: the bodies of Zouaves, 22 April 1915.

RIGHT BELOW: No.8 Casualty Clearing Station, Bailleul, 1 May 1915. British victims of a gas attack at Hill 60, near Ypres.

LOGISTICS

Logistics – the art and science of moving and supplying troops – is an unglamorous but vital facet of warfare. During the First World War, armies used a combination of horse-drawn and motor transport, backed up by light- and standard-gauge railways. Vast quantities of materiel had to be moved; before the French Sixth Army's attack on the Somme in July 1916, ammunition for 552 heavy guns had to be stockpiled. In the autumn of 1918, a robust and flexible logistic system would give the BEF an important advantage over the Germans.

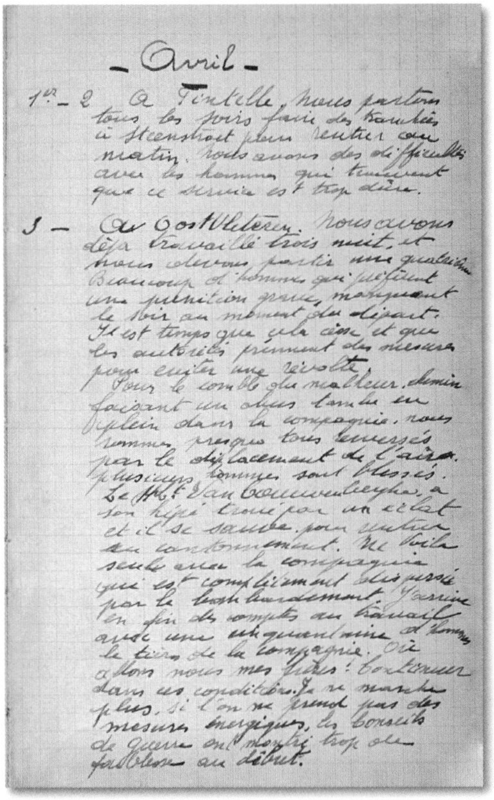

— Avril —

1er – 2 A Tintelle, nous partons tous les soirs faire des tranchées à Steenstraet pour rentrer au matin. Nous avons des difficultés avec les hommes qui trouvent que ce service est trop dur.

3 – Au Oostvleteren. Nous avons déjà travaillé trois nuits et nous devons partir une quatrième. Beaucoup d'hommes qui préfèrent une punition grave, manquent le soir au moment du départ. Il est temps que cela cesse et que les autorités prennent des mesures pour éviter une révolte.
Pour le comble du malheur, chemin faisant un obus tombe en plein dans la compagnie, nous sommes presque tous renversés par le déplacement de l'air. Plusieurs hommes sont blessés. Le Ltt Van Bouwenteghe, a son képi troué par un éclat et il se sauve pour rentrer au cantonnement. Me voila seul avec la compagnie qui est complètement dispersée par le bombardement. J'arrive en fin de compte au travail avec une cinquantaine d'hommes le tiers de la compagnie. Où allons nous mes frères! Continuer dans ces conditions je ne marche plus, si l'on ne prend pas des mesures énergiques, les conseils de guerre ont montré trop de faiblesse au début.

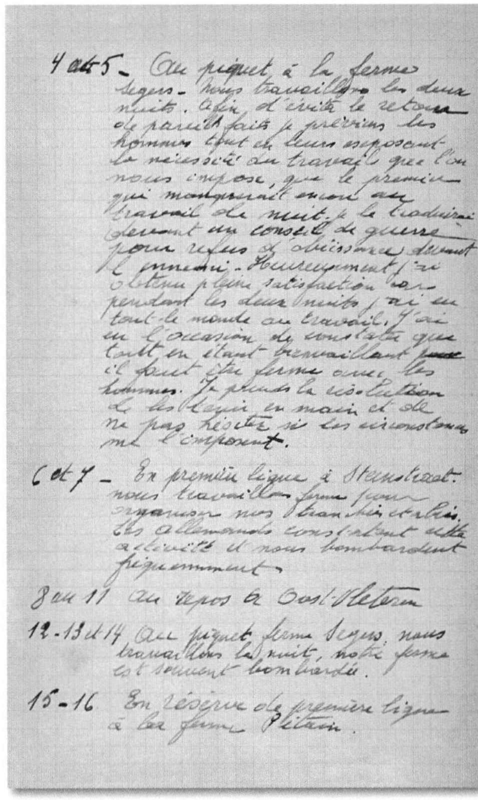

4 et 5 – Au piquet à la ferme Segers. Nous travaillons les deux nuits. Afin d'éviter le retour de pareils faits je préviens les hommes tout en leurs exposant la nécessité du travail que l'on nous impose, que le premier qui manquerait encore au travail de nuit, je le traduirai devant un conseil de guerre pour refus d'obéissance devant l'ennemi. Heureusement j'ai obtenu pleine satisfaction car pendant les deux nuits j'ai eu tout le monde au travail. J'ai eu l'occasion de constater que tout en étant bienveillant il faut être ferme avec les hommes. Je prends la résolution de les tenir en main et de ne pas hésiter si les circonstances me l'imposent.

6 et 7 – En première ligne à Steenstraat. Nous travaillons ferme pour organiser nos tranchées centrales. Les allemands constatent cette activité et nous bombardent furieusement.

8 au 11 Au repos à Oost-Vleteren

12-13 et 14 Au piquet ferme Segers, nous travaillons la nuit, notre ferme est souvent bombardée.

15-16 En réserve de première ligne à la ferme Pétain.

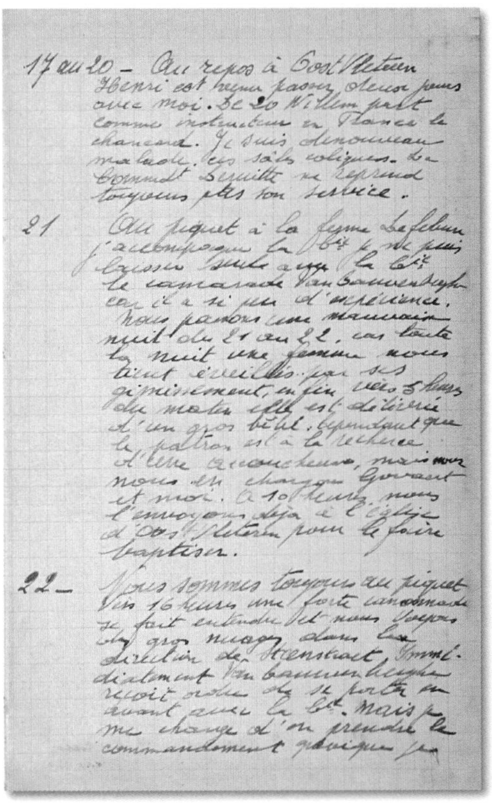

17 au 20 – Au repos à Oost-Vleteren. Henri est venu passer deux jours avec moi. Le 20 Willem part comme instructeur en France le chanceux. Je suis de nouveau malade, mes sales coliques. Le Commandant Dewitte ne reprend toujours pas son service.

21 Au piquet à la ferme Lefebvre j'accompagne la Cie je ne puis laisser seul avec la Cie le camarade Van Bouwenteghe car il a si peu d'expérience. Nous passons une mauvaise nuit du 21 au 22, car toute la nuit une femme nous tient éveillés par ses gémissements, enfin vers 5 heures du matin elle est délivrée d'un gros bébé, cependant que le patron est à la recherche d'une accoucheuse, mais nous en chargeons Govaert et moi. A 10 heures, nous l'envoyons déjà à l'église d'Oost-Vleteren pour le faire baptiser.

22 – Nous sommes toujours au piquet. Vers 16 heures une forte canonnade se fait entendre et nous voyons un gros nuage dans la direction de Steenstraat, immédiatement Van Bouwenteghe reçoit ordre de se porter en avant avec la Cie. Mais je me charge d'en prendre le commandement puisque je

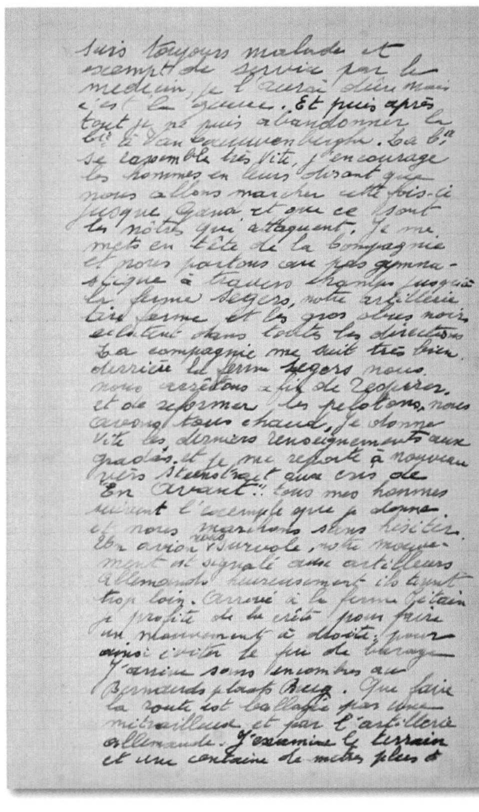

suis toujours malade et exempt de service par le médecin, je l'aurai dire mais c'est la guerre. Et puis après tout je ne puis abandonner la Cie à Van Bouwenteghe. La Cie se rassemble très vite, j'encourage les hommes en leurs disant que nous allons marcher cette fois-ci jusque Gand et que ce sont les nôtres qui attaquent. Je me mets en tête de la compagnie et nous partons au pas gymnastique à travers champs jusqu'à la ferme Segers, notre artillerie tire ferme et les gros obus noirs éclatent dans toutes les directions. La compagnie me suit très bien derrière la ferme Segers nous nous arrêtons afin de reprendre et de reformer les pelotons, nous avons tous chaud, je donne vite les derniers renseignements aux gradés, et je me reporte à nouveau vers Steenstraat aux cris de En avant!! Tous mes hommes suivent l'exemple que je donne et nous marchons sans hésiter. Un avion nous survole, notre mouvement est signalé aux artilleurs allemands heureusement ils tirent trop loin. Arrivé à la ferme Pétain je profite de la crête pour faire un mouvement à droite, pour ainsi éviter le feu de barrage. J'arrive sans encombre au Bernardsplaats Brug. Que faire la route est balayée par une mitrailleuse et par l'artillerie allemande. J'examine le terrain et une centaine de mètres plus à

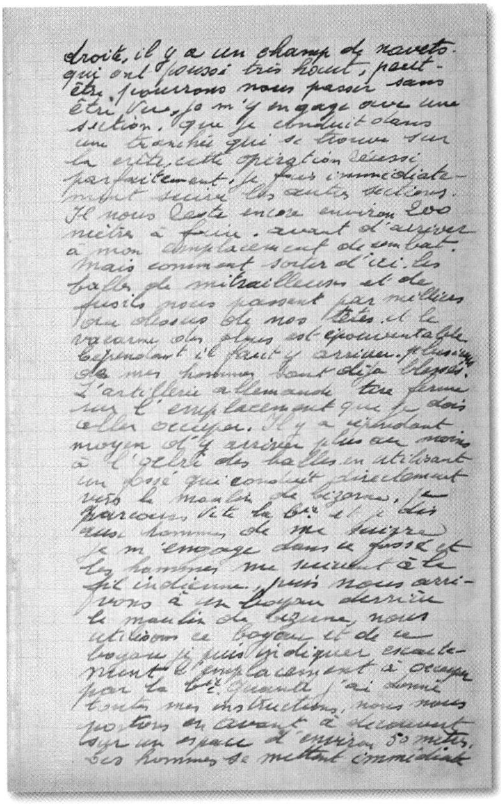
droit, il y a un champ de navets qui ont poussé très haut, peut-être pourrons nous passer sans être vus, je m'y engage avec une section, que je conduis dans une tranchée qui se trouve sur la crête, cette opération réussi parfaitement. je fais immédiatement suivre les autres sections. Il nous reste encore environ 200 mètres à faire avant d'arriver à mon emplacement de combat. Mais comment sortir d'ici. les balles de mitrailleuses et de fusils nous passent par milliers au dessus de nos têtes et le vacarme des obus est épouvantable. Cependant il faut y arriver. plusieurs de mes hommes sont déjà blessés. L'artillerie allemande tire ferme sur l'emplacement que je dois aller occuper. Il y a cependant moyen d'y arriver plus ou moins à l'abri des balles en utilisant un fossé qui conduit directement vers le moulin de bezone(?), je parcours vite la Cie et je dis aux hommes de me suivre je m'engage dans ce fossé et les hommes me suivent à la file indienne. puis nous arrivons à un boyau derrière le moulin de bezone nous utilisons ce boyau et de ce boyau je puis indiquer exactement l'emplacement à occuper par la Cie. Quand j'ai donné toutes mes instructions, nous nous portons en avant à découvert sur un espace d'environ 50 mètres. Les hommes se mettent immédiat

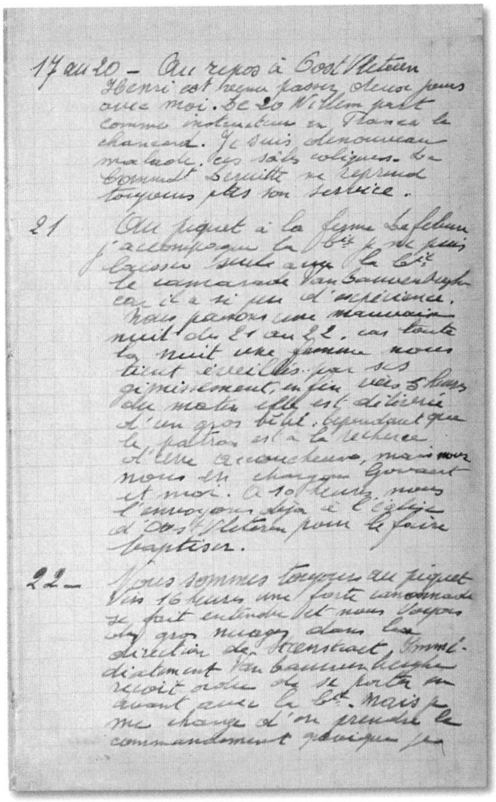
17 au 20 – Au repos à Oost Vleteren Henri est venu passer deux jours avec moi. Le 20 Willem part comme instructeur en France le chanceux. Je suis de nouveau malade, les sales coliques. Le Commdt Devritte(?) ne reprend toujours pas son service.

21 Au piquet à la ferme Lefebvre j'accompagne la Cie je ne puis laisser seule avec la Cie le camarade Van Bauwenhuyghe car il a si peu d'expérience. Nous passons une mauvaise nuit du 21 au 22, car toute la nuit une femme nous tient éveillés par ses gémissements, enfin vers 5 heures du matin elle est délivrée d'un gros bébé. Cependant que le patron est à la recherche d'une accoucheuse, mais nous nous en chargeons Govaert et moi. A 10 heures nous l'envoyons déjà à l'église d'Oost Vleteren pour le faire baptiser.

22 – Nous sommes toujours au piquet. Vers 16 heures une forte canonnade se fait entendre et nous voyons un gros nuage dans la direction de Steenstraat, immédiatement Van Bauwenhuyghe reçoit ordre de se porter en avant avec la Cie. mais je me charge d'en prendre le commandement puisque je

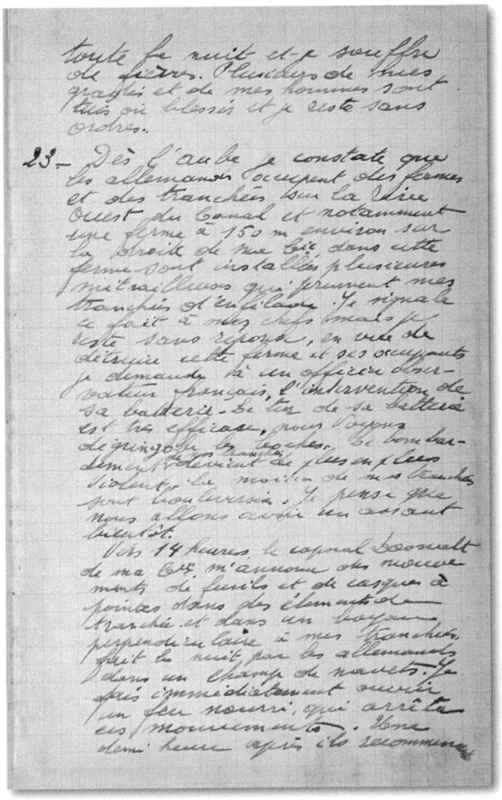
toute la nuit et je souffre de fièvre. Plusieurs de mes gradés et de mes hommes sont tués ou blessés et je reste sans ordres.

23 – Dès l'aube je constate que les allemands occupent des fermes et des tranchées sur la rive Ouest du Canal et notamment une ferme à 150 m environ sur la droite de ma Cie dans cette ferme sont installées plusieurs mitrailleuses qui prennent mes tranchées d'enfilade. Je signale ce fait à mes chefs mais je reste sans réponse, en vue de détruire cette ferme et ses occupants je demande à un officier observateur français, l'intervention de sa batterie. Le tir de sa batterie est très efficace, nous voyons déguerpir les boches. Le bombardement devient de plus en plus violent, la moitié de mes tranchées sont bouleversées. Je pense que nous allons avoir un assaut bientôt.

Vers 14 heures, le caporal Desmalt(?) de ma Cie m'annonce des mouvements de fusils et de casques à pointes dans des éléments de tranchée et dans un boyau perpendiculaire à mes tranchées fait la nuit par les allemands dans un champ de navets. Je fais immédiatement ouvrir un feu nourri, qui arrêta ces mouvements. Une demi heure après ils recommence

LEFT: The first gas attack at Ypres in April 1915 is captured in this account by Lieutenant Toudy of the Belgian Army.

25 SEPTEMBER–13 OCTOBER 1915

AUTUMN 1915 BATTLES

ARTOIS, CHAMPAGNE AND LOOS

Although the summer of 1915 was relatively quiet on the Western Front, there was still plenty of fighting in "minor operations". In the Argonne in late June, a German offensive penetrated 225 m (250 yds) into the lines of XXXII French Corps and took Fontaine-aux-Charmes.

French counter-attacks prevented any further major advance, but by mid-July they had suffered 32,000 casualties. Near Ypres, the Germans used flamethrowers on 30 July to capture Hooge from the British. Actions such as these were in addition to the everyday grind of trench warfare.

Joffre's strategy for the autumn offensive aimed not so much at a clean breakthrough, but at pushing the enemy out of key positions and thus disrupting the continuity of his defences, compelling the Germans into a major retreat. In its final form, Joffre's strategy sought to pinch off the great German salient that had Noyon at its head by attacking from Artois, to the north – Vimy Ridge being a key tactical objective – and from Champagne, to the south. After heated debate, the BEF was committed to a simultaneous supporting attack at Loos, near Lens, despite the opposition of both French and Haig. This was coal-mining country, and the terrain of slag heaps and pit villages would be difficult ground for the British infantry to traverse. Nonetheless, Lord Kitchener, who was still the chief at the War Office, was persuaded that the problems being experienced by the Russians, and the threat of the current French government falling and being replaced by a ministry that would seek peace with Germany, meant that Loos had to go ahead. Haig, whose First Army would carry out the attack, warmed to the concept as he came to believe that the use of poison gas made a victory possible by compensating for lack of artillery. On the other side of No Man's Land, the Germans built additional defences, and waited.

Expectations were high on the day of the great offensive, 25 September 1915. The Allies had a numerical advantage, but the battle demonstrated the extent to which the odds were stacked in the favour of the defender. On some sectors in Champagne the French infantry made some substantial gains. XIV Corps of Pétain's Second Army, attacking across a narrow strip of No Man's Land, punched through the first belt of German defences to a depth of 4 km (2.5 miles). II Colonial Corps in Second Army gained about 3 km (2 miles). At the end of the first day, there was good reason for optimism in the French High Command. On the second day, some more gains were made, although not of the order of those gained on 25 September, and at the inevitable cost in heavy casualties. Thereafter, the battle reverted to attritional slogging.

OPPOSITE: Fatigues and work parties were a never ending part of life on the Western Front. Here French troops fill sandbags behind the lines in Champagne.

BELOW LEFT: British troops advance through a gas cloud on the first day of the Battle of Loos, 25 September 1915.

BELOW RIGHT: A disc grenade, produced to meet the demands of trench warfare. This one contained 65 grams (2.3 oz) of explosive.

THOMPSON ("TOMMY") CAPPER (1863–1915)

General Capper, commander of British 7th Division, died of wounds sustained at the Battle of Loos in September 1915. He joined in the front line fighting on the second day of the battle and was hit by a bullet while organizing an attack, dying at a casualty clearing station on 27 September. Contrary to the myth that generals invariably kept out of harm's way in comfortable chateaux miles behind the lines, Capper was one of eight British generals killed, wounded or taken prisoner during the Loos offensive.

In Artois, too, there was disappointment for the French. D'Urbal's Tenth Army attacked in bad weather, and took some positions on their left, around Arras. But the German positions were very strong, and on the right, south of Arras, the French infantry sustained heavy losses for paltry gains. On 26 September, d'Urbal decided to reinforce success rather than attempt to rescue failure, and attacked on his left. Souchez fell, and on 28 September French troops fought their way on to the crest of Vimy Ridge but were driven back. Fighting continued into October, but the French made no further important gains.

For the BEF's attack at Loos, much depended on the wind's blowing in the right direction to carry chlorine gas over the German trenches. In the early morning of 25 September, Haig had to decide whether or not to order the gas to be released from the 5,000 cylinders that had been installed, and, despite worries about the wind, at 05:15 he gave the order. At 06:30, six British divisions attacked the enemy positions, only for the advancing infantry to find that, on the left and centre, the gas cloud had not delivered the anticipated benefits – indeed, in some places, such as the extreme left, it drifted back on to the attacking troops. For all that, Haig's troops did well. The 9th (Scottish) Division, part of Kitchener's New Army which was raised from volunteers in 1914, seized the powerful Hohenzollern redoubt, while another captured the village of Loos. The German defences were in disarray, and the timely arrival of British reserves could have been devastatingly effective. But the reserves did not reach the battlefield until the following day, when they were decisively repulsed. Loos, like the offensive in Artois and Champagne, ended in disappointment. The outnumbered Germans held off the Allies with relative ease.

"Votre élan sera irrésistible" ("Your élan will be irresistible")

Joffre to his army, September 1915.

OPPOSITE: The grim price of war: French dead after an attack in the Champagne sector.

LEFT: Scots Guardsmen in Big Willie Trench, Loos, October 1915. Three are preparing Mills Bombs (grenades) while others look at the camera.

BELOW: The attack of 46th (North Midland) Division on Hohenzollern Redoubt, 13 October 1915. Note smoke and gas in the centre and left.

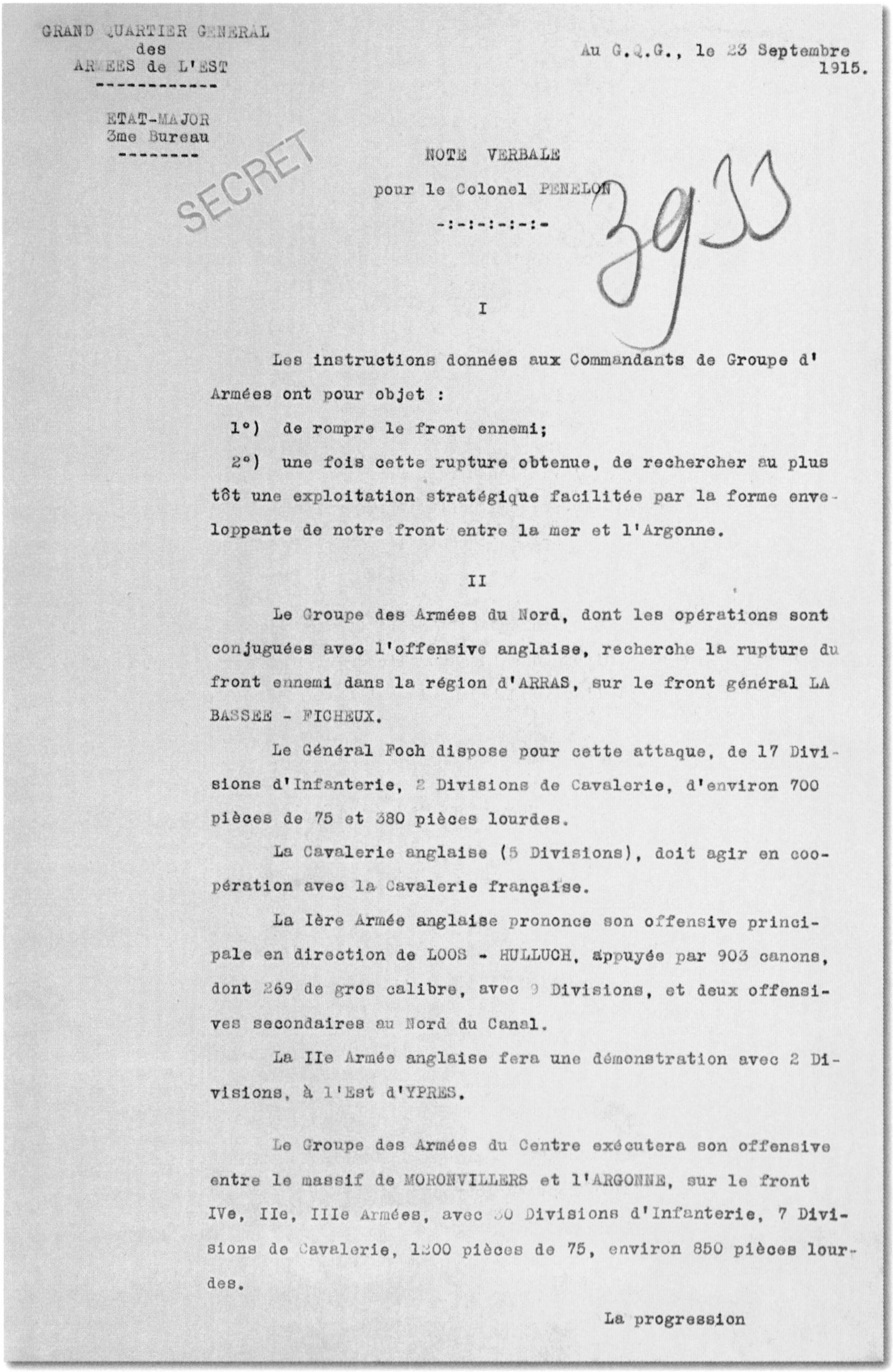

GRAND QUARTIER GENERAL
des
ARMEES de L'EST

ETAT-MAJOR
3me Bureau

Au G.Q.G., le 23 Septembre
1915.

SECRET

NOTE VERBALE

pour le Colonel PENELON

-:-:-:-:-:-

I

Les instructions données aux Commandants de Groupe d'Armées ont pour objet :

1°) de rompre le front ennemi;

2°) une fois cette rupture obtenue, de rechercher au plus tôt une exploitation stratégique facilitée par la forme enveloppante de notre front entre la mer et l'Argonne.

II

Le Groupe des Armées du Nord, dont les opérations sont conjuguées avec l'offensive anglaise, recherche la rupture du front ennemi dans la région d'ARRAS, sur le front général LA BASSEE - FICHEUX.

Le Général Foch dispose pour cette attaque, de 17 Divisions d'Infanterie, 2 Divisions de Cavalerie, d'environ 700 pièces de 75 et 380 pièces lourdes.

La Cavalerie anglaise (5 Divisions), doit agir en coopération avec la Cavalerie française.

La Ière Armée anglaise prononce son offensive principale en direction de LOOS - HULLUCH, appuyée par 903 canons, dont 269 de gros calibre, avec 9 Divisions, et deux offensives secondaires au Nord du Canal.

La IIe Armée anglaise fera une démonstration avec 2 Divisions, à l'Est d'YPRES.

Le Groupe des Armées du Centre exécutera son offensive entre le massif de MORONVILLERS et l'ARGONNE, sur le front IVe, IIe, IIIe Armées, avec 30 Divisions d'Infanterie, 7 Divisions de Cavalerie, 1200 pièces de 75, environ 850 pièces lourdes.

La progression

RIGHT: Plans issued by Joffre's headquarters on 23 September 1915 for the major offensive two days later.

La progression ultérieure de ces Armées sera facilitée par une attaque de la Ve Armée, entre le massif de CRAONNE et la Vallée de l'AISNE, que le Général Commandant le Groupe d'Armées du Centre déclenchera quand il le jugera utile (après l'entrée en action des IVe et IIe Armées).
Forces de la Ve Armée consacrées à cette action : 6 Divisions d'Infanterie, environ 250 canons de 75 et autant de pièces lourdes.

L'aviation a reçu pour instruction de détruire les points les plus importants des voies ferrées utilisables pour les transports des renforts ennemis vers les zones intéressantes, au moyen des escadrilles de bombardement.

Le Groupe de l'Est se tiendra prêt à participer à l'offensive générale quand l'ordre lui en sera donné, en déclenchant l'action d'ensemble qu'il a préparée en WOEVRE.

III

Si les Armées du Nord et du Centre obtiennent la rupture du front ennemi, leur mission sera de pousser l'ennemi droit devant elles et sans arrêt, en direction de l'Est et du Nord, en visant ses communications.

Toute recherche de mouvement latéral ferait le jeu de l'ennemi, en lui laissant le temps d'occuper avec ses réserves les lignes successives qu'il aura préparées.

Le Groupement Ière Armée britannique - Xe Armée visera le front Le QUESNOY - FRASNES-les-BUISSENAL.

Les Armées du Général de Castelnau, le front LE NOUVION-SEDAN.

Les autres Armées Britanniques et la VIe Armée Française participeront au mouvement en avant suivant les circonstances.

La mission de la Cavalerie sera : L a mission ....

1°) D'effectuer une poursuite acharnée sur le plus grand front possible;

2°) De lancer des détachements chargés de procéder à des destructions sur les communications de l'adversaire pour troubler les mouvements de ses réserves et ses ravitaillements.

19 DECEMBER 1915

BRITISH COMMAND

DOUGLAS HAIG TAKES OVER

Sir John French's reputation had been in decline through 1915, and the failure at Loos was the final blow. The last stage, the attack of 13 October, had produced, in the words of the official historian "nothing but the useless slaughter of infantry". French's misuse of the reserves – two New Army Divisions –which were held back well behind the lines on 25 September under his personal control, was seen as a major mistake.

French publicly blamed Haig, a charge that Haig indignantly rebutted. In truth, Haig aimed for a decisive breakthrough while French anticipated a more methodical battle, in which there would be plenty of time to deploy the reserves when needed. The tension between these two concepts was never resolved.

French's clumsy attempt to pass the buck was followed by his replacement by Haig, who became Commander-in-Chief of the BEF on 19 December 1915. A few days later General Sir William Robertson became the Chief of the Imperial General Staff (CIGS), the professional head of the British Army. He was elevated as a means of marginalizing Kitchener's influence as Secretary of State for War, and in tough negotiations Robertson insisted on receiving enhanced powers before he would take the job. Both "Wully" Robertson and Haig were "Westerners" – men who believed in the primacy of the Western Front. They formed a powerful team that in 1916 came into conflict with David Lloyd George, the Liberal politician who succeeded to the War Office after the death of Lord Kitchener in June 1916.

This clash grew more serious when Lloyd George succeeded Asquith as Prime Minister in December 1916. Lloyd George, although a proponent of total war, shrank from Haig's insistence on fighting attritional battles in the West, and at various times tried to clip Haig's wings by attempting to transfer the main effort away from the Western Front; placing him under a French general; and withholding troops from the BEF. Haig and Robertson became more distant in the course of 1917. Robertson had wider strategic vision than Haig, and his job required him to oversee the global British war effort, not just the Western Front. Haig unfairly blamed the CIGS for dispersing troops away from the West, and refused to stand by him when Lloyd George sacked Robertson early in 1918. The Prime Minister's relations with Robertson's replacement, Sir Henry Wilson, deteriorated over time as they too clashed over civil-military issues.

Lloyd George would have liked to sack Haig, but the latter enjoyed support from the Press and the Conservative members of the Coalition government. After the disappointment of the battle of Cambrai in late 1917 (see pages 54–55), and the near disaster of the German Spring Offensive of 1918 (see pages 56–59), Haig lost support and his position became weaker. Curiously, Lloyd George still refused to move against him. In the 1930s, after Haig was dead, Lloyd George in his War Memoirs inflicted lasting damage on the Commander-in-Chief's reputation.

Today, there is a popular perception that First World War generals presided over a series of failed battles in which the same outdated tactics were tried over and again. In reality, soldiers at all levels of the British, French and German Armies responded to the unexpected stalemate by experimentation and innovation, whether it was methods of improvising hand grenades from jam tins, developing techniques of trench raiding or ordering, deploying and working out the tactics for sophisticated new weapons. Haig is often accused of being a military Luddite. Nothing could be further from the truth. He was very keen on technology, being an enthusiastic supporter of tanks and the Royal Flying Corps. If anything, the problem was that Haig expected too much of primitive technology; witness his belief that poison gas could help overcome the major disadvantages faced by the BEF at Loos.

> **"I had only one idea,... to do my utmost to win the war"**
>
> **Douglas Haig in his diary, 14 December 1915**

Underpinning the narrative of the battles on the Western Front was a struggle by the armies to out-think the enemy by using new technology and tactics. In the process, the warfare of 1914 – which essentially looked back to Napoleonic warfare – was transformed into something recognizably modern. The BEF was some way down this track by the time Haig took over.

The great battles of 1916 and 1917 were to result, by 1918, in an all-arms team that included tanks, infantry, artillery, airpower, machine guns and chemical weapons, bound together by modern – if primitive – wireless communications and supported by effective logistics. By then, the Allies had moved decisively ahead of the Germans in the sophistication of their fighting. An updated version of this form of warfare remains in use to the present day.

OPPOSITE: General (later Field Marshal) Sir Douglas Haig, with a Guard of Honour for an Allied general, St Omer, March 1916.

LEFT: Early volunteers for Kitchener's Army, 1914, still in civilian clothes. This unit was the Grimsby Chums (10th Lincolns).

21 FEBRUARY–25 FEBRUARY 1915

THE BATTLE OF VERDUN

OPERATION GERICHT

Even by the standards of the First World War, Verdun has an evil reputation as a battle of pure attrition. In his December 1915 "Christmas Memorandum", Falkenhayn identified Britain as Germany's most dangerous enemy.

At that stage the German High Command had little regard for the British Army, and Falkenhayn saw the French Army as "England's best sword" without which Britain would be neutralized. The final plan – Operation Gericht, or "Law Court" – pitted the German forces against Verdun, a fortress-city which represented the strength and spirit of France, a place with enormous symbolic as well as strategic importance. Historians still argue about Falkenhayn's true aims, but it is probable that, believing a clean breakthrough was impossible, he intended to grind the French down in a series of attritional battles that would force France to come to terms. Historian Jehuda Wallach described this calculated use of attrition as "the degeneration of the art of war". It certainly involved the application of total, ruthless methods to achieve a limited aim – to force France to come to a separate peace and thus destroy the cohesion of the Allied coalition.

The city of Verdun had for many years been an important frontier position which had been fortified by the great engineer and siege-master Sébastien Le Prestre, Seigneur de Vauban in the seventeenth century. After the Franco-Prussian War, Verdun became a key part of the French defences against Germany, blocking the way to the Champagne region and, ultimately, Paris. In 1916, the main fortifications of Verdun consisted of a belt of forts some miles from the city. The French population may have believed that Verdun was a mighty fortress, but the truth was different. Much of its artillery had been removed and sent elsewhere on the Western Front to feed the insatiable demands of the field armies for guns, and the infantry garrison was thinly spread.

Falkenhayn entrusted the attack to Fifth Army, commanded by the Kaiser's eldest son, Crown Prince Wilhelm, with General von Knobelsdorf, as his chief-of-staff and the army's military brain. The offensive began on 21 February 1916. At 07:15, a nine-hour artillery bombardment was heralded by a shell from a heavy naval gun that overshot its target and landed near the Bishop's Palace in Verdun. The guns were able to rain shells onto the Verdun salient from three sides, creating the heaviest bombardment of the war so far, and the defenders suffered terribly. At 17:00, the German infantry began to push forward cautiously, probing for weak spots in the French positions. The plan was for the main infantry attack to begin on the following day, when it was hoped that the French defences would be thoroughly weakened. In the event, the Germans were overly wary, and a major assault might have paid off. General von Zwehl's VII Reserve Corps, which had ignored the instructions for caution and

OPPOSITE: French infantry undergo a German bombardment. Artillery fire turned battlefields such as Verdun into cratered moonscapes.

BELOW LEFT: Colonel Emile Driant in the Bois des Caures. His doomed defence of the position is one of the tragic stories of the battle.

CROWN PRINCE WILHELM (1882–1951)

The eldest son of the Kaiser, Wilhelm held two important commands on the Western Front. As commander of Fifth Army, he was a central figure in the Verdun campaign. From September 1916, he led Army Group Crown Prince. His greatest success was the Aisne offensive of May 1918. Wilhelm showed a surprising streak of realism in his make up, recognizing the futility of Falkenhayn's Verdun strategy. He went into exile at the end of the war, but returned to Germany in 1923.

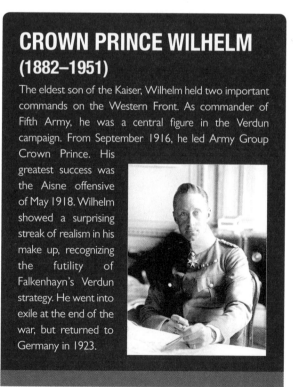

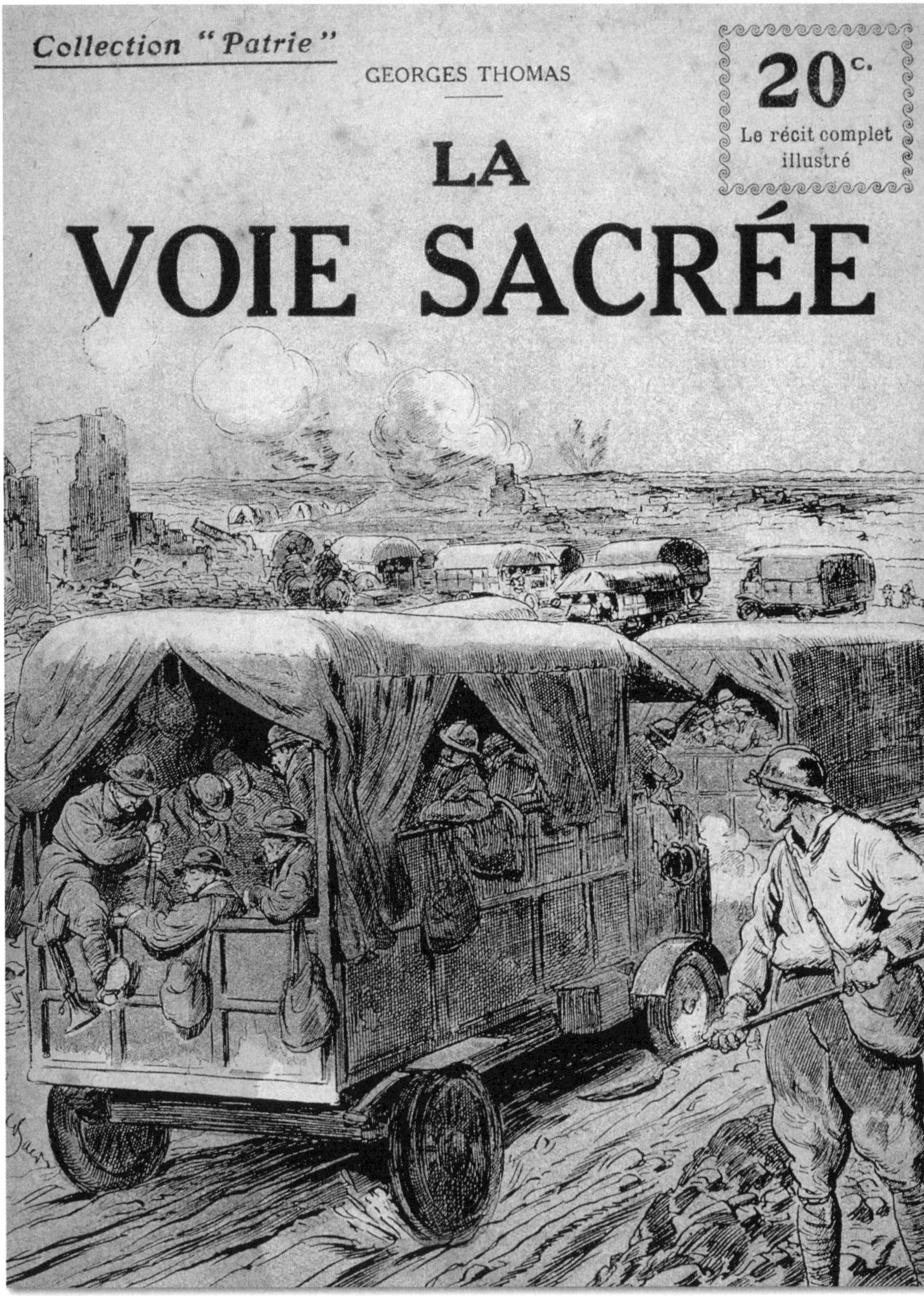
Collection "Patrie"
GEORGES THOMAS
20c.
Le récit complet illustré
LA
VOIE SACRÉE

THE LÉGION D'HONNEUR

The Légion d'honneur is a decoration dating back to Napoleon I. Over 50,000 were awarded during the First World War.

Major Sylvain-Eugene Raynal was awarded the Légion d'Honneur after he volunteered to defend Fort Vaux although he realized it meant almost certain death.

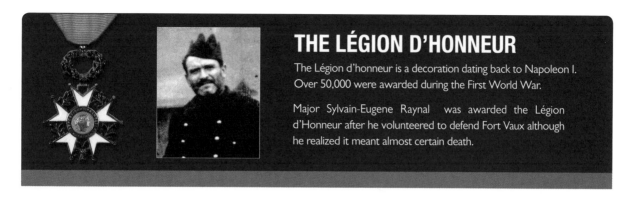

attacked in greater strength than the other two corps, captured the Bois d'Haumont and thus made a significant dent in the French lines.

As it was, the French put up strong resistance. In the Bois des Caures, Colonel Emile Driant's Chasseurs (light infantry) – who were virtually destroyed in the first days of the battle – succeeded in holding up the attacks of German XVIII Corps. Ironically, Driant, a member of the French Chamber of Deputies, had previously raised the issue of the weakness of Verdun's defences, much to Joffre's fury. He was killed on 22 February.

> **"The forces of France will bleed to death"**
>
> **Falkenhayn, December 1915**

By the following day, the French were reaching crisis point. Divisions were simply crumbling under the German pressure, having taken huge losses, and the French second position was falling into enemy hands. General Langle de Cary, Central Army Group commander, decided to abandon the right bank of the Meuse. While this was a sensible military decision, he was overruled by Noel de Castelnau, Joffre's chief-of-staff, acting on his superior's behalf, who saw the potentially disastrous political impact of such a retreat. Instead, Pétain was placed in command of Second Army and began his dogged defence of Verdun.

Recognizing the central place of artillery on the modern battlefield, Pétain brought up additional guns and located them west of the Meuse to help counter the weight of German firepower. He also paid careful attention to logistics. The Verdun sector was supplied by a narrow gauge railway and by the minor road to Bar-le-Duc, the Voie Sacrée, (the "Sacred Way"). Pétain, offered solid, unflashy leadership, understood the poilu (the ordinary French soldier), who in return trusted him. His appointment was a turning point in the battle.

BELOW: The German stick grenade was known to the British as the "potato masher" because of its shape.

LEFT: A French military band marching along La Voie Sacrée, the road that ran from Bar-le-Duc to Verdun.

OPPOSITE: The cover of a wartime book showing troops going to the front along the "Sacred Way". A pioneer is repairing the road.

20 MAY–2 NOVEMBER 1916

THE BATTLE OF VERDUN

THEY SHALL NOT PASS

The fact that the Germans never made a serious attempt to cut the Voie Sacrée, added to the limited numbers of troops committed to the battle and that the Germans attacked only on the right bank of the Meuse, provides strong circumstantial evidence that Falkenhayn had indeed always intended to fight an attritional battle rather than to capture Verdun.

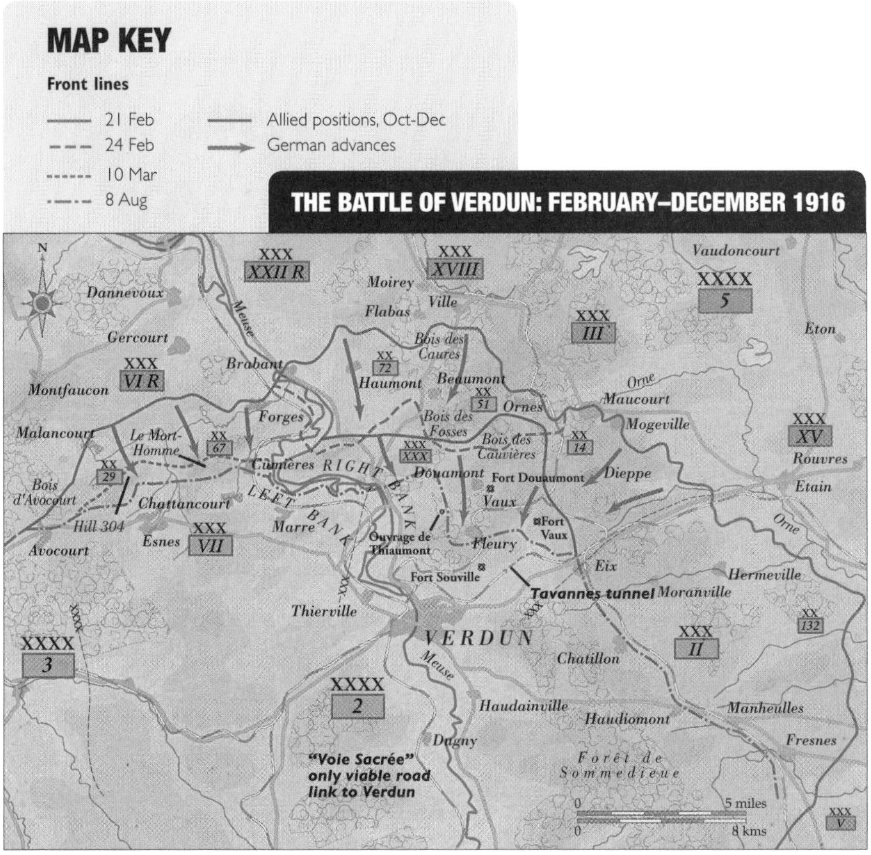

OPPOSITE: Crown Prince Wilhelm speaks to a stretcher-bearer at Verdun. To the British, "Little Willie" was a figure of fun.

If the Germans had put the supply route out of use, the effect on the French Army would have been catastrophic. At the height of the battle, 50,000 tons of supplies and 90,000 troops travelled to Verdun every week along the Voie Sacrée, while trucks took wounded and troops heading out of the line in the opposite direction. This was dubbed the "noria" system, after the word for a bucket water-wheel.

On the day Pétain arrived to take command, the Germans seized one of the key fortifications, Fort Douaumont. Its capture was largely because of a bizarre accident whereby the fort had been left almost defenceless. The Germans seemed on the verge of victory, but Pétain's arrival and massed French artillery fire helped to retard the German advance. Now attention switched to Le Mort Homme ("the Dead Man"), a French-held hill on the left bank of the Meuse from which guns wreaked havoc among the Germans.

By attacking at Verdun, Falkenhayn disrupted Anglo-French preparations for their offensive on the Somme and forced the Allies to dance to his tune. Yet Falkenhayn in turn was about to lose his tenuous grip on events. He sanctioned an attack on the left bank of the Meuse, which not only expanded the geographical scope of the battle, but undermined the whole concept of a limited battle as it played into the hands of Falkenhayn's critics, who sought an outright victory. The fresh attack

CONSTANTIN SCHMIDT VON KNOBELSDORF (1860–1936)

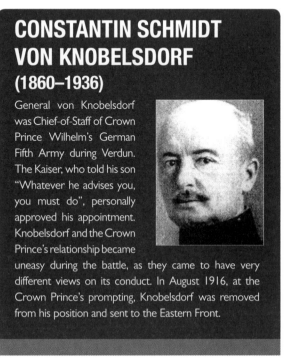

General von Knobelsdorf was Chief-of-Staff of Crown Prince Wilhelm's German Fifth Army during Verdun. The Kaiser, who told his son "Whatever he advises you, you must do", personally approved his appointment. Knobelsdorf and the Crown Prince's relationship became uneasy during the battle, as they came to have very different views on its conduct. In August 1916, at the Crown Prince's prompting, Knobelsdorf was removed from his position and sent to the Eastern Front.

ABOVE LEFT: Bodies in a trench at Le Mort Homme, April 1916. The Germans saw the capture of this position as an essential step.

ABOVE RIGHT: One of the most famous French posters of the War, advertising a war loan, featuring an enthusiastic poilu repeating Pétain's famous slogan: "we'll get 'em!".

brought the Germans some territorial gains, but the defenders clung tenaciously to the Mort Homme. A new phase of the battle began on 9 April when the Germans attacked simultaneously on both banks of the Meuse, but the battle remained, in the Crown Prince's words, a "stubborn to-and-fro contest for every foot of ground". By the end of April, he had came to believe that "a decisive success at Verdun could only be assured at the price of heavy casualties, out of all proportion to the desired gains". Von Knobelsdorf disagreed, and for the moment the Germans continued their attacks. The Mort Homme and the neighbouring Hill 304 fell at last in May, after a huge and concentrated bombardment.

Pétain was promoted to command Central Army Group, and was replaced at Verdun by Robert Nivelle, whose aggressive subordinate Charles Mangin attempted, unsuccessfully, to retake Douaumont in late May. A fresh German push, Operation "May Cup", opened on the right bank on 1 June. Fort Vaux was captured after an epic, seven-day long defence led by Major Raynal, who was forced to surrender as his men were running out of water. The Ouvrage de Thiaumont, one of the last fortifications blocking the way to Verdun city, was captured by the Germans on 8 June. It was promptly retaken, and then captured and retaken another 15 times in the course of the battle. The Germans now went all out to take Fort Souville, 4 km (2.5 miles) from Verdun. On 23 June, after saturating the defenders with new phosgene gas, the German attack broke against the fort, which remained tantalizingly

FORT VAUX

Vaux was one of the smaller forts in the Verdun complex, but its week-long defence became one of the most famous episodes in the whole battle. The garrison commander, Major Sylvain-Eugene Raynal, was taken prisoner and brought to the Crown Prince. As a mark of respect, when Wilhelm saw that Raynal was without his sword, he presented him with another. A carrier pigeon that Raynal sent out from Fort Vaux delivered its message, but then died of gas poisoning. It was decorated for bravery.

just beyond their reach. One last effort, on 11 July, also failed and the Germans went on to the defensive.

By then, the Allies had regained the strategic offensive. The Russian Brusilov offensive, launched on 4 June, forced Falkenhayn to detach divisions to the Eastern Front, and on 1 July the British and French attacked on the Somme, beginning the offensive that Joffre had been demanding for months. The pressure on the French at Verdun eased, but the fighting continued. The failure at Verdun contributed to Falkenhayn's replacement by Hindenburg and Ludendorff at the end of August, and von Knobelsdorf was posted to the Eastern Front. Nivelle, employing massed guns and sophisticated artillery tactics to fight limited battles, retook the Ouvrage de Thiaumont and Douaumont in late October. Fort Vaux fell on 2 November and in one last spasm of action, bemoaned by the Crown Prince as "this black day", on 15 December the French advanced 3 km (2 miles) past Douaumont. The battle was over. It had cost 377,000 French and 337,000 German casualties.

RIGHT: The Verdun Medal. An unofficial Verdun Medal issued to combatants by the city itself. It could not be worn on military uniform.

BELOW: The cheerful crew of a French 105mm gun pause to have their photograph taken, Verdun area, 1916. Their ragged appearance gives a realistic impression of campaign dress, which was often far removed from official uniforms.

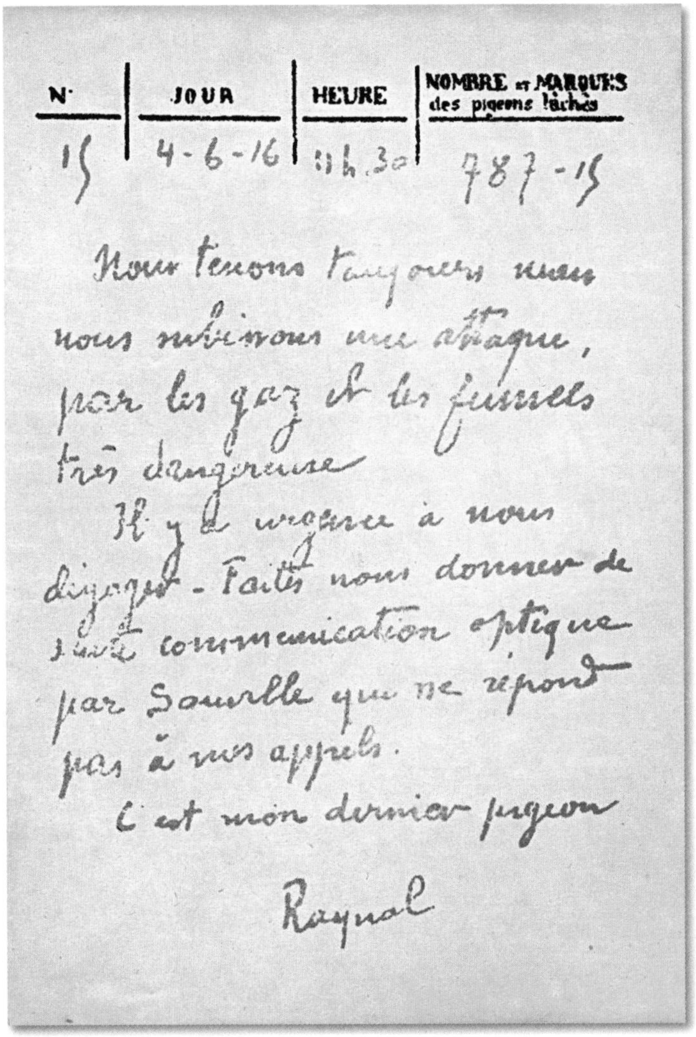

N°	JOUR	HEURE	NOMBRE et MARQUES des pigeons lâchés
15	4-6-16	11h.30	787-15

Nous tenons toujours mais nous subissons une attaque, par les gaz et les fumées très dangereuse

Il y a urgence à nous dégager - Faites nous donner de suite communication optique par Souville qui ne répond pas à nos appels.

C'est mon dernier pigeon

Raynal

ABOVE: Major Reynal's last message, which was sent by carrier pigeon from Fort Vaux on 4 June 1916.

RIGHT: Pétain's order of the day of 10 April 1916, which contains the phrase which passed into history – "*On les aura*" – "we'll get 'em"!

II° ARMEE

Etat-Major

3° Bureau

Au Q.G.A., le 10 Avril 1916.

O R D R E

-:-:-:-

Le 9 Avril est une journée glorieuse pour nos armes. Les assauts furieux des soldats du Kronprinz ont été partout brisés. Fantassins, artilleurs, sapeurs, aviateurs de la II° Armée ont rivalisé d'héroïsme. Honneur à tous !

Les Allemands attaqueront sans doute encore. Que chacun travaille et veille pour obtenir le même succès qu'hier.

Courage. On les aura.

Pétain

EMPIRES AT WAR

FIGHTING FOR "HOME"

Both Britain and France were great imperial powers in 1914, able to draw on the vast human resources of their empires. In August 1914, George V declared war on behalf of the whole British Empire.

The Australian statesman Andrew Fisher promptly pledged to support Britain "to the last man and last shilling", and this reflected a general mood in Australia, New Zealand and Anglophone South Africa and Canada. Imperial ties were still strong, there was much loyalty to the monarch and many still considered Britain as "home". A large number of the men who enlisted had been born in Britain, or were the sons of British migrants. In South Africa, where many Afrikaners had fought against the British only 12 years before, some of them revolted, and others were reluctant to support Britain. Other Afrikaners did rally to the Empire. Jan Christian Smuts, who had fought against the British in the South African War, became a leading member of the War Cabinet. The French-Canadian community were also notably less enthusiastic about fighting for Britain than English-speaking Canadians.

The Australians and New Zealanders earned reputations as good fighting troops in 1915 at Gallipoli. They arrived in France in early 1916, where over the next two years the Anzacs won the respect of friends and enemies alike. The five-division Australian Corps was created in November 1917, and along with the New Zealand Division under General Sir Andrew Russell, played key roles in the Allied victories. The Canadians followed a similar path, first fighting at Second Ypres in April 1915. The four-division Canadian Corps was formed in 1916 and acted as a spearhead formation during 1918. Indian troops (all volunteers) fought in France in 1914–15 as part of the Indian Corps, which included British troops; they were a timely reinforcement to the BEF. Subsequently, the Indian infantry were sent to the Middle East, with the cavalry remaining in France. In all, about 210,000 Canadians, 180,000 Australians, 47,000 New Zealanders and 25,000 Indians were killed or wounded on the Western Front.

Not all the men from the Empire that went to France were fighting soldiers. Chinese from Weiheiwei and Black and Coloured South African labourers did valuable and sometimes dangerous work behind the lines.

One of the strategic problems France faced before the war was that it had a smaller population than its rival Germany: 35 million to 65 million. In a war of mass armies, this put the French at an obvious disadvantage. In La Force Noire, the then Colonel Charles Mangin advocated drawing upon the population of France's sub-Saharan colonies to boost its armies. This controversial suggestion earned him notoriety long before the Nivelle offensive (see pages 42–43). In the event, France did make extensive use of colonial manpower on the Western Front, in Italy, Salonika and at Gallipoli, as well as in colonial campaigns in North Africa. A small such force also fought with the British in Palestine and Syria. A total of 150,000 soldiers from Algeria, 39,000 from Tunisia and 14,000 Moroccans served in the European theatre, in addition to 135,000 Black Africans, 34,000 from Madagascar and 143,000 from Indochina.

Under French law, conscripts from mainland France could normally not serve outside its borders. Control of the Empire was therefore the responsibility of two forces: the Armée d'Afrique and La Coloniale. Both provided units to reinforce the Western Front. They included troops of European origin, such as the élite Coloniale Blanche and the white Chasseurs d'Afrique (African Light Cavalry) and Zouaves (white troops who wore North African-style uniforms). In a class of its own was the Foreign Legion. One of its members was a British colonel, disgraced in 1914 for attempting prematurely to surrender his battalion on the retreat from Mons. He joined the Legion, fought bravely, and was eventually reinstated in the British Army. Black and North African units were often used as storm troops.

The French made far more use of its colonial troops in Europe than the British did of the Indian Army. Indeed, without their help, it is difficult to see the French home army could have coped with the stresses of war. I Colonial Division, fighting alongside the British on the Somme in 1916, made a favourable impression on their allies, as did the Moroccans operating on the flank of 2nd US Division during Second Marne. Probably most impressed of all were the Germans who had to face them across No Man's Land – they paid them a backhanded compliment by being reluctant to take Black and Arab troops prisoner.

OPPOSITE: Zulus of the South African Native Labour Corps prepare to perform a war dance in June 1917. South Africa also provided white combat troops for Western Front service.

LEFT: A dressing station in Tikrit, Mesopotamia in 1917. A Royal Army Medical Corps officer, helped by Indian medical orderlies, tends wounded Turks.

1 JULY–4 SEPTEMBER 1916

THE BATTLE OF THE SOMME

THE BIG PUSH

The Battle of the Somme was a product of coalition warfare, an offensive fought in the sector where the boundary between the British and French forces lay. Haig's aims at the beginning of the battle were mixed. While he hoped to break through the German lines and reopen mobile warfare, he recognized that an attritional, "wearing-out battle" might be all his army could achieve.

By the end of 1 July 1916 – the first day of the Battle of the Somme – 57,470 men of the BEF had become casualties; 19,240 were killed. In the northern part of the battlefront, the British had taken very little ground. However, in their part of the battlefield the French army had taken comparatively light casualties in making significant gains. Alongside them, the British forces in the south had also done well, taking all of their objectives, albeit at a high cost in lives. What had gone wrong in the north?

For the seven days before 1 July, Allied guns had pounded the German positions. In retrospect, the British guns were given too many targets. Massed on a short length of front, artillery could be very effective. Spread out along many miles and given multiple targets, the effect was dissipated. This mistake reflected a further problem in the British plan. Haig sought a breakthrough battle, while Rawlinson, Fourth Army commander and Haig's principal lieutenant on 1 July, wanted to fight a limited bite-and-hold affair. The eventual compromise was neither one thing nor another. To be added to this was the inexperience of the British soldiers – mainly wartime volunteers – and the fact that British war industries were still developing. In both respects, the French were ahead. While the British had only one heavy gun for every 52 m (57 yds) of trench, the French had one to every 18 m (20 yds).

North of the Albert-Bapaume road, there was a depressingly familiar story of troops suffering high casualties for little gain. 1st Newfoundland Regiment suffered losses of nearly 700 men at Beaumont-Hamel. In Sausage Valley, the 103rd (Tyneside Irish) Brigade was reduced to a mere 50 men. There were some exceptions. Near Thiepval, 36th (Ulster) Division advanced deep into German lines, only to be driven back. South of the road, the British did much better. The German positions were weaker, and the

> **"Without our superiority in guns where would we be?"**
>
> **Captain JC Dunn DSO MC and Bar DCM**
> **Medical Officer with the 2nd Royal Welch Fusiliers**

RIGHT: A British officer's whistle. At 7.30 am on 1 July, the blowing of whistles signalled the beginning of the infantry assault on the Somme.

ABOVE RIGHT: The badge of the Newfoundland Regiment, featuring the caribou. This unit became the "Royal Newfoundland Regiment" in 1917.

OPPOSITE: A sentry and sleeping soldiers in a front line trench at Ovilliers. These men are from 11th Cheshires, 25th Division.

HENRY SEYMOUR RAWLINSON
(1864–1925)

General Rawlinson bore the primary operational responsibility for the first day on the Somme. An Eton-educated infantry officer, son of a noted Assyriologist, he saw service in the South African War (1899–1902). He was a reforming Commandant of the Staff College, Camberley and in the First World War he commanded consecutively IV Corps, First Army (temporarily) and the Fourth Army. His finest hour came as commander of Fourth Army in the Allied Advance to Victory in 1918. He died in 1925, when Commander-in-Chief, India.

British benefited from the proximity of their Allies. On XIII Corps front, the German defences crumbled and, arguably, Rawlinson might have exploited this success to produce a victory of sorts out of defeat. For all that, on 1 July 1916 the BEF landed a heavy blow on the German army, which suffered greatly from British artillery fire and was dangerously stretched.

Fayolle's French Sixth Army did very well on 1 July, capturing all of their objectives and taking 4,000 prisoners. I Colonial Corps and XXXV Corps, positioned south of the Somme, deployed 84 heavy batteries; the Germans had only eight. Not surprisingly, Fayolle was frustrated by the inability of the British to push on. The French success on 1 July 1916 poses a fascinating allohistorical: what if, as originally planned, the French Army had taken the lead in the campaign, with the inexperienced BEF able to learn the ropes under relatively favourable conditions?

After 1 July, Haig switched the British main effort to the south of the main road, while the French continued to fight on the southern flank. Rawlinson launched a well-conducted limited attack on 14 July on Bazentin Ridge which briefly opened the possibility of a major advance. Otherwise, in the British sector, the months of July and August were marked by bloody and laborious struggles to wrest ground from determined defenders in places like Delville Wood, High Wood and Pozières, the latter being captured by the Australians on 23 July. The Germans, clinging to a doctrine of refusing to countenance the abandonment of territory, counter-attacked vigorously. Under increasing pressure on the Somme, by the end of July the Germans had been forced to go onto the defensive at Verdun.

Co-ordination between the BEF and the French Army was difficult, and often they appeared to be fighting parallel battles rather than making a combined effort. The French continued to push ahead, nearing Péronne on 2 July. A few days later, Joffre contemplated moving cavalry forward. But lacking sufficient reserves, and with the British failing to keep up and the German defenders recovering their balance, the chances of the French army breaking though diminished. The French continued to advance; for instance on 3 September Sixth Army captured 2,000 prisoners. Joffre pressured Haig to conduct another major offensive on a wide front, believing that the numerous small efforts being made by the BEF were inefficient and costly. By mid-September, the British were ready, and Haig made his second attempt at a break-through on the Somme.

BELOW: British infantry move up through wire, August 1916. By this stage the British were slowly gaining ground but at heavy cost.

ABOVE: The Somme typified the "war of the guns". Here British 8 inch howitzers of 39th Siege Battery Royal Garrison Artillery are in action in August 1916.

BELOW: This German Maxim 1908 model machine gun is mounted on a tripod. Although manufactured in 1918, similar weapons were used on the Somme two years earlier.

BELOW: German dead in a shell hole, the victims of British XVIII Corps' successful attack at the beginning of the Somme Offensive.

MARIE ÉMILE FAYOLLE (1858–1928)

At the beginning of the war, General Fayolle was in retirement, but was recalled to command an infantry division. A gunner by background, he earned Joffre's admiration and rose rapidly as less competent or fortunate commanders were sacked. He commanded French Sixth Army on the Somme in 1916, and in 1917 went on to command an army group. He played a key role in the battles of 1918. Fayolle was created a Marshal of France in 1921.

No 1 Red Cross Hospital
APO. S11
BEF
July 16 France

Dear Coz.

Your delightful letter helped to chase away for quite a time some of the MOTONY that rules life here. I'm afraid I cannot promise to give a very good description of the battle and one's feelings in it partly because the whole thing was so abnormal & partly because prolonged sojourn in bed seems to dull the mind. It was the night of my birthday that we marched from the wood where we had been bivouacking for a day or so before. The boys had had a concert in the evening in the wood. The usual mixture of Lancashire humour & sentimentality 'Tis our brave young hero the gallant General wild ' etc

One loved them all more than ever. Then the rum ration was served & off we marched.

It was a strange march rather trying. One kept wondering what TOMORROW wd bring. We got to the trenches just

2

after daybreak. Whilst filing along the main communication trench we had to pass a gloomy sight 2 or 3 poor figures mutilated by a shell.

Death takes no form more terrible to look upon than when a shell has burst right in a trench – it generally means mutilation.

But we got to our own station where we simply had to wait until Z hour shd arrive (like a Cambridge Boat race)

The day was going to be one of the sunniest that summer brings: the fields even up to edges of the trenches were wonderfully beautiful & rich with flowers. The larks were singing like mad – the louder the bombardment. Our guns had been going all week but about 6.30 they burst out into their loudest & most concentrated ROAR. I soon got the message that 7.30 was the hour.

Strangely enough my spirits were beginning to rise more & more. I felt jovial but nervous & an absorbing

3

excitement made me almost long for Z hour to be & over the top – one of a victorious sweeping army. We My company were not in the first line but had to follow the first battalions dividing into small bodies to sweep up & consolidate the first 3 lines of Boche trenches – not so difficult or dangerous a job as some.

Everything had been worked out mathematically before hand. Zero came & 3 mins after I swarmed the trench ladder followed by a party whom I conducted to their place of entry in the Boche lines.

On the left the ~~Borders~~ Gordons were going over as on parade.

Occasionally a shell wd burst & some poor fellow wd be torn asunder – men dropped out just as you read in books or see in pictures: in the midst of the great tumult there was a strange silence somehow.

4

The excitement of battle was still on me then – I wanted to push on & on.

The Boche lines were smashed to smithereens by our artillery. Then afraid I rather let go the idea of sweeping up the prisoners etc remains just then – one wanted to get on. Some of my poor chaps got hit – one close to me to whom I had just said 'You come along by me. I'm very lucky.' Another's brains were blown out less than a yard off & at the same time a slight sting in my back told me a bullet had just grazed my tunic.

Eventually we got to our destination where were the points we had to consolidate – but unfortunately there didn't seem to be many men left to do much digging. However one got something going. Soon after that a shell dropped in a trench &

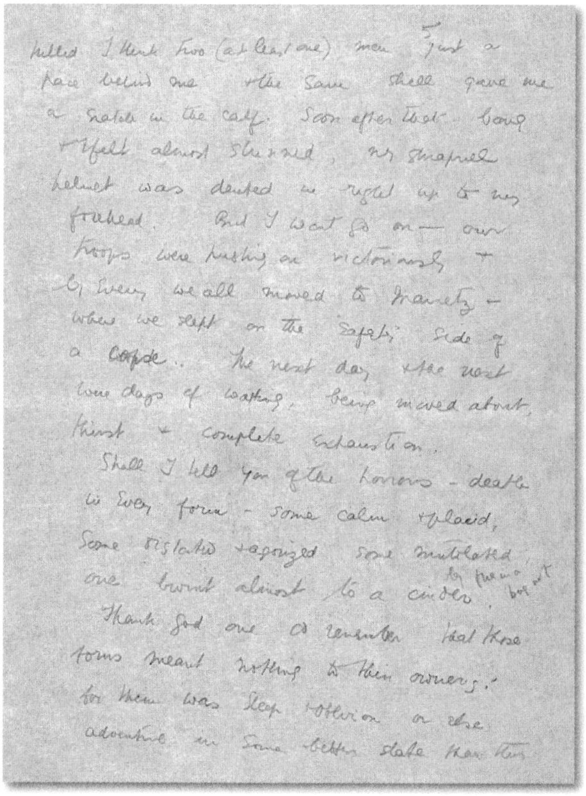

killed I think two (at least one) men 5 just a pace behind me & the same shell gave me a scratch in the calf. Soon after that bang & I felt almost stunned, my shrapnel helmet was dented in right up to my forehead. But I went on — our troops were pushing on victoriously & by evening we all moved to Mametz — where we slept on the 'safety' side of a copse. The next day & the next were days of waiting, being moved about, thirst & complete exhaustion.

Shall I tell you of the horrors — death in every form — some calm & placid, some distorted & agonized some mutilated, one burnt almost to a cinder by flame bayonet. Thank God one could remember that those forms meant nothing to their owners; for them was sleep & oblivion or else adventure in some better state than this

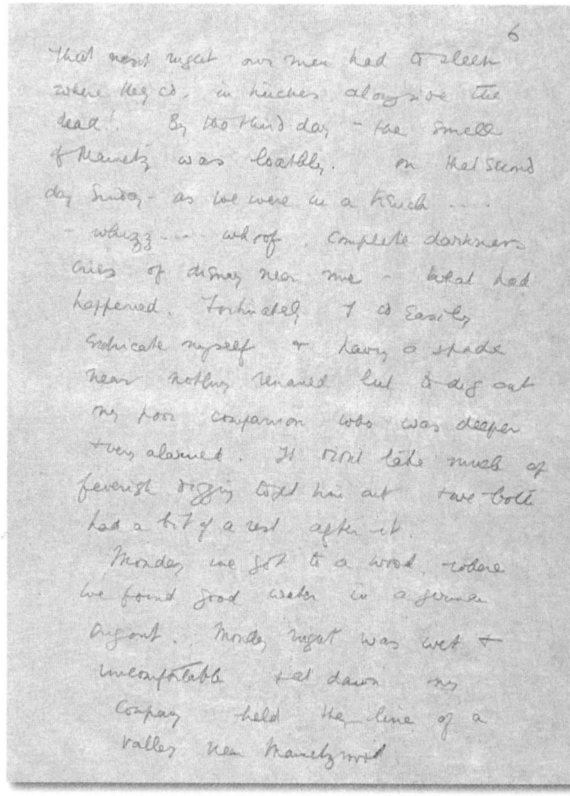

6

That next night our men had to sleep where they could, in trenches alongside the dead! By the third day — the smell of Mametz was loathly. On that second day Sunday — as we were in a trench .... — whizz — whoof. Complete darkness cries of dismay near me — what had happened. Fortunately I could easily extricate myself & having a spade near nothing remained but to dig out my poor companion who was deeper & very alarmed. It didn't take much of feverish digging to get him out & we both had a bit of a rest after it.

Monday we got to a wood where we found good water in a German dugout. Monday night was wet & uncomfortable & at dawn my company held the line of a valley near Mametz wood

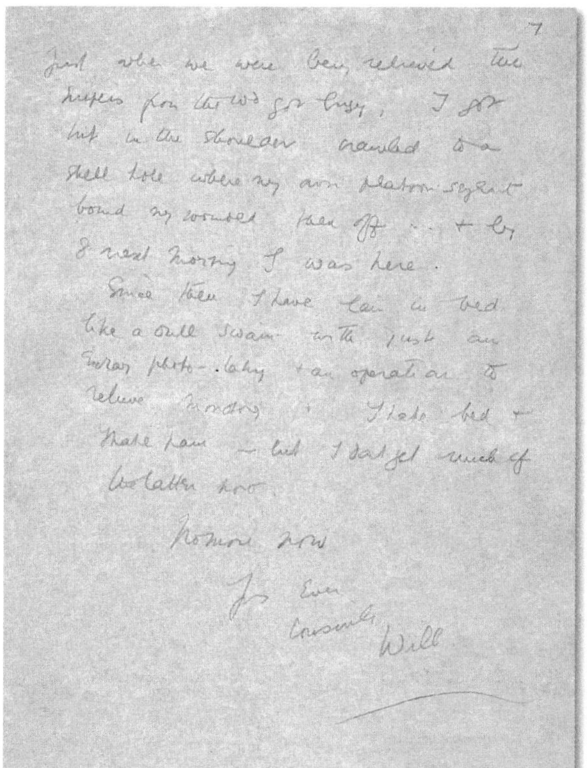

7

Just when we were being relieved the snipers from the wood got busy, I got hit in the shoulder crawled to a shell hole where my own platoon sergeant bound my wound [illegible] off — & by 8 next morning I was here.

Since then I have lain in bed like a dull swan with just an x-ray photo-taking & an operation to relieve [illegible] — I hate bed & make haste — but I don't get much of the latter now.

No more now

Yr Ever
Cousinly,
Will

ABOVE: A letter from Lieutenant Will Mulholland of 21st Manchesters (30th Div) to his cousin describing the events of the first day of The Battle of the Somme.

For his second "Big Push" on the Somme, on 15 September 1916, Haig was able to deploy 32 tanks, a new and secret weapon, although only 24 took part in the action on that day. Their impact was modest, although they made a big impression on the German troops who were confronted by them. Assisted by tanks, 41st Division captured the village of Flers. Many other British divisions also did well, as did the Canadians and New Zealanders. In all, the line advanced about 2.5 km (1.5 miles). By the standards of trench warfare, this was creditable enough, but the Battle of Flers-Courcelette fell a long way short of a breakthrough.

Ten days later, at Morval, a more limited attack on a narrow front did achieve considerable success. Simultaneously, the French army made important gains in the nearby Rancourt sector. On the following day, 26 September, the fortress of Thiepval, which was supposed to have fallen on 1 July, was captured by 18th Division in a well-planned and executed attack. These two attacks, in which British troops had demonstrated that they were absorbing the hard-won tactical lessons of the Somme, pointed the way towards a more successful way of fighting. Unfortunately, Haig misread the message of these limited battles, believing that German resistance was crumbling, and hence he ordered ambitious attacks rather than further bite and hold battles. Subsequent offensives, such as the battle for the high ground around Le Transloy in October, demonstrated that Haig's optimism was misplaced. Although he can be criticized for this, in truth Haig had no alternative but to continue the battle as he was under pressure from Joffre. As autumn arrived the weather deteriorated, with sticky Somme mud adding to the troops' woes.

During this time, the French continued to attack on the Somme, committing Micheler's Tenth Army to the fighting in September. However, co-operation with the BEF, already poor during Flers-Courcelette, broke down. In later offensives the French, like the British, tended to neglect large-scale well co-ordinated battles in favour of smaller, disjointed actions. The French suffered heavily in engagements such as those at Sailly-Saillisel, St Pierre-Vaast, and in the Rancourt sector. "On the 16th, 18th, 21st and 22nd of October," Joffre candidly admitted in his memoirs, "a series of small attacks followed one another without great results." One problem was that that the "fragmentary … attacks" of the French played into the hands of the Germans. Under the new team of Hindenburg and Ludendorff, who replaced Falkenhayn at the end of August, new tactics had been introduced. Gone were rigid trench lines.

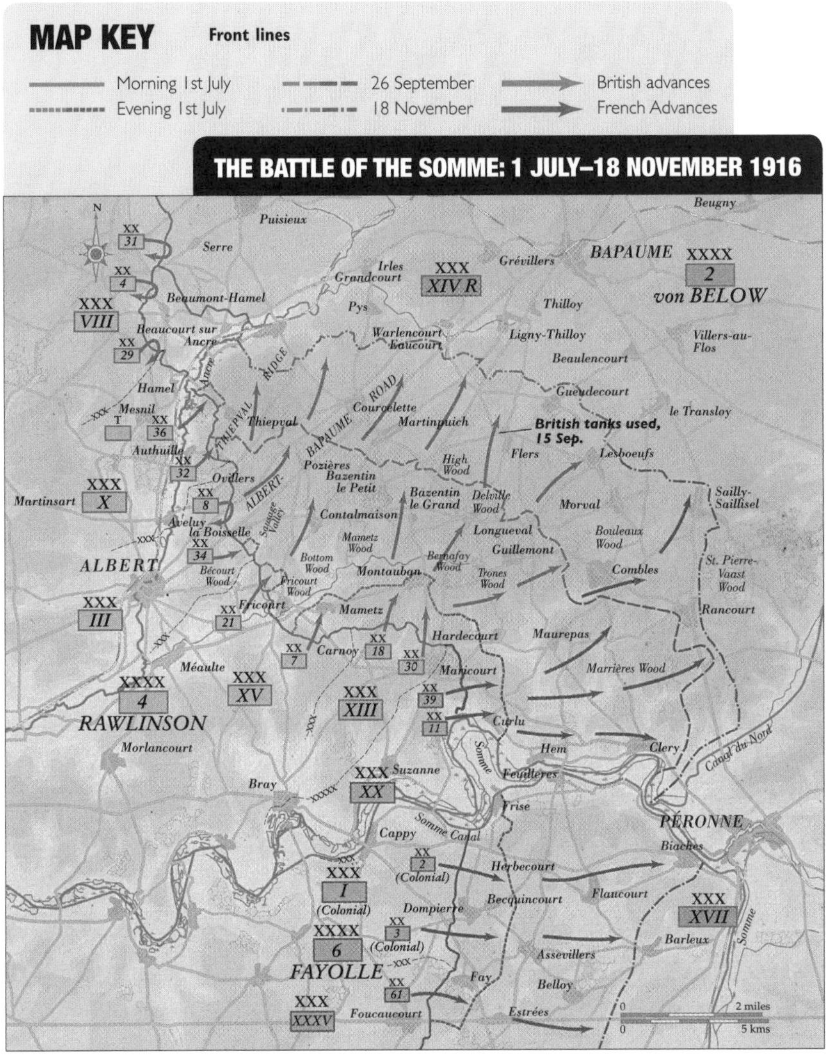

OPPOSITE: "Clan Leslie", a Mark I tank on 15 September 1916, the day of the first tank action in history.

Now German positions had depth, with machine guns in shell-holes to break up enemy attacks. The British, too, experienced problems in dealing with these new defensive methods.

The final phase of the Somme returned the focus of the action to the northern extremity of the battlefield, which had seen relatively little action since the early stages of the offensive. On 13 November, General Sir Hubert Gough, commander of British Fifth Army, launched the Battle of the Ancre. Gough applied many of the lessons of the previous months. His plan was reasonably limited; there was a sufficient number of guns, including 282 heavies; the field guns fired a "creeping barrage", a relatively flexible curtain of shells that moved ahead of the infantry (the failure to use such methods on 1 July had been a contributory factor to the British setbacks); and staff work showed a distinct improvement over the earlier months of the battle. While not completely successful, the Fifth Army took most of its objectives, including Beaumont-Hamel and Beaucourt villages.

Losses on the Somme were shockingly high. The British suffered 420,000; the French 200,000. German losses were probably in the region of 450,000 to 600,000. The battle is customarily portrayed as a British defeat. It was not. While not a victory in the conventional sense of the word, the attrition was in favour of the Allies, and the BEF's bloody apprenticeship meant that it ended the year as a more effective army than it had been at the beginning. The German High Command was well aware of the serious consequences of the Somme; it had discounted the British army, but now realized that it was a major force that stacked the odds against a German victory on land. Instead, 1917 was to see an attempt to use the U-boat fleet to starve Britain out of the war. This failed, and served to bring the USA into the war instead. British generalship and tactics were often poor on the Somme, but the overall result was a success for Allied arms.

STRATEGIC CHOICES

THE WAR ON OTHER FRONTS

The single most important factor influencing Allied strategy was the presence of German troops on French and Belgian soil. For France, the absolute priority was to expel the invaders. Britain went to war partly to prevent Germany from becoming the dominant power in Europe, which meant supporting France, but also to keep the Channel coast out of the hands of its principal naval rival.

Thus, for both states the Western Front was of primary importance. However, the war was also a global conflict. France and Britain had huge empires, and in places Germany and her ally Turkey either posed a threat or offered an opportunity for expansion. Moreover, an important group of the British decision-making elite, horrified by the losses and stalemate of the Western Front, favoured an "indirect" strategy: using sea power to attack the enemy's periphery.

A principal foundation of Allied strategy was control of the sea. For the most part, the powerful German battle fleet was kept bottled up in harbour. Only once was there a full-scale clash between the British and German fleets. Although the Germans had the best of the fighting on the day, Jutland (31 May 1916) was a British strategic victory. The German fleet retreated and never came out in such strength again. The most significant German naval threat was the U-boat (submarine). The Allied war effort depended on supplies from North America, and in 1917 U-boats came dangerously close to causing unsustainable losses to Allied merchant shipping. That the Allies weathered the crisis was a strategic success of the first magnitude.

In spring 1915, the Allies tried a new strategy by attacking Turkey. The initial attempt by ships to force the Dardanelles – the strategically vital waterway that connects the Mediterranean and Black Seas – failed, and amphibious landings on the adjacent Gallipoli peninsula rapidly became bogged down. For eight months, British, Indian, Australian, New Zealand, French and French colonial troops fought in trench warfare conditions against a tough and determined Turkish enemy. The strategy, although imaginative, was hopelessly over-ambitious, and the execution of the campaign was poor. The failure of Gallipoli discredited such grand-scale uses of sea power for the rest of the war. However, Allied interest in the Balkans continued. Largely at French insistence, a force was sent to the Greek port of Salonika in October 1915 to counteract the defeat of Serbia. It remained pinned into a narrow area until September 1918, when a highly successful offensive by French, British and other Allied troops broke out and inflicted a major defeat on Bulgarian forces.

Germany's overseas colonies, in Africa, the Pacific and China, were quickly overrun. In East Africa, however, Colonel Paul Lettow-Vorbeck kept up a highly successful guerrilla campaign that tied down large numbers of British Empire troops. Further north, Allied troops repelled an attempted Turkish invasion of Egypt in 1915, and then, by stages, captured Sinai, Palestine and Syria. Jerusalem fell on 9 December 1917, and in the following September, Allenby's forces

OPPOSITE: French troops at Gallipoli, 1915. On 25 April the French made a diversionary landing on the mainland of Asia Minor.

BELOW: British battlecruisers at the Battle of Jutland, 31 May 1916. *HMS Lion* (flagship of Admiral Beatty) ahead of *HMS Princess Royal* and *HMS Queen Mary.*

BELOW INSET: A surfaced German submarine torpedoes a merchant ship. U-Boats preferred to attack on the surface if at all possible.

won the battle of Megiddo, effectively destroying Turkish power in the region. Arab forces led by Colonel T E Lawrence ("of Arabia") played an important but subsidiary role in the campaign. British and Indian troops attacked Turkish-held Mesopotamia (modern Iraq) as early as November 1914. Originally intending just to secure Basra at the head of the Persian Gulf, the British were gradually drawn further inland. A substantial force was besieged at Kut and surrendered to the Turks in April 1916. This was one of the worst Allied military disasters of the war. Subsequently, a better-equipped and commanded force captured first Baghdad (March 1917) and in 1918 most of the rest of the country.

Italy entered the war in 1915. While superficially attractive as an alternative to the Western Front for the main Allied effort, practical difficulties and the resistance of "Westerner" generals and politicians prevented this transfer of effort being realized. However, after the Italian defeat at Caporetto on 24 October 1917, British and French forces were sent to Italy in November, and they participated in the great victory of Vittorio Veneto (October 1918).

ABOVE: The landing at V beach, Gallipoli (25 April 1915) taken from *SS River Clyde*. Infantry are pinned down on the shore.

The Germans too made strategic choices. From 1915 to 1917 they mainly stayed on the defensive in the West and concentrated on knocking Russia out of the war. Without the huge efforts of the Russian army, the Allies could not have survived until the British mass mobilization bore fruit in 1916. The defeat of Russia in 1917 was an enormous blow to the Allies, but they were fortunate to survive until American manpower helped restore their advantage over the Germans.

LAWRENCE OF ARABIA (1888–1935)

One of the most glamorous figures to emerge from the war, Colonel Thomas Edward Lawrence was a pre-war archaeologist who served as liaison officer with Emir Faisal Ibn Hussein during the Arab Revolt against the Ottoman Turks (1916–18). T E Lawrence himself claimed to have been the effective leader of the revolt. A highly complex man, author of several books and a leading theorist of guerrilla warfare, "Lawrence of Arabia" died in a motorcycle accident in 1935. He was immortalized in a film by David Lean in 1962.

"Damn the Dardanelles! They will be our grave!"

Admiral "Jacky" Fisher, 1915

ABOVE: British artillery in Mesopotamia (modern day Iraq). This theatre posed some of the greatest logistic challenges of the war.

BELOW: An Austrian infantryman in silhouette on the mountains on the Italian Front. This theatre witnessed bitter attritional fighting on inhospitable battlefields.

FRENCH CHANGE OF COMMAND

THE APPOINTMENT OF NIVELLE

By the end of November 1916, activity died down on the Western Front, and the generals prepared to renew the offensive in the New Year. Haig and Joffre consulted on plans but in mid-December Joffre, the man who had sacked so many generals, was himself dismissed.

He was still popular, so his sacking was dressed up as a promotion to strategic adviser to the government and he was elevated to Marshal of France. But in reality Joffre's power was at an end, and he was reduced to a ceremonial role for the rest of the war. The enormous moral capital Joffre had amassed through his steady, calm generalship in 1914 had been eroded by the huge casualties and the continuing deadlock. Despite the sanguinary efforts of 1915, despite Verdun, despite the Somme, the invading Germans were still firmly camped on French soil, at their closest only 65 km (40 miles) from Paris. The politicians had had enough. It was time for a change.

Change took the form of General Robert Nivelle who was appointed as de facto French Commander-in-Chief on the Western Front. From the beginning he wielded a new broom. Articulate and persuasive in French and English (his mother was British), Nivelle had a very different personal style from Joffre. Initially, Haig, who had had a sometimes turbulent relationship with Joffre, thought Nivelle "a most straightforward and soldierly man". In the context of French military politics, where Catholic piety was a handicap, Nivelle had good credentials as a Protestant. Above all, he promised success. Nivelle had come to prominence as a result of his successes at Verdun, which had been based on the techniques of the set-piece attack. Massed artillery fire covered the advance of the infantry, who were set limited objectives. This had worked well in small-scale actions, but now he persuaded his superiors that the same methods could be used to achieve the elusive breakthrough on the Western Front which would reopen mobile warfare and lead to a decisive victory. At his first meeting with Haig, Nivelle made it clear that he intended to disregard existing plans. Haig noted in his diary that the new French commander was "confident of breaking through the Enemy's front now that the Enemy's morale is weakened". The key was for the attack to achieve surprise "and go through in 24 hours".

Nivelle found a key supporter in London as well as in Paris. David Lloyd George, who had become Prime Minister in December 1916, distrusted Haig and Robertson and was opposed to a fresh British offensive on the Western Front. As the leader of a coalition government, however, he was too weak politically to move against the senior generals. He fell for Nivelle's eloquence, and so decided to push for the BEF to be placed directly under the French command: this would marginalize Haig and effectively reduce him to an administrative role. The prospect of getting a firmer grip on their ally appealed to some senior French commanders, and Lloyd George conspired with Nivelle and others to present Haig with a fait accompli. This was duly delivered at a meeting at Calais on 26 February, ostensibly called to discuss transportation. Haig and Robertson were predictably furious that their own prime minister wanted to hand the BEF over to foreign generals. As one of the participants at the conference, the British liaison officer Brigadier General Edward Spiers (known after the war as Spears), later wrote, "Seldom in history can Englishmen have been asked to subscribe to such abject conditions … such as might be imposed on a vassal state."

Haig and Robertson fought back, and the end result was an uneasy compromise. Haig remained in operational control of the BEF but was placed under Nivelle's command for the forthcoming operation. Crucially, the British Commander-in-Chief was given the right of appeal to London if he objected to Nivelle's orders. This was a long way short of what Lloyd George and Nivelle had wanted, and came at a high price. The Calais plot destroyed what remained of the trust between Lloyd George and the two most important generals in the British army. Unity of command was certainly desirable, but a shotgun marriage was not the sensible way to achieve it. Haig did not know how deeply Nivelle had been involved in the conspiracy, and he remained correct in his dealings with him. The French change of command had avoided a major breach between the Allies, but had precipitated the worst clash between the British military and government of the entire war.

OPPOSITE: Foreground, left to right: Albert Thomas (French Munitions Minister), Haig, Joffre and Lloyd George, 1916. By the end of the year, Joffre had been "kicked upstairs".

LEFT: France's transition to a total war economy from 1914 to 1918 was impressive. Factory workers are soldering the fins onto bombs.

9 APRIL–16 MAY 1917

THE BATTLE OF ARRAS

ALLIED OFFENSIVE

The 9 April 1917 was the most successful day that the BEF had enjoyed since the beginning of trench warfare. The BEF committed to battle as the first stage of an Anglo-French operation, with the French Nivelle Offensive beginning on 16 April (see pages 78–81).

After a heavy artillery bombardment, 14 British and Canadian divisions of General Sir Edmund Allenby's Third Army attacked on a 23,000-m (25,000-yd) front near Arras. For an army that on the Somme had become used to gains that were meagre at best, the results of the day's fighting were hugely encouraging. The Canadian Corps – which was commanded by a British officer, General Sir Julian Byng and included a number of British troops – captured the daunting high ground of Vimy Ridge, while further south British forces made some important gains. The 4th and 9th (Scottish) Divisions of XVII Corps pushed 5.5 km (3.5 miles) into the German positions and dug in on the German Third Line. This was the longest single advance achieved by a British formation under conditions of trench warfare. VI Corps pushed forward about 3.25 km (2 miles); Battery Valley, complete with German artillery, fell to 12th and 15th (Scottish) Divisions. The village of Neuville-Vitasse fell as VII Corps advanced 1,800 m (2,000 yds). Not surprisingly, on the afternoon of 9 April, Haig wrote to King George V on a note of triumph.

The first day of Arras was a successful example of a limited battle founded on careful planning and preparation. Twelve tunnels were dug under Vimy Ridge which allowed troops to move up to the front line safe from artillery fire. Light railways brought supplies and ammunition to the front line, and troops trained in the new tactics that had emerged from the Somme, were thoroughly rehearsed in the roles they were to play on 9 April. The artillery preparation lasted for five days – Allenby had wanted a shorter bombardment, but Haig overruled him – and was thorough and effective. The effectiveness of much of the German artillery was sharply reduced by British fire, with many German gunners killed or forced to take shelter. At Vimy Ridge, the artillery fire plan was masterminded by a British gunner, Lieutenant Colonel Alan Brooke, who was to rise to become Churchill's principal military adviser in the Second World War.

The seizure of Vimy Ridge was a particularly impressive operation, where the infantry-artillery combination was highly successful, and four Victoria Crosses were awarded. Vimy Ridge has since become a symbol of the birth of Canadian nationhood, and a beautiful memorial was inaugurated in 1936. It is sometimes said that the Canadians succeeded in capturing Vimy Ridge where the British had failed. This is inaccurate; since the British had taken over the sector, they had mounted no major operation against the Ridge. Despite the fact that the German defence-in-depth tactics did not work well here – the German commanders made mistakes and the terrain did not lend itself to these methods – in many places the Germans fought very effectively. The Canadian Corps emerged from Vimy with its reputation as an élite formation greatly enhanced.

The first day of the battle demonstrated that the BEF had matured greatly since July 1916, but it was unable to capitalize on its success. The weather was poor, and Allenby did not receive reconnaissance reports from Royal Flying Corps (RFC) aircraft. He wrongly believed

OPPOSITE: A ditched tank surrounded by curious British infantrymen, possibly of 4th Division, on the Fampoux Road, Battle of Arras, April 1917.

ABOVE: A Canadian cap badge which incorporates the maple leaf, the symbol of the Canadian nation.

JULIAN HEDWORTH GEORGE BYNG
(1862–1935)

General Byng, a British officer from a smart cavalry regiment (10th Hussars), was a great success in command of the Canadian Corps. The Corps was nicknamed "The Byng Boys" after a popular musical show. Vimy Ridge was his finest achievement, and he took the title of Viscount Byng of Vimy when he was ennobled. In late 1917, he was promoted to command Third Army, which he led with success until the end of the war. He became Governor-General of Canada in 1921.

that Third Army was facing a retreating enemy and ordered that "risks must be taken freely". In reality, German reserves were arriving on the battlefield as the Allied advance slowed down. The infantry were moving out of range of the field artillery, which was struggling to get forward over ground which had been cratered in the initial attack. This starkly revealed the problem of artillery-driven limited offensives – it was very difficult to maintain operational tempo. The battle congealed, and although bloody actions continued for a month – the Australians had particularly gruelling fights in two actions at Bullecourt in April and May, and a general attack on 23 April gained over 2 km (more than a mile) – Allenby's optimism was proved to be chimerical.

Arras was the product of coalition politics, a battle that Haig never wanted to fight. Nevertheless, it demonstrated that the BEF was now capable of conducting an effective limited battle and that the German line could be broken, knowledge which was to influence Haig and GHQ in their planning for Third Ypres later in 1917 (see pages 90–91). Arras was the shortest but most intense of the BEF's major offensives under Haig. The daily loss rate of 4,076 was higher than that at the Somme or Passchendaele. In all, 150,000 of the BEF's solders became casualties, along with over 100,000 Germans.

ABOVE: Australian infantry cleaning their rifles in a second-line trench near Bullecourt, May 1917, while serving in Gough's Fifth Army.

BELOW: Following the success of the initial attack, Canadian troops advance on Vimy Ridge. Note the German prisoners in the foreground.

OPPOSITE BELOW: A group of German prisoners. The doctor is treating a man in a litter constructed from a groundsheet and a pole.

EDMUND HENRY HYNMAN ALLENBY (1861–1936)

General Allenby was Haig's exact contemporary. Both were cavalrymen, and while there was never an open breach, the two never worked together entirely easily. After Arras, to his disgust, Allenby was sent to command the Egyptian Expeditionary Force. Ironically, the move away from trench stalemate to conditions of open warfare was the making of him. In 1917 and 1918, Allenby fought a series of successful battles against the Turks in Palestine, and today his popular reputation stands in stark contrast to that of Haig.

16 APRIL–20 APRIL 1917

THE NIVELLE OFFENSIVE

BUILD UP TO A MUTINY

The battle launched on the Aisne on 16 April 1917 is known to history as "the Nivelle Offensive". It is a monument to one man's folly. When he was briefed on Nivelle's plans, General Lyautey, a veteran of French colonial conflicts who was serving as Minister of War, thought them ridiculous.

Likewise, Nivelle's principal subordinates expressed reservations. Nivelle planned to smash through the enemy front by heavy artillery fire followed by infantry attacks, which he believed would lead to a decisive defeat of the Germans. Moreover, he asserted that, unlike battles of the past, this one would be time limited. Nivelle promised that if, by some mischance, the troops did not break through, he would call off the battle rather than allow it to become a lengthy attritional struggle.

The initial objective of the offensive was the ridge of the Chemin des Dames in Champagne, an area that was no stranger to warfare. It was a tough prospect for the attackers: the Germans had taken maximum advantage of the high ground and strengthened it to create an immensely strong belt of trenches and strong-points designed according to the principles of elastic defence. To add to the problems of the French army, the element of surprise was soon lost. Nivelle himself was unbelievably indiscreet, and before long rumours of the offensive were being reported in the French press, which was assiduously read by the Germans. In any case, a set of preliminary "Instructions" for the attack fell into German hands as early as 15 February. All this merely confirmed the build up they could see with their own eyes. The Germans reinforced the threatened sector, the number of divisions there rising from 18 divisions in January to 42 in March.

Micheler's Reserve Army Group, (Fifth, Sixth and Tenth Armies under Mazel, Mangin and Duchêne respectively) was entrusted with the main attack, with Pétain's Central Army Group playing a secondary role. Originally, Franchet d'Espèrey's Northern Army Group was to have attacked as well, but the planned German withdrawal to the Hindenburg Line in February-March 1917 had made this plan redundant. The British, of course, were to attack at Arras a week earlier. Morale among the troops was generally high, but curiously, as the date of the attack neared, Nivelle's confidence sagged, and thanks to a change of government, his political support waned.

On 16 April, the attack began. For days beforehand the French guns pounded the German defences. The French artillery observers were hampered by poor weather and enemy strength in the air; this was the period known to the British pilots as "Bloody April". The resulting bombardment was heavy – Micheler's artillery fired 11 million shells – but inaccurate and ineffective. Since Nivelle's method depended heavily on artillery blasting a way for the infantry through the German positions, this was a disastrous start to the attack. The French infantry struggled through the in-depth defences, finding wire uncut, machine-gun posts untouched, and the German reserves virtually unscathed. Even so, some of the French infantry did well. By 20 April, part of Sixth Army had pushed forward about 6.5 km (4 miles) and taken 5,300 prisoners.

OPPOSITE: Craonne, the scene of one of Napoleon's victories in 1814, also witnessed heavy fighting in the Nivelle Offensive 103 years later.

BELOW: Although the French army's morale was in a delicate state after the Nivelle Offensive, nevertheless, here the 313 Infantry move up to the trenches on 7 June 1917.

By the end of the battle, Nivelle's troops had taken 29,000 enemy prisoners and had carved out a salient 6.5 km (4 miles deep) and 26 km (16 miles) wide. Judged by the standards of 1917, this was a limited success. But the huge French losses – 134,000 casualties of which 30,000 were fatalities – incurred in a few days and the failure of Nivelle's ambitious plans to come even remotely close to achievement meant the attack was written off as a ghastly failure, and the Chemin des Dames gained the sinister reputation it holds in France to this day.

The morale and cohesion of the French army was badly shaken. Swathes of divisions were affected by "collective indiscipline", that is, by mutiny, which broke out almost as soon as the Nivelle

> **"We demand peace, peace"**
>
> **French soldier, June 1917**

Offensive began. Some acts of defiance were relatively minor, such as the shouting of slogans or smashing of windows. Others threatened the very disciplinary fabric of the French army. Troops refused to obey orders to return to the trenches and gathered in crowds to air their grievances and even express revolutionary sentiments. The failure of the Nivelle offensive was the trigger for the mutinies, but the causes were deeper, reaching back to the huge losses since 1914, to the soldiers' discontent with their conditions, and their lack of faith in their officers. The mutinies were at their worst in June, but over the next few months General Philippe Pétain, who replaced Nivelle, rebuilt the army's fragile cohesion. Fortunately for the Allies, the Germans did not take advantage of the French army's most traumatic period of the war.

ABOVE: Scenes of carnage at Craonne, after the French attack of 16 April 1917.

BELOW RIGHT: A French F1 hand grenade.

BELOW LEFT: King George V decorates General Philippe Pétain with the Order of the Bath on 12 July 1917.

HEALING THE ARMY

On being appointed Commander-in-Chief on 17 May, Pétain energetically addressed the bread-and-butter issues that underlay the soldiers' grievances. He introduced more frequent leave, better food and improved welfare facilities. He also mounted several small-scale operations, carefully planned and backed by massed artillery, to demonstrate that battlefield success was possible. Pétain, however, made it clear that his strategy had changed, announcing that he intended to "wait for the Americans and the tanks". The French Army would no longer bear the principal burden of the war on the Western Front.

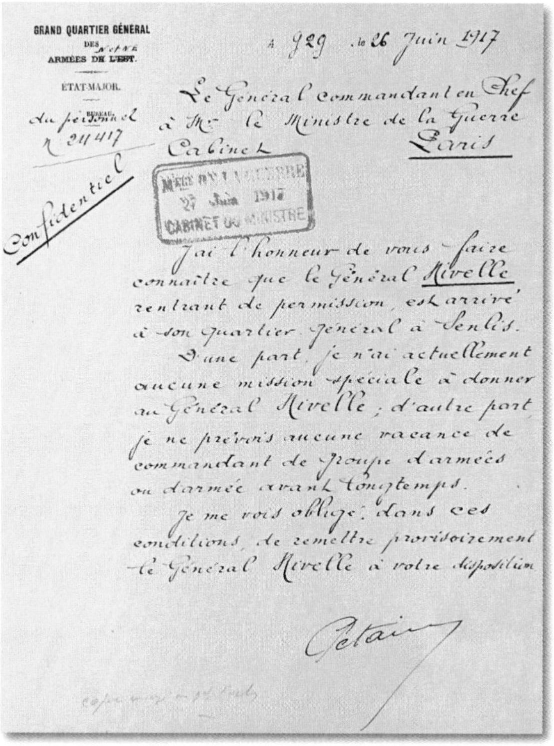

GRAND QUARTIER GÉNÉRAL
DES ARMÉES DU NORD ET DU NORD-EST
ÉTAT-MAJOR.
du personnel
N 24417

Confidentiel

à 929 . le 26 Juin 1917

Le Général commandant en Chef
à Mr le Ministre de la Guerre
Cabinet
Paris

MINISTÈRE DE LA GUERRE
27 Juin 1917
CABINET DU MINISTRE

J'ai l'honneur de vous faire connaître que le Général Nivelle rentrant de permission, est arrivé à son quartier général à Senlis.

D'une part, je n'ai actuellement aucune mission spéciale à donner au Général Nivelle ; d'autre part je ne prévois aucune vacance de commandant de groupe d'armées ou d'armée avant longtemps.

Je me vois obligé, dans ces conditions, de remettre provisoirement le Général Nivelle à votre disposition

Pétain

LEFT: On 26 June 1917 General Pétain sent this letter to the Minister of War indicating that he could not employ Nivelle.

BELOW: Pétain's policy for dealing with mutinies was set out in this telegram to Army Groups and Armies.

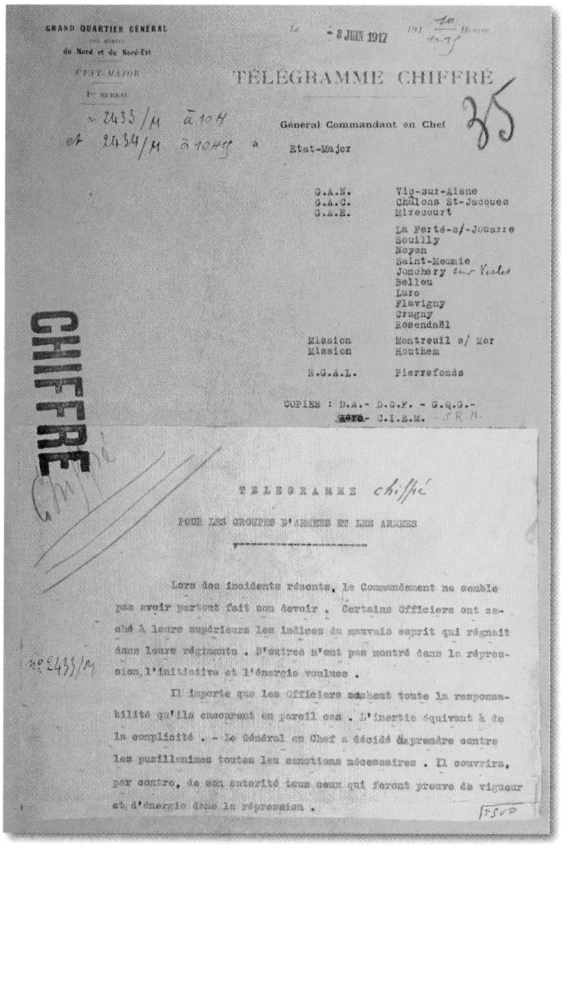

GRAND QUARTIER GÉNÉRAL
DES ARMÉES
du Nord et du Nord-Est
ÉTAT-MAJOR
1er BUREAU
N 2433/M à 10 H
et 2434/M à 10 H 15

Le – 8 JUIN 1917 191 10 Heure 10.15

TÉLÉGRAMME CHIFFRÉ

85

Général Commandant en Chef

à

Etat-Major

G.A.N.	Vic-sur-Aisne
G.A.C.	Châlons St-Jacques
G.A.E.	Mirecourt
	La Ferté-s/-Jouarre
	Souilly
	Noyon
	Saint-Memmie
	Jonchery sur Vesles
	Belleu
	Lure
	Flavigny
	Crugny
	Rosendaël
Mission	Montreuil s/ Mer
Mission	Houthem
R.G.A.L.	Pierrefonds

COPIES : D.A.- D.C.F. - G.Q.G.-
Aéro- C.I.E.M. - S.R.A.

CHIFFRE

Chiffré

TELEGRAMME chiffré

POUR LES GROUPES D'ARMEES ET LES ARMEES

N° 2433/M

Lors des incidents récents, le Commandement ne semble pas avoir partout fait son devoir . Certains Officiers ont caché à leurs supérieurs les indices du mauvais esprit qui régnait dans leurs régiments . D'autres n'ont pas montré dans la répression, l'initiative et l'énergie voulues .

Il importe que les Officiers sachent toute la responsabilité qu'ils encourent en pareil cas . L'inertie équivaut à de la complicité . - Le Général en Chef a décidé de prendre contre les pusillanimes toutes les sanctions nécessaires . Il couvrira, par contre, de son autorité tous ceux qui feront preuve de vigueur et d'énergie dans la répression .

TSVP

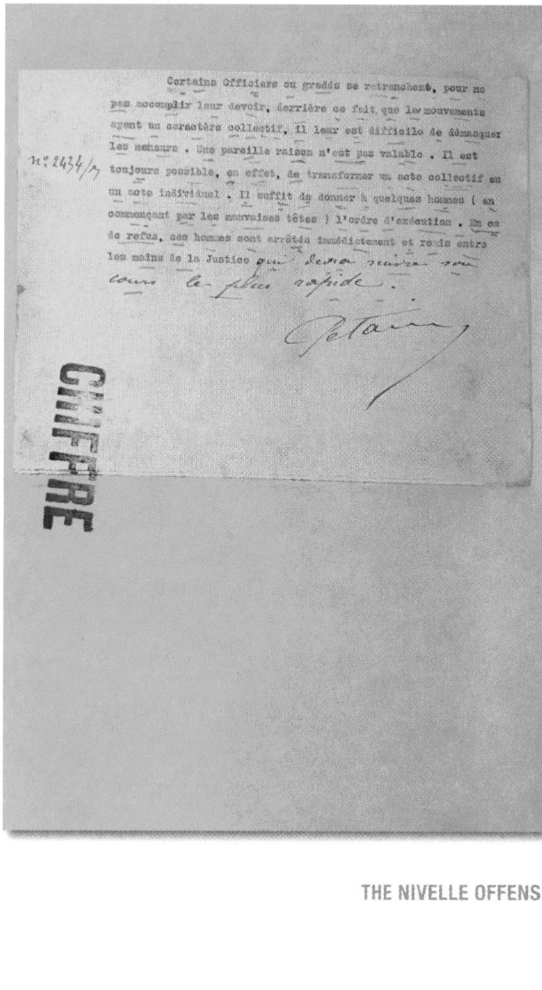

N° 2434/M

Certains Officiers ou gradés se retranchent, pour ne pas accomplir leur devoir, derrière ce fait que les mouvements ayant un caractère collectif, il leur est difficile de démasquer les meneurs . Une pareille raison n'est pas valable . Il est toujours possible, en effet, de transformer un acte collectif en un acte individuel . Il suffit de donner à quelques hommes (en commençant par les mauvaises têtes) l'ordre d'exécution . En cas de refus, ces hommes sont arrêtés immédiatement et remis entre les mains de la Justice qui devra suivre son cours le plus rapide .

Pétain

CHIFFRE

7 JUNE–14 JUNE 1917

THE BATTLE OF MESSINES

MINE WARFARE COMES OF AGE

Ever since he became Commander-in-Chief, Douglas Haig had wanted to fight a major battle in the Ypres area. Unlike on the Somme, here there were important strategic objectives.

A relatively short advance would threaten the major German communications centre at Roulers. This would open the enticing prospect of reducing the threat to the Channel ports, on which the BEF depended for supplies. It also would allow the BEF to threaten the German-held Belgian coast. The Admiralty were extremely worried about the risk posed by German U-Boats and surface warships. While capturing the ports such as Ostend would not eliminate the German naval threat, it would certainly help to reduce it.

The first stage of the offensive was an attack against Messines Ridge. This key position had been lost to the Germans in 1914, and General Sir Herbert Plumer's Second Army was given the task of winning it back. He formed an effective team with General Sir "Tim" Harington, his Chief of Staff, who described Plumer's methods as being underpinned by three Ts: "Trust, Training and Thoroughness". Plumer was popular with his men, who gave him the nickname "Daddy". His methodical approach and his insistence on extensive training for operations were very evident in his preparations for Messines. For months, a series of mines had been dug under Messines Ridge. Each consisted of a tunnel, laboriously bored under No Man's Land by specialized mining companies, packed with explosive. It was, even by the standards of the Western Front, dangerous work. Aside from the normal perils of working deep beneath the ground, miners faced the continuous fear that the enemy might explode a small charge in the mine shaft and bury them alive. Alternatively, German miners, engaged in their own tunnelling, might break into a British working party, in which case a hand-to-hand struggle would take place beneath

SIR HERBERT PLUMER (1857–1932)

General Plumer was the ultimate safe pair of hands on the Western Front. He commanded in the ever-dangerous Ypres Salient from 1915, except when he was sent to take command of British forces in Italy for a period in late 1917 to early 1918. His methodical approach to offensive operations paid dividends at Messines and in the middle phase of Passchendaele, albeit at a heavy cost in the lives of British and Empire soldiers. His reputation remains high among historians.

OPPOSITE: Wytschaete village (known as "Whitesheet" to the British), captured on 7 June 1917 and photographed a day later.

BELOW: In 1917 the Germans often used "flexible" defensive tactics in which outlying parties were deployed in shell holes to break up attacks.

the ground. In the event, 24 mines were excavated. On average, each mine contained about 21 tons of high explosive, but the largest charge was roughly double that size. No wonder that on the eve of the battle Harington said "I do not know whether we will change history tomorrow, but we shall certainly alter the geography."

Nine divisions were to be used for the initial assault. These included the Catholic, Nationalist 16th (Irish) Division and the Protestant, Unionist 36th (Ulster) Division, fighting alongside each other for the first time. As at Arras, the preliminary artillery bombardment was highly successful. The British had twice as many heavy guns as the Germans, and had a five-to-one advantage in other guns. British artillery fired 3.5 million shells between 26 May and 6 June. The German artillery suffered badly even before the mines were detonated, meaning that when the British and Anzac infantry attacked, they did so under highly favourable conditions. The commander of German XIX Corps contributed to the defenders' problems when he rejected a solution to pull out of the Messines sector.

Nineteen of the mines were detonated at 03:10 on 7 June 1917. The force of the explosion was tremendous, leaving many of those defenders that survived the blast shocked and easy targets for the Allied infantry that advanced under an accurate barrage. The attackers rapidly captured their objectives: Messines village fell to the New Zealanders; and the Wytschaete area was occupied by 16th and 36th Divisions. In the fighting, the BEF demonstrated how proficient they had become at combined arms tactics, with 72 tanks accompanying the infantry. The battle was effectively won on that first day, although the fighting continued spasmodically for a week. The Germans mounted a number of counterattacks from 8 June to 14 June, but none succeeded in dislodging the British. Ironically, the worst loss of life for the BEF came not in the initial assault but on subsequent days, when the Germans shelled British troops crowded

ABOVE: Engineers (sappers), such as these Australians, and tunnellers played a crucial role in the preparation and execution of the Battle of Messines.

WILLIAM "WILLIE" REDMOND (1861–1917)

Major William Redmond was in his 50s when he was kill ed at Messines. Brother of John, the leader of the constitutional Irish National Party, Willie was one of some 210,000 Irishmen who served in the British Army in the First World War. Given the level of Irish involvement in the battle, fittingly, Messines was many years later chosen as the site of an Irish "Peace Tower". Curiously it was erected in the sector over which the New Zealand Division attacked in June 1917.

LEFT: Plunging the handle generated an electrical charge down the wires connected to the two knobs on the box and set off an electric detonator in the explosive.

BELOW: Lancashire Fusiliers in a trench opposite Messines clean a Lewis light machine gun. Note the gas alarm horn and sandbags.

onto the newly captured ridge, causing heavy casualties.

Messines was Plumer's masterpiece, and it is not surprising that when he was ennobled after the war, he took as his title Plumer of Messines. The battle showed that, by June 1917, the BEF had become highly proficient at limited, set-piece battles. However, Haig controversially judged that Plumer was not the right man to command the next stage of the Flanders offensive. Haig believed a breakthrough was possible and placed Hubert Gough, renowned as a "thruster", in charge of the push. Logistic problems and the time needed for Anthione's French First Army to arrive meant that six weeks elapsed between Messines and the beginning of the Third Battle of Ypres.

17 JULY–18 AUGUST 1917

THIRD YPRES

ATTEMPTING THE BREAKTHROUGH

Haig hoped that the Third Battle of Ypres would prove decisive. The BEF would break out of the Salient, and trigger a landing on the Belgian coast by British 1st Division, which had been secretly training for the operation.

On 17 July, the Allied guns began a preliminary bombardment of the German positions. Haig had 3,091 guns at his disposal, and nine infantry divisions of Gough's Fifth Army were to be committed to the first phase of the campaign, officially known as the Battle of Pilckem Ridge. Just as in the First and Second Battles of Ypres, British and French troops were to fight alongside each other. General François Anthoine's French First Army of six divisions (and more than 900 guns) was slotted into the line on the British left flank. Plumer's Second Army guarded Gough's other flank.

On the other side of No Man's Land, the troops of German Fourth Army were deployed in a very strong defensive system based around a series of miniature fortresses, known to the British as "pillboxes". The essence of German defensive tactics was flexibility. The front line was defended lightly, with pillboxes used to slow the enemy advance, while counter-attack troops would hit the attackers as they became over-extended and vulnerable. In spite of some sensible suggestions from GHQ for a more limited approach, Gough believed that his Fifth Army could rapidly overcome the German defences and so planned for an ambitious advance of up to 5,500 m (6,000 yds). This was to reach the German Third Position, after which further fighting would carry Fifth Army out of the Salient altogether.

The infantry attack began at 03:50 on 31 July, as the artillery fire reached a crescendo. The assault was supported by tanks, and thanks to a major aerial offensive commenced on 11 July, British and French

OPPOSITE: The armies of 1917 were heavily dependent on horses for transportation. Here, a British 18-pounder field gun moves up on the first day of Third Ypres, 31 July 1917.

ABOVE: German barbed wire obstacles. The introduction of advanced shell fuses in 1916–17 improved the ability of artillery to cut wire.

FRANÇOIS PAUL ANTHOINE (1860–1944)

General Anthoine commanded the French First Army in the Ypres salient during the "Passchendaele" offensive of 1917. In his memoirs, Gough blamed Anthoine's inability to get his guns in place for the delay of the start of the battle from 25 to 31 July. Anthoine benefitted from the mass clearout of senior commanders in 1914, rapidly progressing from a staff job to high command. After Third Ypres, Anthoine was appointed chief-of-staff to Pétain, the French commander-in-chief. Anthoine was sacked, probably unfairly, in mid-1918.

aircraft had superiority in the air. Initially, the attack made progress. Anthoine's infantry had been carefully trained for the operation, and were supported by a mass of heavy artillery; French First Army gained about 3,200 m (3,500 yds); the left-hand British formation, XIV Corps, advanced about the same distance. The Guards Division, which in a brilliant preliminary operation on 27 July at Boesinghe had crossed the Yser Canal and seized positions on the German bank, took 600 prisoners. The advance was reasonable in the circumstances, but still only about half what Gough had hoped to achieve. In the centre and on the right, the picture was much gloomier. Here, the German defensive tactics worked well. The advancing British infantry were caught off balance by the German counter-attack units and forced back as much as 1,800 m (2,000 yds). Allied losses amounted to about 17,000. In spite of some modest success achieved, Gough's ambitious plan had failed.

In the early evening of 31 July, it began to rain. The ground, badly churned up by shelling, which had severly damaged the drainage system, turned to thick mud. The weather is an ever-present and unpredictable factor in military operations. Frequent statements by subsequent writers to the contrary, rain in these quantities could not have been predicted; Flanders was not regularly subject to a "monsoon" in August. Major operations had to be halted on 2 August, and were not recommenced until 16 August when the Battle of Langemarck began.

This phase of fighting lasted only two days and was a bigger failure than 31 July. Langemarck village itself was captured, but the Gheluvelt Plateau, the possession of which was critical if the BEF was to make a substantial advance, remained in German hands. Haig had made it clear that the ridge, which dominated the battlefield, had to be taken as a priority, but Gough had not made it his

CROWN PRINCE RUPPRECHT OF BAVARIA (1869–1955)

The Ypres sector came under the Army Group of Crown Prince Rupprecht, son of the King of Bavaria. Under the German system, royal personages often received high military positions. Unlike some of his peers, Rupprecht was a highly effective commander and thoroughly merited his promotion to lead an army group. If history had turned out differently 200 years earlier, Rupprecht might have been commanding British forces. When his mother Queen Marie Theresa died shortly after the war in February 1919, he became the Jacobite Pretender to the British throne.

OPPOSITE: In the conditions in the Ypres salient, pack mules came into their own, though many were killed by shell fire. This photograph was taken on 31 July 1917.

BELOW: One of the iconic images of the Third Battle of Ypres: stretcher-bearers struggle in the mud near Boesinghe, 1 August 1917.

priority. The battle spluttered into a number of small-scale actions rather than being joined up into a coherent offensive. Fifth Army's progress was stymied by a combination of heavy German fire and tenacious defence, poor weather and difficult ground, and failure to concentrate artillery. It all seemed a far cry from the heady days of Messines, only two months earlier. The main operation was halted on 18 August, but smaller actions continued.

In London, the War Cabinet came close to ordering the halt of the entire offensive, but Haig won the day. Clearly, however, something had to change. Haig did not readily admit to making errors, but when in mid-August he relegated Gough to a supporting role and made Second Army the principal attacking force, he implicitly acknowledged his mistake.

20 SEPTEMBER–10 NOVEMBER 1917

PASSCHENDAELE

TAKING THE RIDGE

With Plumer in charge, British fortunes began to improve. Haig proved amenable to Plumer's request for a three-week delay to ensure everything was ready. At 05:40 on 20 September the Battle of the Menin Road began.

THIRD BATTLE OF YPRES: JULY–DECEMBER 1917

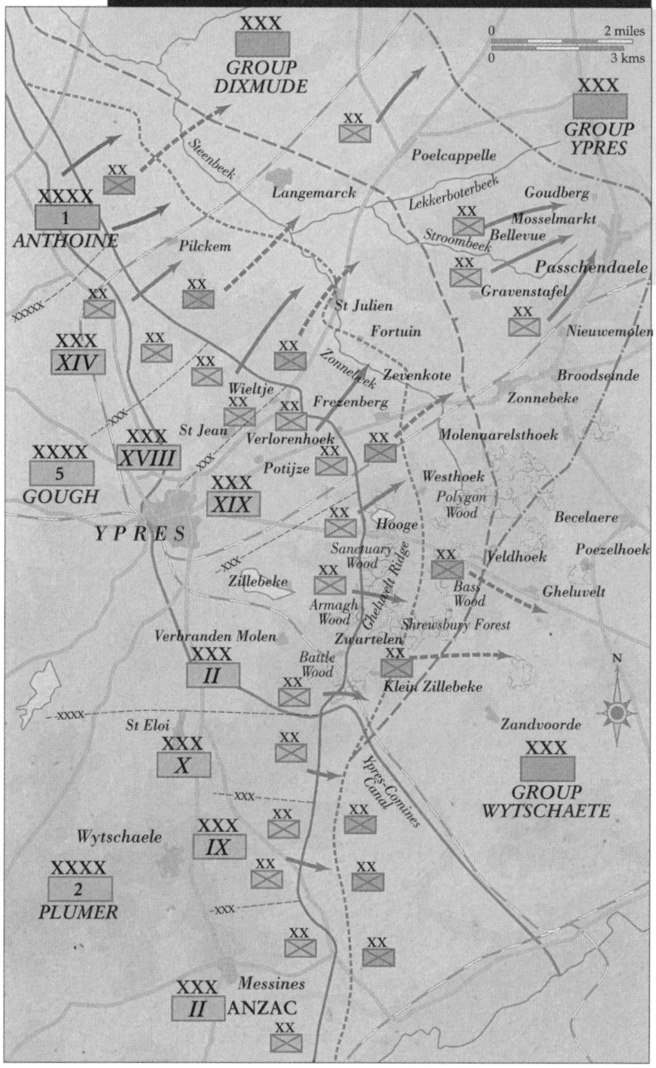

MAP KEY

- Morning, 31 July
- Evening, 31 July
- 20 September
- 7 December
- British advance
- German retreat

ARTHUR CURRIE (1875–1933)

General Currie was a pre-war businessman and part-time Canadian Militia officer. He did well as a brigade and divisional commander, and in 1917 replaced Byng as the first Canadian at the head of the Canadian Corps. The hallmark of Currie's generalship was careful, meticulous preparation, and it helped turn his Corps in toan exceptionally effective formation. When tasked by Haig with capturing Passchendaele Ridge, he stated that it could be done but at the cost of 16,000 casualties. He was right on both counts.

Four divisions attacked, each on a narrow frontage, with further divisions guarding the flanks of the main assault. The infantry's objectives were limited, some 1,450 m (1,600 yds) away, and the attackers advanced behind a deep and complex artillery barrage. Pillboxes proved death traps to any German infantry caught in them, as by now the BEF had evolved sophisticated tactics for tackling defensive positions. German counter-attacks were negated by British firepower – the infantry did not advance out of artillery range – and special units held in reserve. Menin Road was a clear, if costly, victory for Plumer's British and Australian troops.

On 26 September, Plumer began the process all over again. The battle of Polygon Wood repeated the formula of the Menin Road. The pattern of massing combat power on a relatively narrow front, formidable artillery support, and limited advances was the epitome of the bite and hold operation. Ludendorff highlighted the acute problems that it posed the defenders: "We might be able to stand the loss of ground, but the reduction of our fighting strength was [on 26 September] again all the heavier… The depth of penetration was limited so as to secure immunity from our counterattacks, and the latter were then broken by the massed fire of artillery." The Germans tried different tactics, reinforcing the front lines, but with little success.

OPPOSITE: Heavy usage took its toll on artillery. The barrel of an 8-inch Howitzer is lowered into place, 26 September 1917.

Plumer's hammer swung for a third time on 4 October and delivered another smashing blow. In preparation for the Battle

ABOVE: A testament to the power of artillery to cause devastation: the Passchendaele battlefield, with shell holes, mud and shattered trees.

LEFT: A potentially lethal sliver of metal from a shell.

of Broodseinde, the guns were moved forward (Second Army fielded 796 heavy and medium guns, and over 1,500 field guns and howitzers). To avoid predictability, on this occasion there was no full-scale preliminary artillery bombardment. This time it was to be primarily an Anzac battle: 3rd Australian Division, the New Zealand Division and 1st and 2nd Australian Divisions were deployed side by side, with British formations protecting the flank. The Germans also planned a major attack on 4 October, and as the Anzac infantry assembled for the assault, they were caught in a German bombardment. However, the Germans suffered much more heavily from the British barrage that at 06:00 rained down on the defenders' positions. Packed into the front line and deployed for attack rather than defence, many Germans were killed or wounded either by the shelling or by Allied infantry advancing with fixed bayonets. Following the setback, Plumer's assault rapidly got back on track, and by the evening the Germans were counting the cost of what their official history referred to as a "black day". Their luck was about to turn, however. The weather had mostly been fine during the period of Plumer's attacks. On the night before Broodseinde it began to rain, and once again the ground was turned into a morass. Believing that the Germans were on the verge of defeat now that much of the Gheluvelt Ridge had been captured, Haig elected to fight on.

The next battle, Poelcappelle, was launched on 9 October. The moonscape created by shelling in previous battles, the rain and the mud hindered the preparations, which were incomplete when the infantry went over the top. The terrible conditions meant that many were exhausted by the time they reached British front line. The artillery bombardment was simply inadequate. Not surprisingly, the result was few gains for heavy losses. The same was true of the First Battle of Passchendaele (12 October). Haig's decision to push on was – and is – highly controversial, but he did not want to leave the Germans on the ridge at Passchendaele to dominate the battlefield over the winter. Writing to Pétain in October, General Anthoine stated that Haig had failed to admit the lack of success, and feared his own French First Army would suffer casualties in a fruitless battle. For the sake of the alliance, Pétain insisted that First Army fight on. The key objective of Passchendaele Ridge eventually fell to the Canadian Corps in the Second Battle of Passchendaele, which ended on 10 November. The bad conditions made Passchendaele (the name popularly given to the entire campaign) infamous. The losses were heavy – 245,000 British, 8,500 French, perhaps 230,000 German. Haig argued that the attritional effect on the Germans made the battle worthwhile. Under extreme pressure, the German High Command considered withdrawing from the Ypres salient, which would have been a significant strategic victory for Haig. A senior German general argued that the Allied Offensive at Ypres, had prevented the Germans from taking advantage of the poor state of the French army after Nivelle's unsuccessful offensive earlier in the year.

RIGHT: German soldiers surrender to British infantrymen in 1917.

BELOW: An example of the "iron harvest" of unexploded shells which still lie in fields in France and Belgium.

12. 20.7.17 – 16.11.17

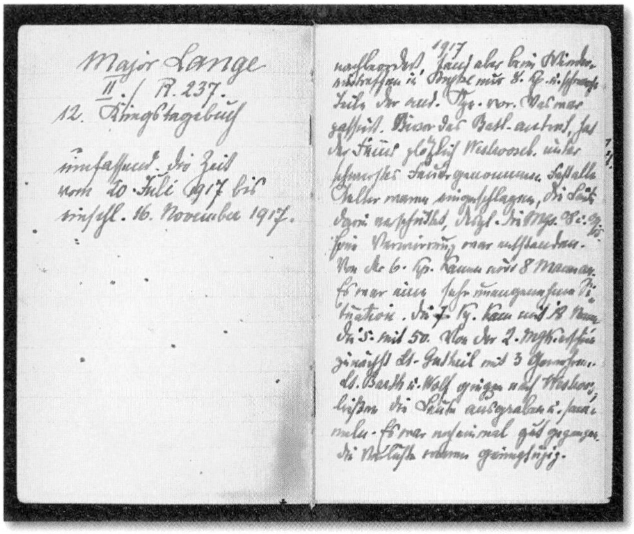
Major Lange
II./R.237.
12. Kriegstagebuch
umfassend die Zeit
vom 20. Juli 1917 bis
einschl. 16. November 1917.

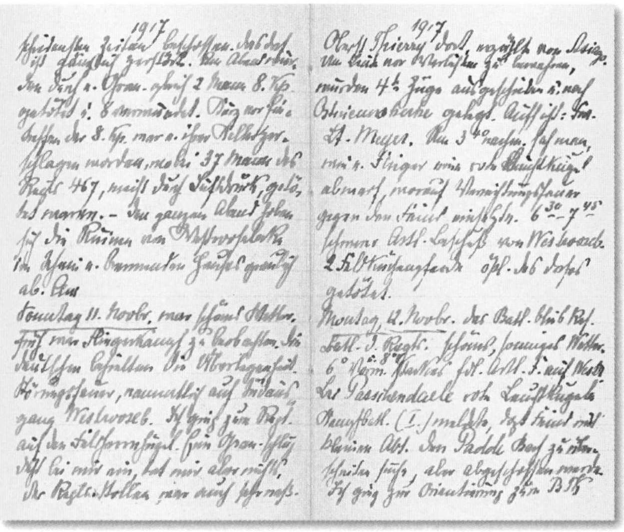

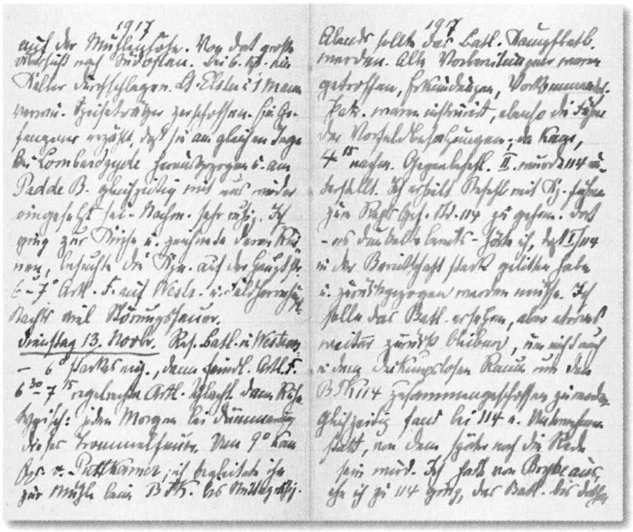

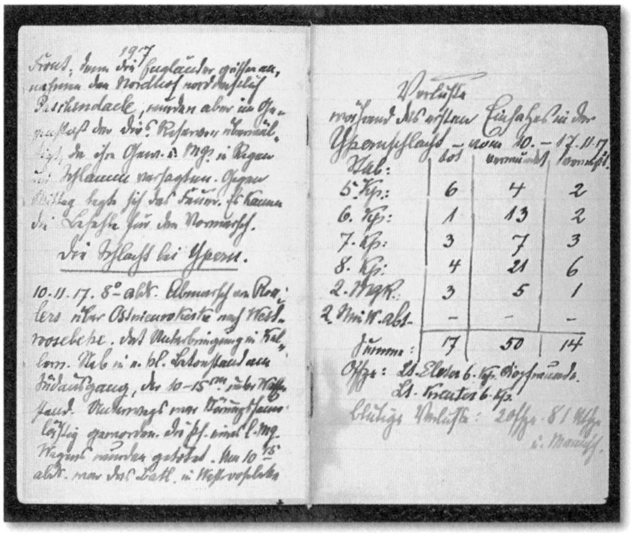
Verluste
tot
verwundet
vermisst
5. Kp.: 6 4 2
6. Kp.: 1 13 2
7. Kp.: 3 7 3
8. Kp.: 4 21 6
2. MGK: 3 5 1
Summe: 17 50 14

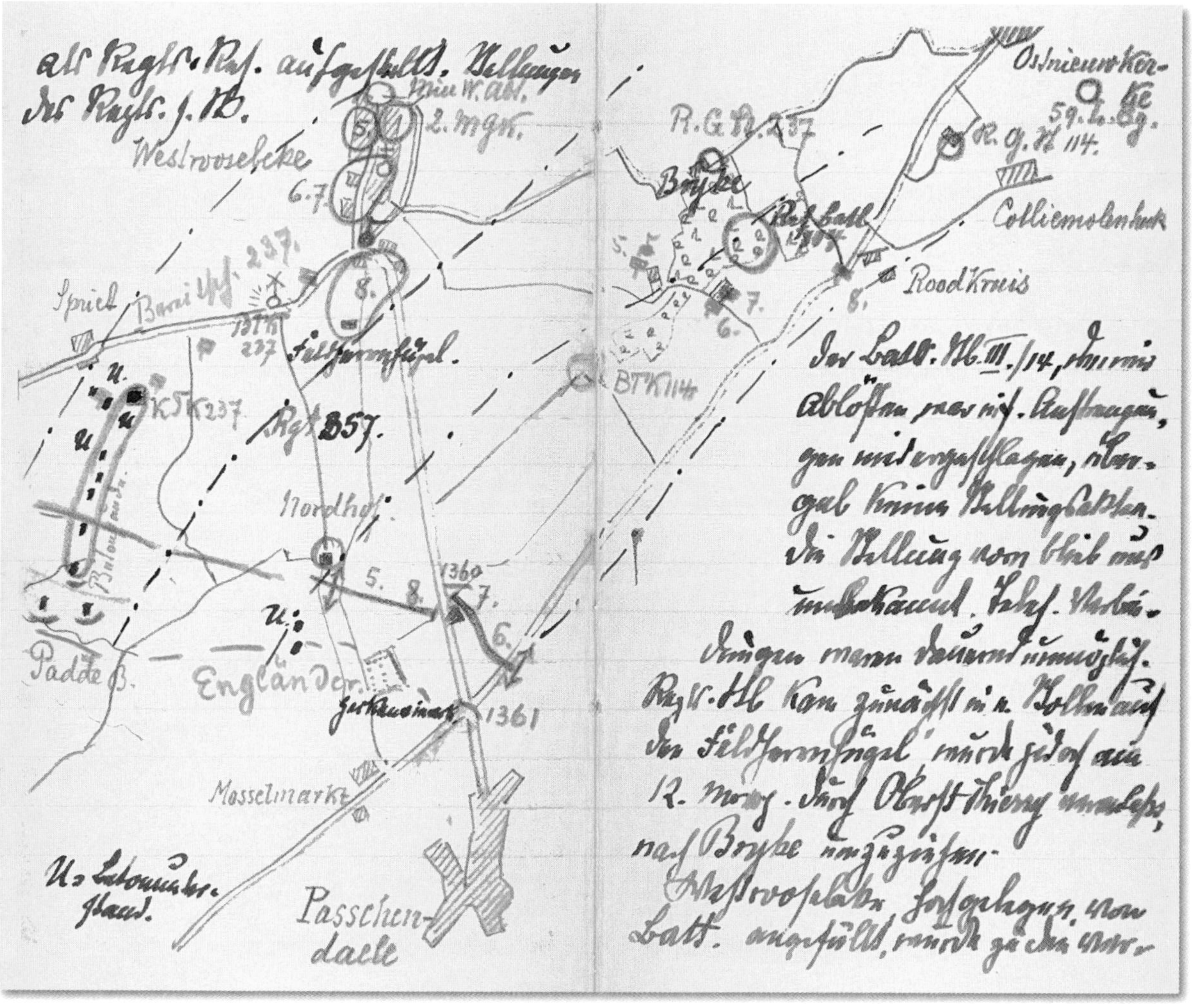

LEFT AND ABOVE: Excerpts from the diary of Major Rudolf Lange, the commander of 2nd battalion, 237 Reserve Infantry Regiment, during the Third Battle of Ypres.

RIGHT: A letter from 2nd Lieutenant M S S Moore of 15th Hampshires describing the action for which he was awarded the Victoria Cross. He won it on 20 September 1917 during an action at "Tower Hamlets" in the Ypres salient.

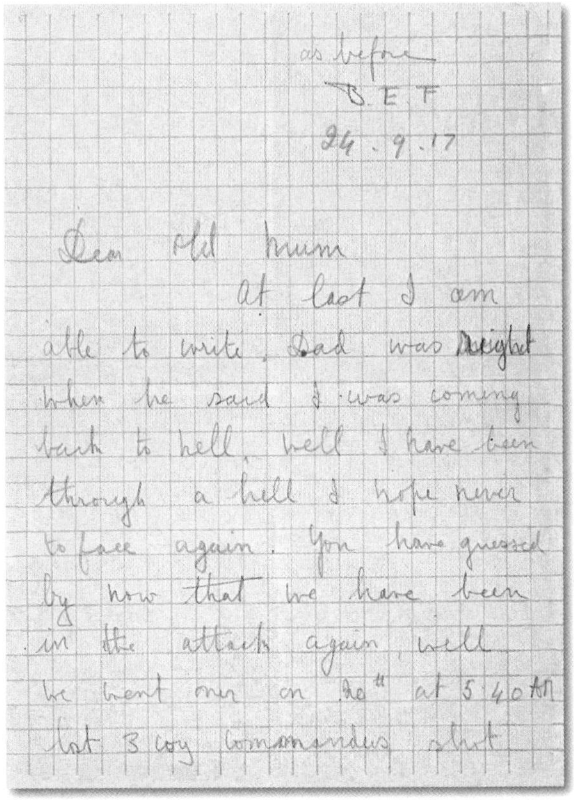

as before
B.E.F
24.9.17

Dear Old Mum
At last I am able to write. Dad was right when he said I was coming back to hell, well I have been through a hell I hope never to face again. You have guessed by now that we have been in the attack again, well we went over on 20th at 5.40 AM lost 3 Coy Commanders shot

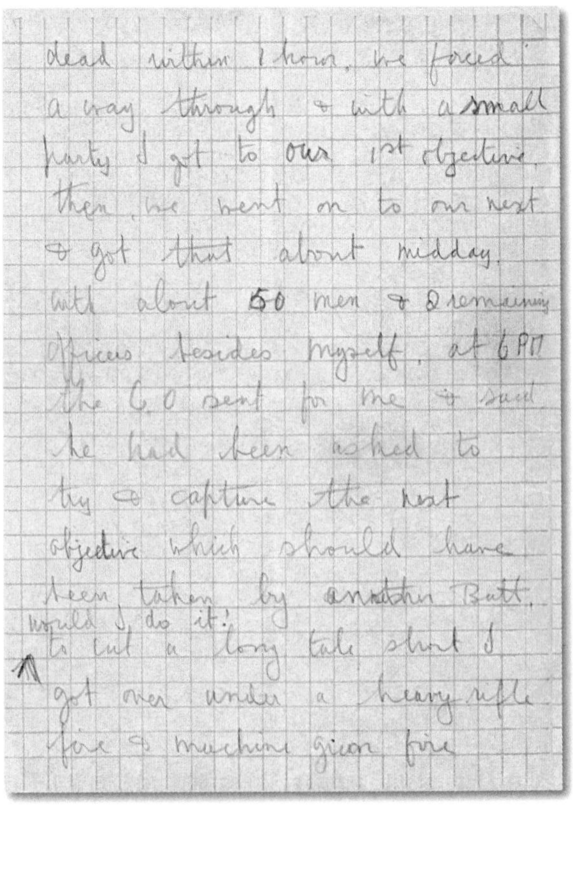

dead within 1 hour, we forced a way through & with a small party I got to our 1st objective, then we went on to our next & got that about midday. with about 50 men & 2 remaining officers besides myself. at 6 PM the C.O sent for me & said he had been asked to try & capture the next objective which should have been taken by another Batt. would I do it? to cut a long tale short I got over under a heavy rifle fire & machine gun fire

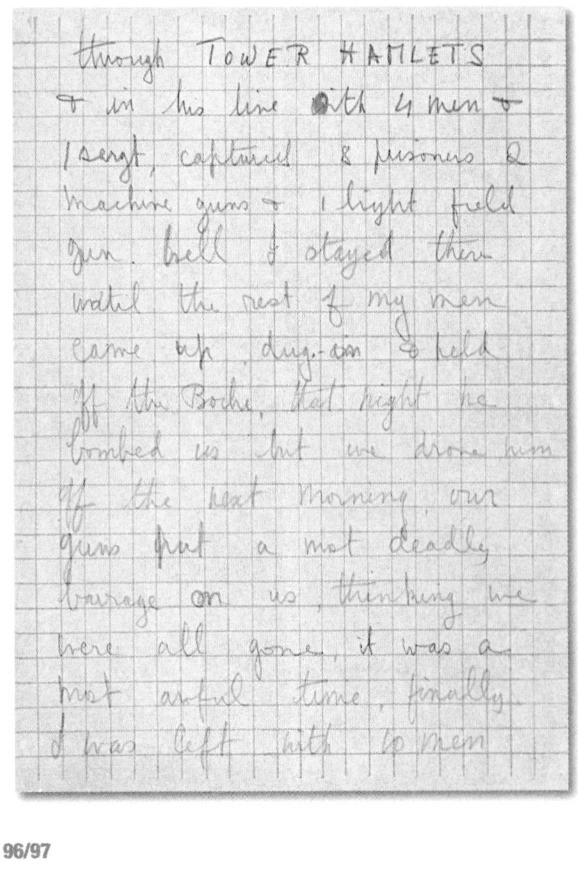

through TOWER HAMLETS & in his line with 4 men & 1 sergt, captured 8 prisoners 2 machine guns & 1 light field gun. Well I stayed there until the rest of my men came up, dug-in & held off the Boche, that night he bombed us but we drove him off the next morning, our guns put a most deadly barrage on us, thinking we were all gone, it was a most awful time, finally I was left with 10 men

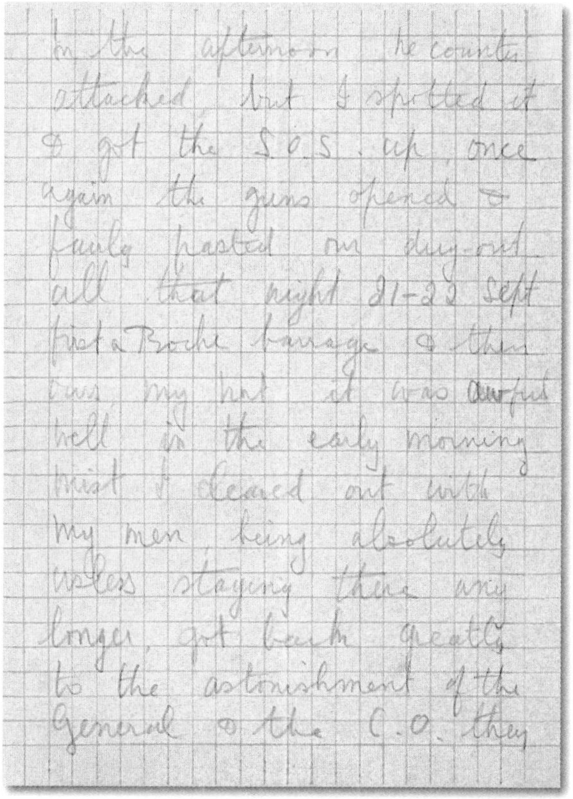
In the afternoon the counter
attacked, but I spotted it
& got the S.O.S. up, once
again the guns opened &
fairly pasted our dug-out
all that night 21-22 Sept
first a Boche barrage & then
ours my hat it was awful
Well in the early morning
mist I cleared out with
my men being absolutely
useless staying there any
longer, got back greatly
to the astonishment of the
General & the C.O. they

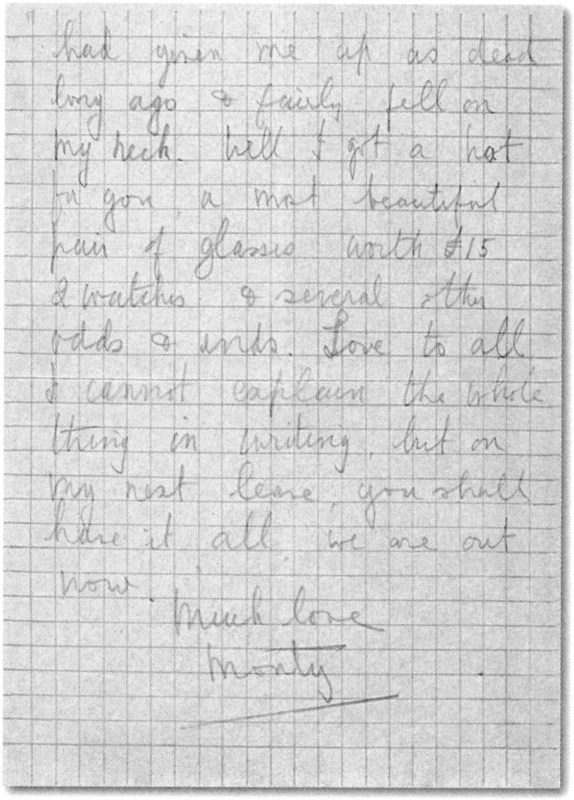
had given me up as dead
long ago & fairly fell on
my neck. Well I got a lot
for you, a most beautiful
pair of glasses worth £15
2 watches & several other
odds & ends. Love to all
I cannot explain the whole
thing in writing, but on
my next leave, you shall
have it all. we are out
now.
Much love
Monty

TRENCH LIFE

A SOLDIER'S LIFE FOR ME

It is a popular myth that the soldiers spent all their time in the trenches. One British regimental infantry officer calculated that in 1916 he was under fire for 101 days, spending 65 days in the front line.

The rest of his time was split between periods in reserve, in rear areas, on leave, and on instructional courses. He spent 12 separate periods in the trenches, and was involved in fighting four times, only one of which was a "direct attack". This pattern held true, with variations, for all armies, although some sectors of the Western Front were more dangerous than others. A French infantry unit at Verdun in May 1916 was likely to see more action than one holding positions near the Swiss frontier. The Ypres Salient was an active sector throughout the war, while for much of 1915 the Somme was generally quiet – although anywhere near the front line random death or wounding was an ever-present threat, whether from sniping, or from "marmites" (as a heavy German shell was known to the French; the British called it a "Jack Johnson", after a Black American boxer).

The trenches themselves evolved during the war. At the end of 1914, they were little more than a series of holes in the ground protected by a little barbed wire. The following years were to see the trench systems become much more elaborate. Duckboards were laid on trench floors, sandbags on the parapet, and barbed wire grew from a few strands festooned with tin cans (a crude early warning system) into dense belts. The men sheltered in "dugouts". In general, German trenches were more elaborate with deeper dugouts than their British or French equivalents. The Germans, sitting on occupied territory, were usually content to hold what they had, while the British and French saw the trenches as jumping-off points for offensives. By the time of the Somme in 1916, defensive systems usually consisted of three parts: fire, support and reserve trenches. Later this set-up was replaced by a much looser defensive system, with front-line posts held lightly, and the main defences further back.

When the troops were not involved in major operations, trench life was a matter of constant work parties, carrying out such tasks as repairing wire, observation, and – since much activity took place at night – trying to snatch naps. Soldiers fought a constant and losing battle against the lice that infested their clothes and the rats that inhabited the trenches. All armies carried out patrols and raids: to gather information; intimidate the enemy; and, supposedly, to inculcate fighting spirit in the troops. These could be highly dangerous. The British were probably the keenest on raiding, while the French had a more pragmatic approach.

Out of the line, soldiers trained, provided work parties that often involved heavy manual work, and had a limited amount of leisure time. Sport was popular, and in the BEF this ranged from simple football kickarounds to elaborate Divisional Horse Shows with gambling (another popular, but illegal, pastime) on the side. Estaminets, a type of café-bar, were ever present. Over a simple meal and rough wine, men could relax, gossip, tell stories, or perhaps sing. For the soldier who simply wished to read or write a letter, organizations such as the YMCA provided some quiet rooms. Toc H, at Poperinghe, provided a Christian haven in which rank was ignored. At the other end of the scale, soldiers could go to brothels, some officially sanctioned, and visit prostitutes. Many French soldiers had a marraine de guerre – a sort of female pen-friend who provided a home for the soldier when on furlough.

The factors that maintained a soldier's morale under such terrible conditions were many and varied: tobacco and alcohol; belief in the cause; pride in the unit; religious faith; superstition; paternal officers; mail from home; leave; baths; and periods away from the front line – all these things were important. The British army was particularly good at sustaining morale by enforcing a "bureaucracy of paternalism" – ensuring that officers inspected soldiers's feet for signs of trench-foot, and providing baths behind the lines, for example – while French morale suffered because of the lack of such a system, with near-disastrous results in 1917. German soldiers in 1918 were badly affected by news from home of the poor conditions being endured by their families. Trench life was hard for everyone, although officers generally had superior facilities. That the morale of soldiers survived so well under the circumstances is testimony to the astonishing ability of the human being to endure the most extreme conditions.

OPPOSITE: A British Soldier using a trench periscope. Note he has removed his helmet to use it.

LEFT: A posed photograph of British and French soldiers mingling at a Church Army hut.

19 JULY–23 OCTOBER 1917

LOCAL ACTIONS

FROMELLES, HILL 70 AND LA MALMAISON

The fighting on the Western Front encompassed local as well as major actions, some of which had major consequences. Others were futile. This was true of the Australian Imperial Force (AIF)'s first taste of action in France after arriving from the Middle East in March 1916.

MAP KEY

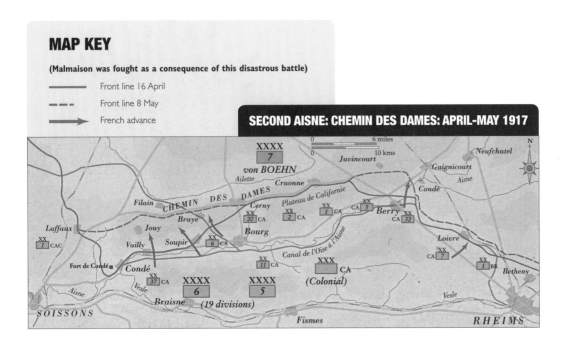

(Malmaison was fought as a consequence of this disastrous battle)

Front line 16 April

Front line 8 May

French advance

SECOND AISNE: CHEMIN DES DAMES: APRIL-MAY 1917

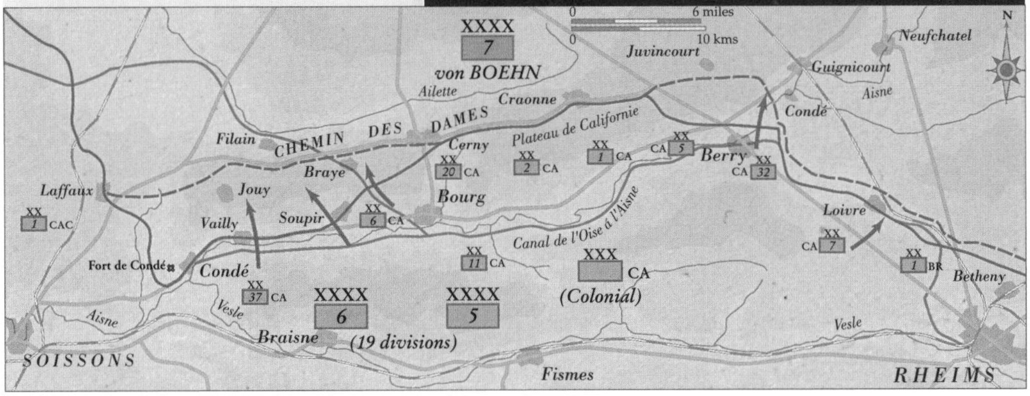

The newly created and inexperienced 5th Australian Division under Major-General J. W. McCay was initially sent to the quiet Armentières sector, known as "the nursery", to learn the ropes. But on 19 July 1916, 5th Australian Division and British 61st Division were committed to an ill-thought-out operation at the village of Fromelles, on ground fought over in 1915. This was a diversion intended to support the Somme offensive by pinning the Germans to their trenches, diverting German reserves, and making clear that the British would not be confining operations to the Somme area.

OPPOSITE: During the Battle for Hill 70 in August 1917, a wounded soldier is brought in on a stretcher by German prisoners of war.

While this was sensible in theory, in practice Fromelles was too obviously an isolated diversion, and had little impact on the German High Command.

Virtually every aspect of the execution of the attack was bungled. The ground which the Australians and British were sent to contest was terribly bare and dominated by the Sugar Loaf, a formidable German strongpoint. The preparations were rushed, the troops and many of the commanders involved were inexperienced and command blunders were made at various levels. In spite of some initial success, such as the capture of part of the German front line by the 2/7th Royal Warwicks, and much heroism, by the troops, Fromelles was a disaster, the only results the slaughter of troops and

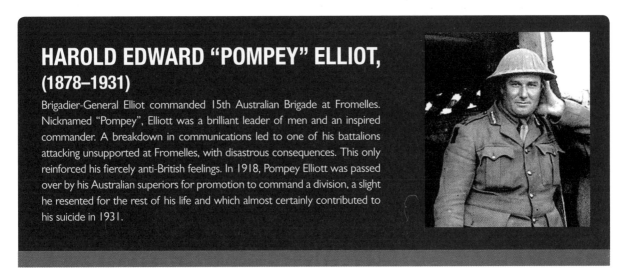

HAROLD EDWARD "POMPEY" ELLIOT, (1878–1931)

Brigadier-General Elliot commanded 15th Australian Brigade at Fromelles. Nicknamed "Pompey", Elliott was a brilliant leader of men and an inspired commander. A breakdown in communications led to one of his battalions attacking unsupported at Fromelles, with disastrous consequences. This only reinforced his fiercely anti-British feelings. In 1918, Pompey Elliott was passed over by his Australian superiors for promotion to command a division, a slight he resented for the rest of his life and which almost certainly contributed to his suicide in 1931.

LEFT: Action shot of the Battle for Hill 70, near Lens, taken by a Canadian official photographer. Note the bursting shells.

ABOVE: The Rising Sun badge was worn by Australian soldiers in both world wars. Introduced in 1904, along with the slouch hat on which it was worn, it came to typify the "digger".

embitterment of Anglo-Australian relations.

Hill 70 was very different from Fromelles. During Third Ypres in 1917, the Canadian Corps were tasked with attacking this rise near Lens, partly as a diversion from the main operation, but also to seize a key position for future use. The original British plan for an assault on Lens itself was altered by General Arthur Currie, the Canadian Corps commander, to become an attack on the vital high ground to the north of the city. The battle lasted 10 days (15–25 August 1917), and cost the Canadians over 9,000 casualties. Currie prepared for the battle in his trademark meticulous fashion, using many of the methods that had proved successful in the capture of Vimy Ridge earlier that year: detailed planning; a creeping barrage; smoke screens; thoroughly rehearsed infantry. An essential element of his plan was to prepare for the inevitable German counter-attacks, and ensure that they were broken up by heavy Canadian fire. This was a sophisticated form of bite-and-hold.

Three Canadian divisions attacked at dawn on 15 August, with a fourth in reserve. The attackers rapidly secured their objectives. At 09:00 the German counter-attacks began; in all there were 21 attempts to retake the hill. Although the Canadians suffered severely – including casualties from mustard gas – they held their ground. Hill 70 is rightly remembered as one of the Canadian Corps's finest feats of arms, with five German divisions that could otherwise have fought at Ypres being engaged and defeated.

Several months later in 1917, the French army carried out a similarly successful minor operation at Fort La Malmaison, on the Chemin des Dames. This formed part of a series of "healing battles" ordered by Pétain to nurse the French Army back to health after the trauma of the Nivelle offensive and the Mutinies (see pages 42–43). Successful limited attacks had already been carried out at Verdun in mid-August 1917. As Ludendorff later noted, "The French Army was once more capable of the offensive. It had quickly overcome its depression."

The Malmaison attack was well planned, limited in scope and, above all, designed to reduce French losses to a minimum. Sixth Army, under General Maistre, was heavily reinforced with artillery, but Pétain refused to allow the infantry of Tenth Army to attack, in order to minimize the chance of casualties. The point of attack was selected in such a way that a relatively short advance would make a sizeable portion of the German defences untenable.

The preliminary bombardment began on 17 October, and the infantry attacked before dawn on 23 October, supported by tanks and aircraft. The crushing weight of artillery fire helped the French infantry on to their objectives. The infantry pushed forward to a maximum depth of 6 km (3.72 miles), and took 11,000 prisoners at a cost of some 12,000 French casualties. The Germans were forced to abandon the Chemin des Dames ridge, the scene of so much fighting in earlier battles (see page 43). Like the Canadians at Hill 70, and Plumer at Ypres, Malmaison demonstrated how effective well-planned, artillery-heavy, limited offensives could be.

OPPOSITE: Canadian troops receiving drinks at a makeshift canteen close to the frontline, before the assault on Hill 70.

ABOVE: French troops overlooking German positions during the Battle of Malmaison in 1917. Malmaison was an outstandingly successful attack.

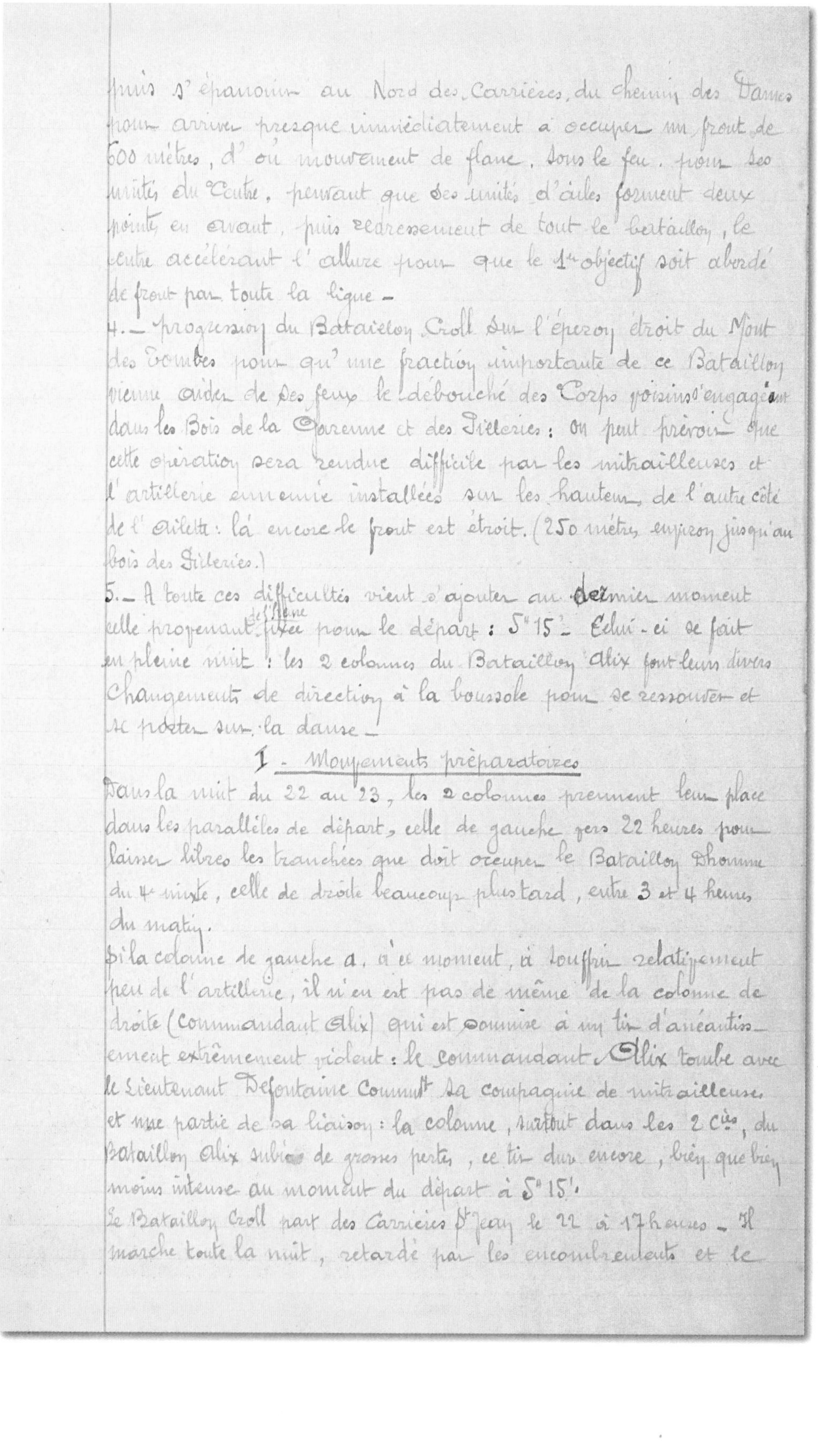

puis s'épanouir au Nord des Carrières du chemin des Dames pour arriver presque immédiatement à occuper un front de 600 mètres, d'où mouvement de flanc, sous le feu, pour les unités du Centre, pendant que les unités d'ailes forment deux pointes en avant, puis redressement de tout le bataillon, le centre accélérant l'allure pour que le 1er objectif soit abordé de front par toute la ligne –

4. – Progression du Bataillon Croll sur l'éperon étroit du Mont des Tombes pour qu'une fraction importante de ce Bataillon vienne aider de ses feux le débouché des Corps voisins s'engageant dans les Bois de la Garenne et des Tilleries : on peut prévoir que cette opération sera rendue difficile par les mitrailleuses et l'artillerie ennemie installées sur les hauteurs de l'autre côté de l'Ailette : là encore le front est étroit. (250 mètres environ jusqu'au bois des Tilleries.)

5. – A toute ces difficultés vient s'ajouter au dernier moment celle provenant de l'heure fixée pour le départ : 5h15 – Celui-ci se fait en pleine nuit : les 2 colonnes du Bataillon Alix font leurs divers changements de direction à la boussole pour se ressouder et se porter sur la danse –

I. – Mouvements préparatoires

Dans la nuit du 22 au 23, les 2 colonnes prennent leur place dans les parallèles de départ, celle de gauche vers 22 heures pour laisser libres les tranchées que doit occuper le Bataillon Dhomme du 4e mixte, celle de droite beaucoup plus tard, entre 3 et 4 heures du matin.

Si la colonne de gauche a, à ce moment, à souffrir relativement peu de l'artillerie, il n'en est pas de même de la colonne de droite (Commandant Alix) qui est soumise à un tir d'anéantissement extrêmement violent : le commandant Alix tombe avec le Lieutenant Defontaine Commt la compagnie de mitrailleuses et une partie de sa liaison : la colonne, surtout dans les 2 Cies du Bataillon Alix subit de grosses pertes, ce tir dure encore, bien que bien moins intense au moment du départ à 5h15'.

Le Bataillon Croll part des Carrières St Jean le 22 à 17 heures – Il marche toute la nuit, retardé par les encombrements et le

RIGHT: War diary of French 76 Brigade, 38th Division for the successful action at Malmaison, 23 October 1917.

mauvais état du Boyau B³ et ne gagne ses emplacements (1 Cie Pardeune et 1 section de mitrailleuses Creuzet dans la tranchée Larrouy - 3 Cies Sabarthe Lacquier, Bourgeois et Bénazet-Domali et les sections de mitrailleuses des Gazels dans les places d'armes du Plateau des Roches) qu'entre 3 heures ½ et 4 heures ½ du matin -

Enfin, comme il est dit plus haut, à 4h45 toutes les troupes sont en place et prêtes à donner l'assaut, leur enthousiasme est grandissant -

II. Exécution de l'attaque

A 5 heures 15 l'attaque générale est commencée dans une obscurité complète.

A.- 4ème Bataillon.-

Ce bataillon doit encercler et pénétrer dans les carrières de Bohéry pour permettre aux Bataillons Alix et Holl de prononcer leur mouvement vers le Nord en toute sécurité : Au centre de ces carrières un très gros amas de déblai formant "Cavalier" domine le plateau sur lequel ces 2 Bataillons doivent s'avancer ; les 4 Compagnies convergent sur le blockhauss Central des Carrières -

Colonne ou ½ Bataillon de gauche.- A l'heure H, la colonne de gauche (ordres du Commandant Pélaudeau) se porte en avant, prend son dispositif d'attaque en marchant et serre sur le barrage - Ses différentes fractions serrent les unes sur les autres et marquent un temps d'arrêt en attendant la marche du barrage - Pendant cette marche, le Sous-Lieutenant Brie commandant la section de gauche reçoit une grenade en pleine tête qui le met hors de Combat -

Dès que le barrage devient mobile, les sections de tête bondissent sur la Fourragère Jaune qu'elles enlèvent sans résistance sérieuse -

La section de gauche traverse la rancune et se porte à la carrière de Jouy où elle capture des petits groupes de prisonniers qui avaient résisté à la grenade -

La section de droite (Sarcelet) se porte au Blockhauss 4038 qui est fortement occupé - Elle l'attaque à la grenade et au lance-flammes et fait des prisonniers ; aidée par la 1ère section Domali qui l'a débordée à droite -

La section Sarcelet se porte ensuite aux Carrières 4 et 3 où elle capture des groupes ennemis dissimulés dans des trous d'obus.

La 3ème section Memerat encercle les Carrières vers le Nord et vient attaquer le blockhauss de l'isthme qui se défend énergiquement avec : mitrailleuses, grenades, fusils - Après une lutte acharnée elle capture

20 NOVEMBER–5 DECEMBER 1917

THE BATTLE OF CAMBRAI

THE FIRST MASSED TANK ASSAULT

Ironically, the bitter slogging match at Passchendaele, the epitome of attrition, was followed by the return of mobile warfare to the Western Front. The Battle of Cambrai, which began on 20 November 1917, was initially planned as a large-scale tank raid.

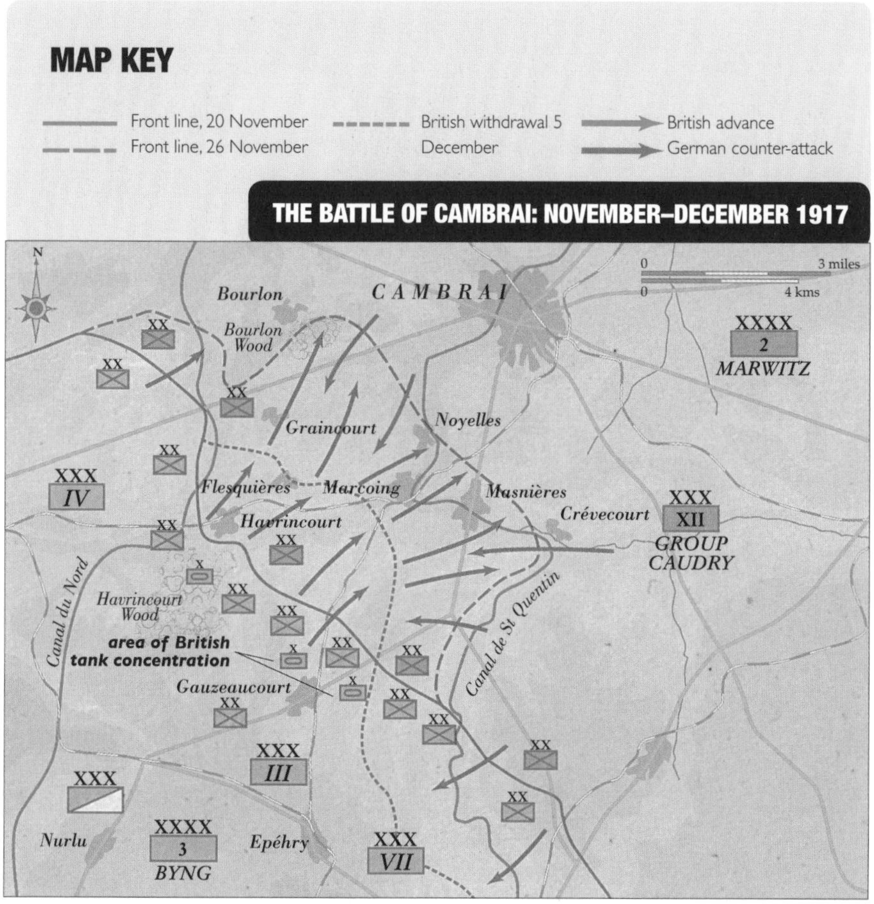

OPPOSITE: A British tank at Cambrai. The rhomboid shape of the early tank is still featured on the badge of the Royal Tank Regiment.

BELOW: A cap badge of the Tank Corps. This replaced the badge of the Machine Gun Corps, of which the first tank formations were technically a part.

With some notable exceptions, the performance of the tanks in the Third Battle of Ypres had been disappointing, which was unsurprising given the poor terrain and the weather. The commander of the Tank Corps, Brigadier General Hugh Elles, and his Chief-of-Staff, Colonel J. F. C. Fuller, believed that the country around Cambrai offered more scope to show what the tank could really do. As Third Ypres dragged, on the idea of a fresh offensive away from Passchendaele grew more attractive to Haig and GHQ. The crushing defeat inflicted on the Italians at Caporetto in October 1917 provided further reasons for a new attack, as a major effort on the Western Front might divert German attention from the Italian front. The original idea of a raid, in which the capture of territory was unimportant, grew into a major offensive by General Sir Julian Byng's Third Army designed to break through the Hindenburg Line (the extensive system of defensive fortifications built by the Germans in northeastern France in 1916–17) and take Cambrai itself. With this stage successfully completed, GHQ would judge the best way to exploit the victory – perhaps an advance on Douai.

There were two novel features about the attack. The attack would take place without a preliminary bombardment or even the guns firing preliminary shots to establish the range. The latter was a revolutionary suggestion, based on the fact that gunnery techniques were now sufficiently sophisticated to allow "shooting off the map". This meant that the tell-tale signs that an offensive was imminent would not be needed and surprise could return to the battlefield. The second novelty was the use of tanks, not thinly spread out in support of infantry formations, but concentrated to gain the maximum advantage from the shock of the assault. A total of 378 fighting tanks were deployed, accompanied by a further 98 for transporting supplies. Haig concentrated 19 infantry divisions on the Cambrai front, plus cavalry formations. Pétain sent three French infantry and two cavalry divisions to the area. If a major success did materialize there, the Allies would be hard pressed to exploit it, given the insufficient numbers of reserves available. The ravages of Passchendaele and the need to send reinforcements to Italy left precious few troops available for Cambrai.

The initial attack was highly successful. At 06:20 the tanks rumbled forward, accompanied by infantry, under the cover of a bombardment. The Germans were caught by surprise, and at first it seemed that the attack was unstoppable. The tanks crushed barbed wire and dropped fascines (bundles of wood) into trenches to allow them across. Third Army broke through the Hindenburg

JOHN FREDERICK CHARLES FULLER (1878–1966)

Colonel Fuller, as Chief of the Staff of the Tank Corps, was a major architect of the Cambrai plan. After the war he was an influential writer, lambasting British high command in the Great War (not always fairly) and making important contributions to the development of armoured warfare. A visionary military thinker, "Boney" Fuller was a man of extremes: at various times he embraced the occult and fascism. His views on tanks on the Western Front were partisan in the extreme.

Line and the possibilities seemed limitless. The cavalry passed through the gap and did relatively well, but given the shortness of daylight hours in late November, its effect was limited. Only on the left flank, on the front of 51st (Highland) Division, where the tanks got too far ahead of the infantry at the village of Flesquières, was there a major setback.

Tanks in the First World War were effectively a one-shot weapon. Mechanical failure and casualties from enemy action meant that the tank force was savagely reduced, and only 92 remained as "runners" three days after the beginning of the battle. With the Allies unable to reinforce the initial success, and with the Germans rushing reserves to the battlefield, the fighting became bogged down on the left flank in a seesaw struggle for Bourlon Wood. This was back to attritional slogging, the antithesis of mobile warfare. Worse was to come, because on 30 November General von der Marwitz's German Second Army launched a counter-attack, giving a taste of the tactics – stormtroopers, hurricane bombardments and low-flying aircraft – that were to be employed to great effect in the German's March 1918 offensive. The British reeled under the impact, and Haig sanctioned a withdrawal – he could not afford another lengthy attritional battle. Some of the gains of 20 November were retained but most were lost. German casualties equalled British losses of about 45,000.

The ringing of the bells in England to celebrate a victory had been premature. Haig's credibility as a commander suffered more as a result of disappointed expectations at Cambrai than it did because of Passchendaele. For those who had eyes to see, Cambrai was a very significant battle. It indicated that the tactical advantage, which for so long had lain with the defender, now rested with the attacker. Trench warfare was on the verge of ending for good.

OPPOSITE BELOW: A crowded rear area scene, Battle of Cambrai, 22 November 1917, with cavalry, infantry, bicyclists and motorcyclists.

ABOVE: A chainmail mask worn by tank crews to protect the face from metal fragments flying around the tank.

BELOW: The perils of "Hyacinth": infantrymen with a tank of H Battalion Tank Corps in a German trench near Ribécourt, 20 November 1917.

BRIGADIER GENERAL HUGH JAMIESON ELLES
(1880–1945)

Aged 37, Elles (below, front left) commanded the Tank Corps at Cambrai. He served as a staff officer from 1914, being wounded at Second Ypres in 1915. A Royal Engineer by profession, Elles's obvious competence attracted the patronage of both Haig and Robertson. At Cambrai, he personally led the attack in his Mark IV tank Hilda. This was a conscious return to old-style heroic leadership. Elles had a forceful personality and he made an outstanding contribution to the development of the Tank Corps.

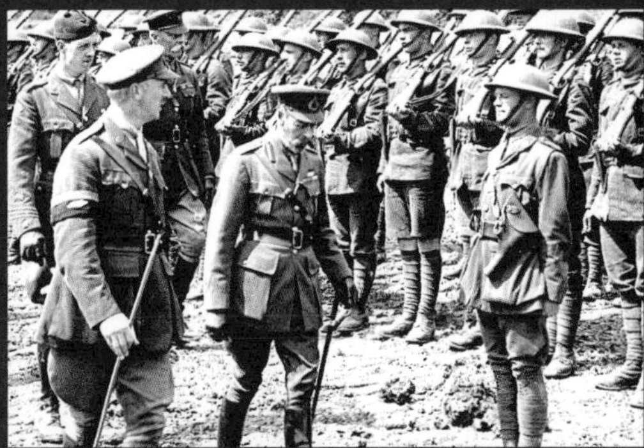

21 MARCH–5 APRIL 1918

GERMAN SPRING OFFENSIVE

HOLDING OUT AGAINST OPERATION MICHAEL

If 1917 had been a year of frustration and stalemate for the Western Allies, for the Russians it had been a year of disaster. Military setbacks on the Eastern Front had helped to trigger the liberal revolution in March 1917. By the end of the year, further defeats and the Bolshevik seizure of power all but removed Russia from the war.

The British and French, suffering from manpower shortages, would be able to field only 156 divisions in early 1918 to the Germans' 192. From the perspective of the German High Command, this offered the chance to mass its forces in the West and seek a knockout blow before American troops could arrive in overwhelming numbers. In a meeting at Mons on 11 November 1917 (in retrospect, both the venue and date are richly ironic), the decision was taken to gamble on a strike in the West. Later, Ludendorff confirmed that the target would be the British Fifth and Third Armies. The codename for the attack was Operation Michael.

The Allies, aware that they had lost the strategic initiative, went on to the defensive. Haig was forced to reduce the size of British divisions from 12 battalions to nine. He was misled by German deception and, realizing he could not be strong everywhere, chose to keep the bulk of his forces in the north, defending the critical areas that led to the Channel ports. In the event, this was to prove to be the correct decision. In the short term, however, Gough's Fifth Army stationed at the southern extremity of the British line and which bore the brunt of the attack, was dangerously weak, with only 12 infantry divisions covering a 68-km (42-mile) front from south of Flesquières to La Fère.

At 04:40 on 21 March 1918, Michael began with a furious hurricane bombardment of British positions in the St-Quentin sector orchestrated by Colonel Bruchmüller. Overwhelmed by the fire of nearly 10,000 guns and trench mortars, five hours later waves of German stormtroopers from Second and Eighteenth Armies assaulted the British defences. The British, having spent most of the previous three years on the offensive, were unused to defending. They misunderstood the principles of defence in depth, massing too many soldiers in the front positions which were supposed to be lightly held. Morale was poor in some units, and by the end of the day, Fifth Army was in serious trouble. Materially aided by thick fog, the Germans captured the British Forward Zone, taking some 500 guns and 21,000 prisoners. Worse, the stormtroopers got through III Corps's Battle Zone, where attackers were supposed to be stopped. However, in places Fifth Army fought well and the Germans did not reach all their

OPPOSITE: German stormtroopers. Tactical developments on both sides of No Man's Land had produced a revolution in infantry tactics by 1918.

ABOVE: The Allies in retreat, Omiecourt, March 24 1918: huts and stores are destroyed as gun teams move to recover their weapons.

FERDINAND FOCH (1851–1929)

If any one individual can be said to have been essential to the Allied victory in 1918, it was Foch. He successfully carried out the difficult job of holding together an international coalition in the face of many competing agendas, being prepared to overrule both Haig and his countryman, Pétain. Deservedly appointed a Marshal of France in August 1918, he said – truthfully – "I am conscious of having served England as I served my own country." He formed a good team with Haig in the final offensives.

OSKAR VON HUTIER (1857–1934)

General von Hutier, commander of German Eighteenth Army in 1918, came to prominence on the Eastern Front. At Riga, in September 1917, his Eighth Army had given an early demonstration of the methods that would be used in March 1918: a short bombardment without previously registering the guns, arranged by Bruchmüller; followed by the infantry using infiltration tactics (although the Russians put up little resistance). This approach became known as "Hutier tactics", although Hutier himself had little influence on their development.

objectives. To the north, British Third Army stubbornly held out south of Arras against German Seventeenth Army's attack.

The attack made further progress on 22 and 23 March as Gough's Fifth Army fell back. Ludendorff, frustrated that his plan was lagging behind schedule, gave Hutier's Eighteenth Army, which had made the most ground, the lead role, although it had been intended to act as a flank guard. Ludendorff's new plan dissipated the strength of his attack, although it threatened to separate the British from the French. It would have been better to continue to aim for the critical communications centres which, if captured, might have crippled the BEF's ability to fight on. Paradoxically, the severe threat forced the Allies to agree to unity of command, a factor that was greatly to improve their command performance. Fearful that the French would give priority to defending Paris over maintaining contact with the BEF, on 26 March the British supported Foch's appointment as overall Allied commander.

Byng's British Third Army decisively defeated another major attack near Arras on 28 March. Operation Michael was slowing down; as the Allies recovered, French reserves arrived, and German infantry outran their artillery support. The German attempt to take the critical rail-hub of Amiens was halted on 4–5 April at Villers-Bretonneux, 16 km (10 miles) from the key city of Amiens, by Australian and British troops. Ludendorff, recognizing that Michael had run out of steam, halted the offensive. It had gained a great deal of ground, but the possession of a bulge into the Allied lines some 65-km (40-miles) deep proved difficult to defend and in the long run more trouble than it was worth. Haig's forces had suffered tactical defeat – Gough paid for it with his job – but the BEF was still very much in the fight. Moreover, Ludendorff had failed to break the link between the French and British armies. The trench deadlock had been broken, and open warfare restored. Who could best take advantage – the Germans or the Allies?

"Holding out – Boche all around within fifty yards – can only see fifty yards, so it is difficult to kill the blighters"

Message from Commander of 7th Battalion Royal West Kents, 21 March 1918

BELOW RIGHT: Two days before the fall of the town, German and British wounded are unloaded from a British hospital train near Bapaume.

BELOW LEFT: The Germans on the advance, March 1918: reserves move across the old Somme battlefield.

RIGHT: A German poster celebrating the success of the 1918 spring offensive, boasting of prisoners and equipment captured and ground gained.

Der erste Monat
deutsche Westoffensive!
127000 Gefangene
1600 Geschütze
ca 200 Tanks
Viele 1000
Maschinen=
gewehre
Ungeheure
Mengen an
Munition u.
zahlreiche
Flugzeuge
Geländegewinn
4100 □Kilometer
DER KANAL
Paris
Klischees und Druck von Dr. Selle & Co. G.m.b.H., Berlin SW 29

9 APRIL–9 JUNE 1918

GERMAN SPRING OFFENSIVE

OPERATION GEORGETTE TO THE SECOND MARNE

There was little respite before Ludendorff's next attack was launched. Operation Georgette (or the Battle of the Lys) opened on 9 April with the now-familiar hurricane bombardment, and infantry of German Sixth Army drove into Allied positions south of Ypres.

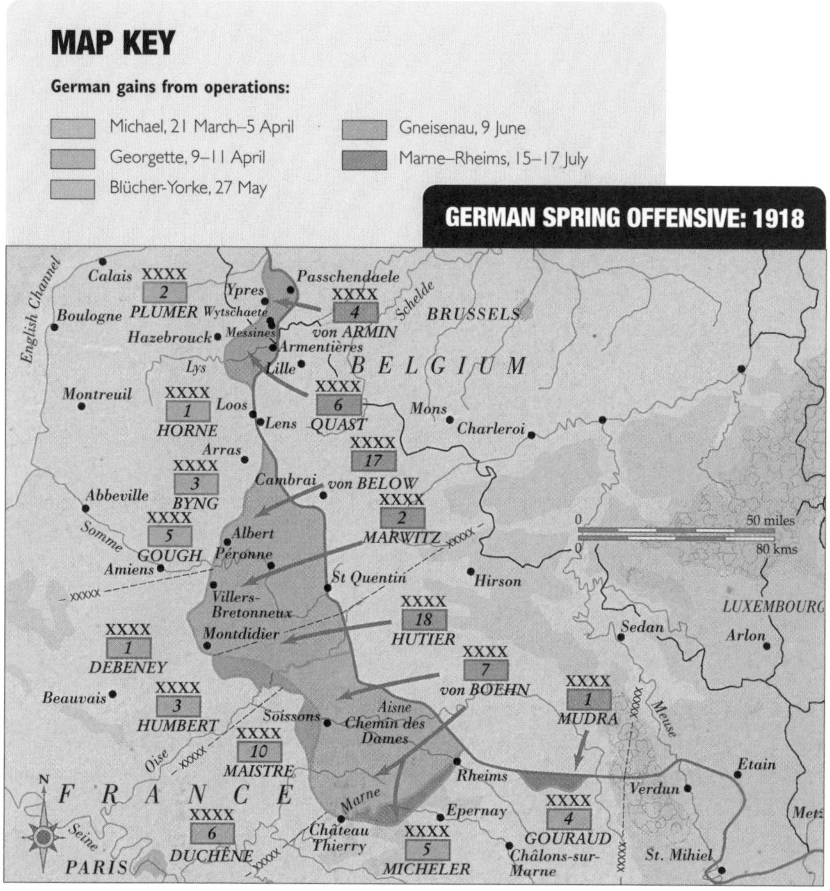

OPPOSITE LEFT: The spring offensive saw fighting under conditions very different from the trench warfare of earlier years: British soldiers defend Bailleul, 15 April 1918.

BELOW: A German Stahlhelm (steel helmet). The first model was introduced in 1915, and was gradually improved during the war.

The objective was Hazebrouck, a major communications centre whose capture would imperil the entire British situation. This threat was, potentially, much more dangerous than that posed by Operation Michael, as it would put the Channel ports directly at risk.

A Portuguese division gave way, but on its flanks British divisions held on, ensuring that the advance of about 5.5 km (3.5 miles) was funnelled on a relatively narrow front. To the north, on the following day, German Fourth Army smashed into British Second Army. The defenders gave some ground and the British were forced to abandon Armentières to the enemy. The villages of Messines and Wytschaete – the scene of so much heavy fighting in previous years – also fell into German hands. The seriousness of the situation can be judged from the fact that on 11 April Haig, not a man given to grand gestures, issued his famous "Backs to the Wall" order.

The Allies survived – just. Foch, whose authority as Allied commander was enhanced on 14 April as a response to the crisis, sent French divisions, including Micheler's French Fifth Army, up to support and relieve the British. Some British divisions were moved to quiet parts of the front. Although Haig wanted more help, he sourly noted in his diary that Foch was "very disinclined to engage French troops in the battle". Foch instead took a hard, calculating look at the situation and decided to keep plenty of French divisions in reserve. He believed that the British could hold on in Flanders, and rightly suspected that the Germans would attack further south. Plumer, after much heart searching, abandoned the positions on the Passchendaele Ridge, won at such a high cost the previous autumn.

On the other side of No Man's Land, Ludendorff was becoming frustrated with the failure to push on. A German account of the fighting of 17 April recorded that the "foremost waves were compelled to return to their jumping-off trenches, suffering severe losses. There they lay the whole day under the heaviest fire." Georgette, like Michael before it, was becoming stalemated. On 25 April, a further crisis arose when the Germans captured Mount Kemmel, the highest feature on the Ypres Salient, which had been held by three French divisions. This setback caused some inter-Allied tension, but the Germans were unable to take advantage. Five days later, the battle came to an end. Both sides had paid a heavy price (from 21 March to 30 April, 332,000 Allied casualties, 348,000 German), but Ludendorff had failed to break through.

On 24 April, even before the Lys had ended, the Germans began

another attack aiming at Amiens. Once again, a clash at Villers-Bretonneux was critical, where two Australian brigades took the lead in mounting a counter-attack and pushing the Germans back. However, for his next offensive Ludendorff turned his attention to the French, aiming to exhaust their reserves. In the early hours of 27 May, a hurricane bombardment, heavy even by Bruchmüller's standards, opened on the Chemin des Dames, held by General Duchêne's French Sixth Army (which included British IX Corps, sent south for a "rest"). The Allies were badly deployed; being forward of the defensible line of the Aisne with their forward positions crammed with troops. Attacking in overwhelming force, the Germans quickly smashed through the Allied defences and crossed the Aisne, advancing 16 km (10 miles) in a day. The situation was stabilized only when the Germans reached the Marne on 3–4 June. Although alarming to the Allies, the Germans had merely acquired another tract of unrewarding territory, as Foch was shrewd enough to realize. Some Allied reserves (including US divisions) had been rushed to the sector, but not enough to make life easier for the Germans elsewhere. Another German offensive had started well but then run into the sand.

HAIG'S ORDER
11 APRIL 1918

Haig's "Backs to the Wall" message of 11 April 1918 was an uncharacteristically dramatic gesture that demonstrates how bleak the situation appeared from the perspective of GHQ. Some British soldiers commented later that they were unaware of the seriousness of the position until they read Haig's message.

OPPOSITE TOP: By 1918, warfare had become well and truly "three-dimensional". Here, British infantry man machine guns delpoyed in an anti-aircraft role on 1 May 1918 at Haverskerque.

OPPOSITE MIDDLE: One of the most evocative images of the war: British solders blinded by gas, April 1918.

OPPOSITE BELOW: Haig greets "The Tiger", the French Premier, Georges Clemenceau.

ABOVE: A pair of German binoculars and case. These items were much sought after by Allied troops as war trophies.

RIGHT: The huge and ungainly German A7V tank was 7 m (7.6 yds) long and had a crew of up to 18.

BELOW: A column of French troops, led by some grizzled poilus, pass a Britsh band resting by the side of the road.

THE GERMAN TANK

On 24 April 1918, at Cachy, three German A7V tanks fought an action against three British Mark IV tanks. After two British machine-gun armed "female" tanks had been forced to pull back, Lieutenant Frank Mitchell's Mark IV "male", armed with a 6-pounder gun drove back an A7V, which overturned, and caused the crew of another to abandon their tank. This action, fought during the clash at Villers-Bretonneux, which prevented the Germans from moving on Amiens, was the first confrontation of armoured fighting vehicles in history.

THE WAR IN THE AIR

THE START OF MODERN WARFARE

Powered flight was very new in 1914 – the Wright brothers' first flight had taken place only 11 years before. German, French and British aircraft all went to war in 1914, but they were primitive and their potential was barely recognized. By 1918, the aircraft had emerged as a powerful weapon indispensable to modern warfare.

OPPOSITE: A German observer manning the machine gun. Both sides made extensive use of two seater aircraft.

LEFT AND ABOVE: French ace René Fonck (right) and the British Captain Albert Ball VC (above) sitting in the cockpit of his SE5 aircraft in April 1917. Ball achieved 17 of his 44 kills in an SE5. Fonck survived the war but Ball was killed on 7 May 1917.

Virtually all of the military roles of the aircraft had been developed. Air power was one of the major reasons why the First World War was different to the wars of the past, instead pointing the way to the wars of the future.

Before the war, military men had viewed aircraft with a mixture of interest, scepticism and doubt. Foch made some dismissive comments in 1910, but at an exercise in the following year the French army used airplanes for reconnaissance and – in a portent of the future – to direct artillery fire. Any initial reservations Haig might have had about aircraft vanished after he was comprehensively beaten in pre-war manoeuvres by a force that used aerial reconnaissance. In August 1914, the value of aircraft was demonstrated graphically when Allied aircraft detected the swing of von Kluck's army inside Paris. The counter-stroke that led to the Battle of the Marne was the result (see pages 14–15). Once trench stalemate set in, aircraft completely took over reconnaissance, traditionally the cavalry's role. In order to keep the prying eyes of the enemy's aircraft away from the trench systems, other aircraft were sent up to shoot them down or drive them away. Yet more aircraft were then deployed to protect the reconnaissance aircraft and fight enemy fighters, and so the modern battle for control of the air was born.

The aircraft of 1914 were crude in comparison to what was available only four years later, and were maids of all work. Eventually, specialist machines were introduced. Artillery spotting was left to large platforms like the British R.E. 8, while fighter planes evolved in a very different direction. Most early planes were unarmed, and air combat only took place if a pilot or observer brought a rifle with them. Even when machine guns were fitted, they were difficult to use. The invention of the interrupter gear in 1915, which permitted a machine gun to fire through the propeller arc, created the modern fighter. By the late period of the war, fighters such as the fast and manoeuvrable French Spad XIII, the British Sopwith Snipe, and the German Fokker D-VII dominated the skies. Arguably the D-VII was the finest fighter aircraft of the war. All three were a far cry from the first dedicated fighters such as the Fokker E-I "Eindekker" (monoplane) of 1915. Individual ace fighter pilots had rather different styles. For the British, Captain Albert Ball VC was a lone hunter, stalking his prey through the skies. The German ace Manfred von Richthofen fought as part of his "flying circus". On the French side, René Fonck was a skilled tactician who studied the techniques of enemy pilots.

Specialized bomber aircraft were also developed. The British DH-4, French Caudron G-4 and German A.E.G. G-IV came into this category.

ABOVE: Royal Flying Corps pilot's "wings": a badge issued to qualified pilots.

And yet this was not the end of the roles performed by aircraft during the war. Ground attack, contact patrols (i.e. attempting to locate and communicate with ground troops during battles), photographic reconnaissance; interdiction bombing; and even dropping supplies by parachute were all roles fulfilled by aircraft during the war. Away from the Western Front, they were used at sea and for strategic bombing of enemy cities.

Even the humble balloon had a role. Tethered behind the lines, with an observer in a basket armed with binoculars and a telephone, the Kite Balloon was an important means of spotting for the artillery. Balloons and aircraft made indirect fire possible – gunners could now accurately shoot at things that they could not see. This apparently simple development transformed warfare by making artillery far more effective. The year 1916 was crucial; for the first time, in the Battles of Verdun (see pages 46–49) and the Somme (see pages 74–79), the struggle for the air became an absolutely essential part of the overall battle. Dominance in the air see-sawed between the belligerents. The 1917 Battles of Arras (see pages 82–83) and the Nivelle Offensive (see pages 84–85) coincided with a period of German air superiority that became known to the British as "Bloody April". In the last phase of the war, the Allies had the upper hand, not least because of weight of numbers.

Air combat made huge advances during the First World War. In recognition, in April 1918 the British created the world's first independent air force, the Royal Air Force, from the army's Royal Flying Corps and the Royal Naval Air Service.

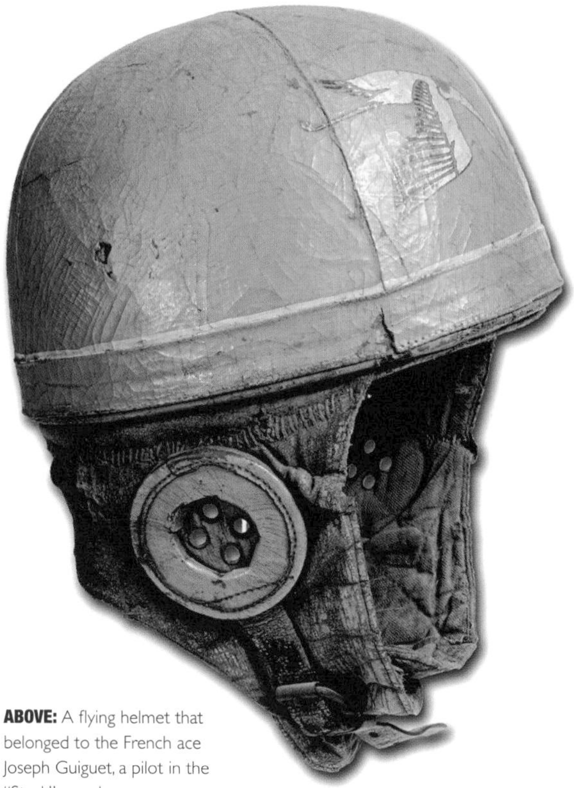

ABOVE: A flying helmet that belonged to the French ace Joseph Guiguet, a pilot in the "Stork" squadron.

BELOW LEFT: A French bomb, designed for dropping from aircraft.

BELOW: A red armband of the type worn by members of the French Air Service in the First World War.

ALLIED ACES

An ace was a pilot with five or more kills. The highest scoring Allied ace was René Fonck, with at least 75 victories. Other French aces included Georges Guynemer, of the French "Stork" squadron with 53 kills and Charles Nungesser (45). Billy Bishop VC, a Canadian, was the leading British Empire ace credited with 72 victories. Edward "Mick" Mannock may have exceeded Bishop's total with 73 kills, but only 47 are officially recognized. The leading American ace was Eddie Rickenbacker with 26 kills.

OPPOSITE BOTTOM: Capitaine Georges Guynemer in front of his Spad SVII aeroplane. He went missing on a patrol in September 1917.

RIGHT: The Blue Max, properly "Pour le Merite" (For Merit) was an award instituted by King Frederick the Great of Prussia in 1740. During the First World War it was awarded to pilots who shot down eight, and later 16, enemy planes.

BELOW: Royal Air Force Sopwith Camels of B and C flights, 201 Squadron in August 1918.

MANFRED ALBRECHT VON RICHTHOFEN (1892–1918)

Von Richthofen was the highest scoring pilot of the war, with 80 kills. Nicknamed the Red Baron from his aristocratic lineage and red-painted aircraft, he achieved a legendary status in his lifetime that has continued to the present day. He came to prominence in the second half of 1916, and was appointed leader of his "Flying Circus" Jagdstaffel (fighter squadron) 11 in January 1917. He was shot down near Amiens on 21 April 1918. There is some mystery over his death, but most likely Richthofen was hit by ground fire.

BELOW: A bi-lingual guide to aircraft recognition dating from the first half of the war.

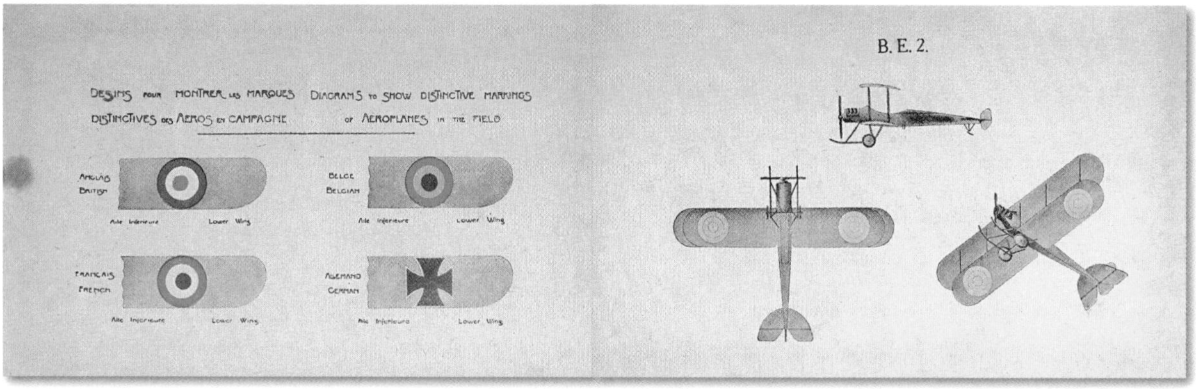

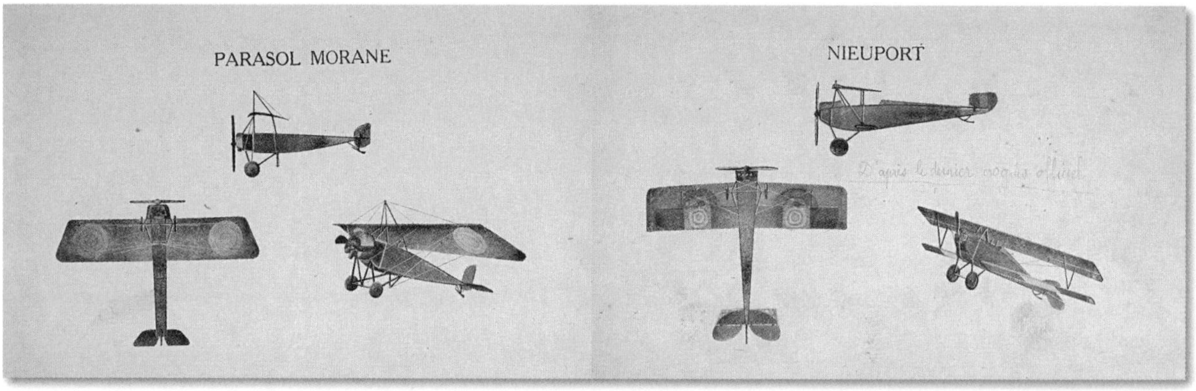

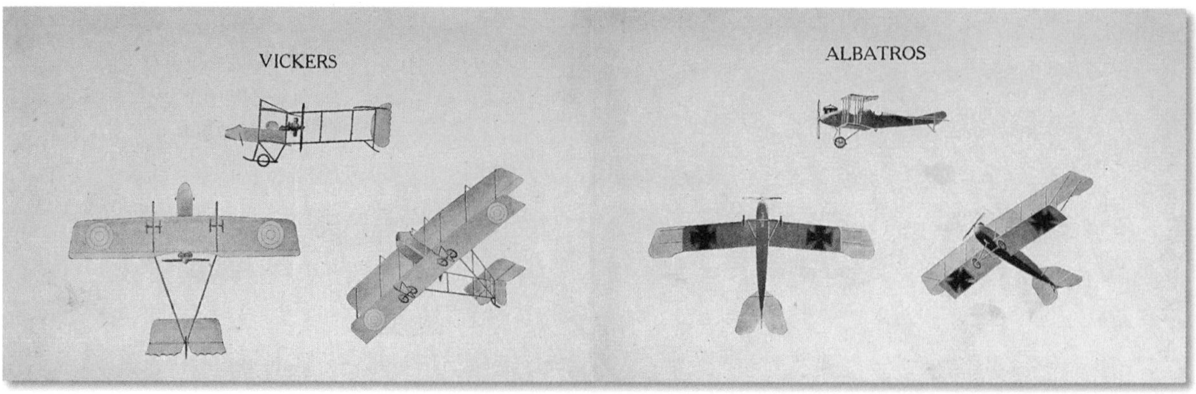

ABOVE: An FE2B, viewed from above. The FE2B was introduced as a fighter in 1915, and was used for bombing later in the war.

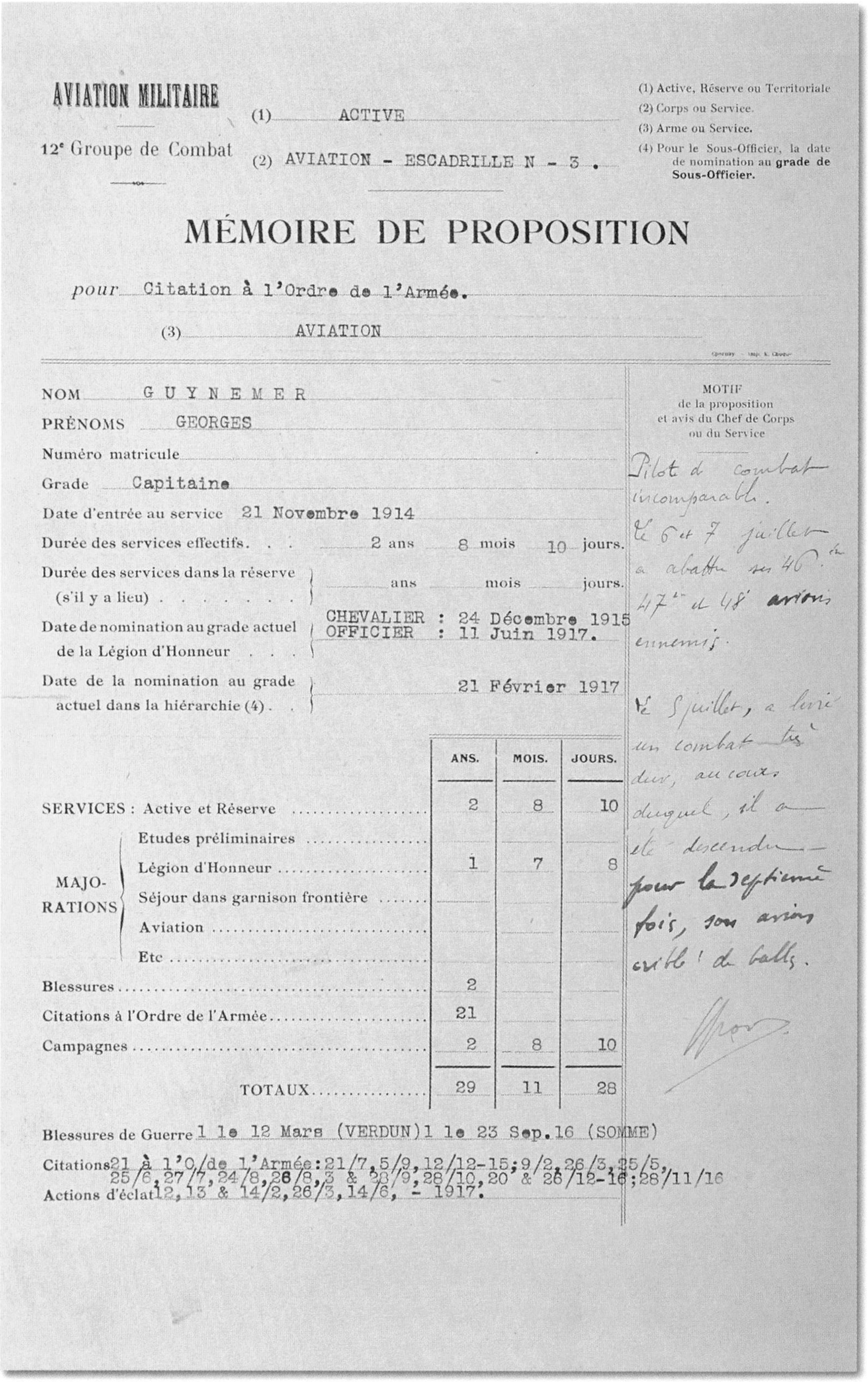

AVIATION MILITAIRE

12e Groupe de Combat

(1) ACTIVE

(2) AVIATION - ESCADRILLE N - 3 .

(1) Active, Réserve ou Territoriale
(2) Corps ou Service.
(3) Arme ou Service.
(4) Pour le Sous-Officier, la date de nomination au **grade de Sous-Officier.**

MÉMOIRE DE PROPOSITION

pour Citation à l'Ordre de l'Armée.

(3) AVIATION

NOM G U Y N E M E R

PRÉNOMS GEORGES

Numéro matricule

Grade Capitaine

Date d'entrée au service 21 Novembre 1914

Durée des services effectifs. . . 2 ans 8 mois 10 jours.

Durée des services dans la réserve (s'il y a lieu) . . . . ans mois jours.

Date de nomination au grade actuel de la Légion d'Honneur . . . CHEVALIER : 24 Décembre 1915 OFFICIER : 11 Juin 1917.

Date de la nomination au grade actuel dans la hiérarchie (4) . . 21 Février 1917

		ANS.	MOIS.	JOURS.
SERVICES : Active et Réserve		2	8	10
MAJORATIONS	Etudes préliminaires			
	Légion d'Honneur	1	7	8
	Séjour dans garnison frontière			
	Aviation			
	Etc			
Blessures		2		
Citations à l'Ordre de l'Armée		21		
Campagnes		2	8	10
TOTAUX		29	11	28

Blessures de Guerre 1 le 12 Mars (VERDUN) 1 le 23 Sep.16 (SOMME)

Citations 21 à l'O/de l'Armée: 21/7,5/9,12/12-15;9/2,26/3,25/5, 25/6,27/7,24/8,26/8,3 & 28/9,28/10,20 & 26/12-16;28/11/16

Actions d'éclat 12,13 & 14/2,26/3,14/6, - 1917.

MOTIF de la proposition et avis du Chef de Corps ou du Service

Pilot de combat incomparable. Le 6 et 7 juillet a abattu ses 46e 47e et 48e avions ennemis.

Le 5 juillet, a livré un combat très dur, au cours duquel, il a été descendu pour la septième fois, son avion criblé de balles.

RIGHT: In this Citation Georges Guynemer is described as "*Pilot de combat incomparable*". The Citation lists his service and decorations.

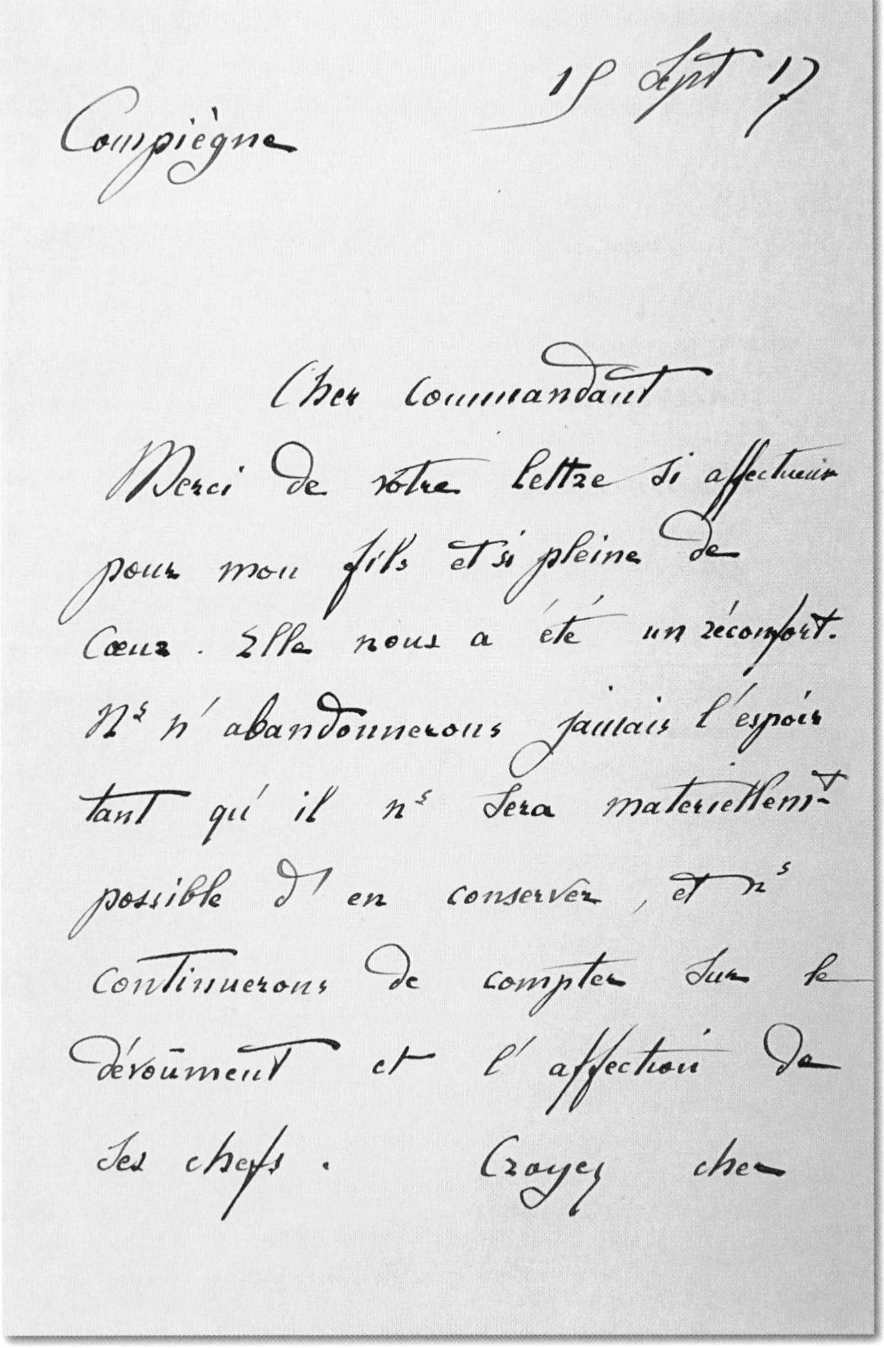

15 Sept 17

Compiègne

Cher Commandant

Merci de votre lettre si affectueuse pour mon fils et si pleine de cœur. Elle nous a été un réconfort. Ns n'abandonnerons jamais l'espoir tant qu'il ne sera matériellemt possible d'en conserver, et ns continuerons de compter sur le dévoument et l'affection de ses chefs. Croyez cher

ABOVE: A letter sent to Guynemer's parents after his death.

9 JUNE–18 JULY 1918

SECOND BATTLE OF THE MARNE

THE LAST GERMAN OFFENSIVE

At the end of the Germans' Chemin de Dames offensive, American troops saw a considerable amount of fighting, notably in the Belleau Wood battle (6 June). This was a warning that there was little time left for the Germans to defeat the Allies before US troops arrived in France in vast numbers.

MAP KEY

Front lines

- 18 July
- 20 July
- 28 July
- 6 August
- American Advance

THE SECOND BATTLE OF MARNE: SHOWING AMERICAN INVOLVEMENT: 18 JULY–6 AUGUST 1918

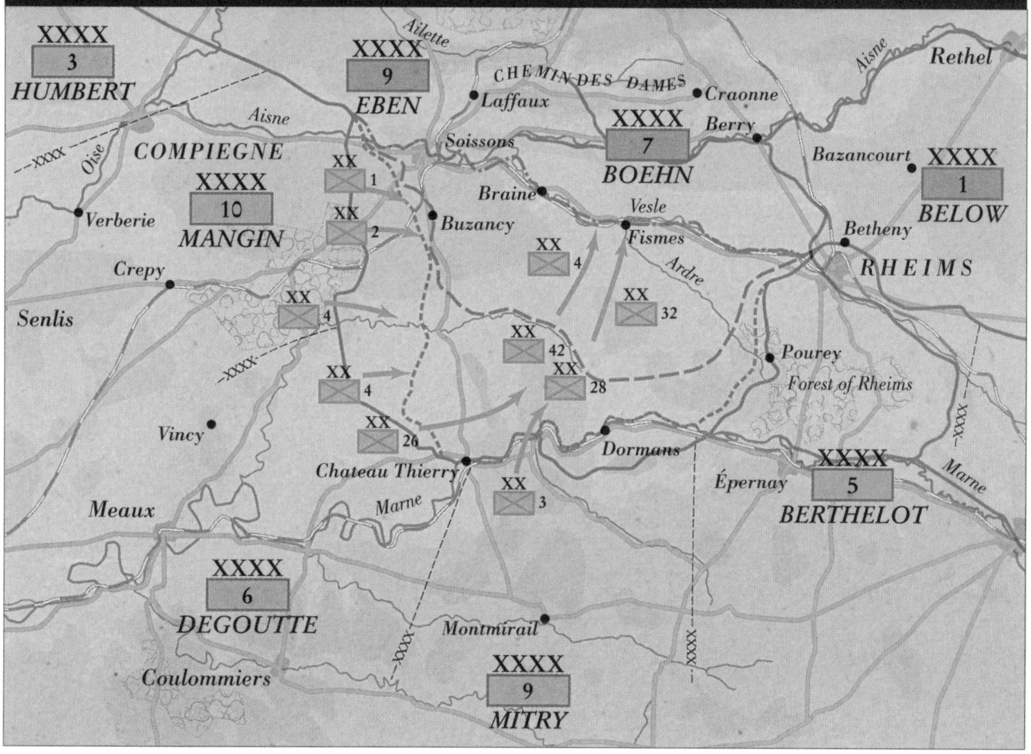

On 9 June, Ludendorff stuck again, this time against Humbert's French Third Army in the River Matz sector between Noyon and Montdider. Again, the German aim was to wear out French reserves before striking in Flanders. The attackers made spectacular gains, 10 km (6 miles) on the first day, but two days into the battle the French launched a counter-offensive under General Charles Mangin, who had been out of favour since the Nivelle Offensive (see pages 84–85). After an hour-long bombardment, Mangin's forces, which included several US Divisions, supported by ground-attack aircraft and 144 tanks, went into action. The Germans were halted, and the main battle was over by 14 June.

German High Command continued to put their faith in a planned attack by Rupprecht in Flanders, Operation Hagen, but felt that a preliminary offensive aimed at exhausting French reserves was necessary. Allied intelligence picked up signs of German activity on the Marne and in Flanders, leading to some inter-Allied disputes about where reserves should be sent. In the meantime, Mangin's Tenth Army made gains around Soissons (28–29 June), an attack that sowed the seeds for a much bigger offensive several weeks later. On the eve of the Second Battle of the Marne, the Allies had concentrated Maistre's and Fayolle's army groups, mostly comprising French divisions but also nine US, two Italian and two British. Against this, the Germans could bring First and Third Armies to attack to the east of Reims, aiming for the River Marne, 25 km (15 miles) away. To the west of the city, Seventh and Ninth Armies had to cross the Marne and link up with the eastern arm of the attack.

From the beginning, some things went wrong for the Germans. The element of surprise was lost because prisoners betrayed the time and date of the attack (03:50 am on 15 July). This allowed the Allies to open a disruptive counter-bombardment 90 minutes before German zero hour. Moreover, unlike during the defence of the Aisne on 27 May (see pages 104–05), the French defenders understood the purpose of defence in depth. French Fourth Army under General Gouraud, a Gallipoli veteran, fought a model defensive battle; the attackers were harried by fire in the outpost

OPPOSITE: In this posed image, French troops take up a defensive position in a ruined church near the Marne, 1918.

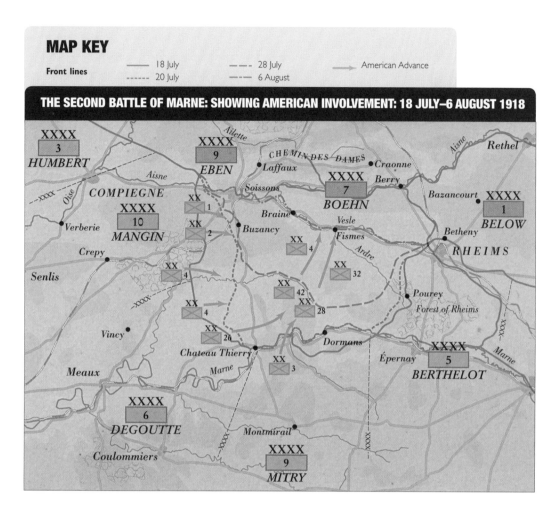

zone and then defeated in the main killing ground. In the western sector, initially the Germans had greater success. The Italians took a battering and were replaced by British 51st (Highland) and 62nd Divisions, which had just arrived in the area. Making good tactical use of a smokescreen, the German Seventh Army fought their way across the Marne at Dormans, and once on the far bank advanced 6 km (4 miles). This caused consternation in some parts of the French High Command. Clemenceau was furious with Foch, and Pétain, the commander of the French Army, was worried by this development. Foch, by contrast, was calm, overruling Pétain's desire to postpone a planned counter-offensive.

Mangin attacked the western flank of the bridgehead on 16 July and gained some ground. Hemmed into a shallow salient, unable to break out, the six German divisions that had crossed the Marne were in a dangerous position and lost heavily from shelling and bombing. But this was just the preliminary to a much larger French attack on 18 July. For this, Mangin massed 18 divisions, backed by another seven. However, it was Degoutte's French Sixth Army on Tenth Army's flank that struck the first blow, 45 minutes earlier at 04:35. Disoriented from this surprise attack, the defenders were wholly unprepared when Mangin's troops joined the battle. The Germans were pushed back 6 km (4 miles) in the face of French artillery, infantry and tanks. Tenth Army took 15,000 prisoners and 400 guns. Pressure grew on the German salient as French Fifth and Ninth Armies came into action later, and increased steadily over the next few days as more troops (including two more British divisions, 15th (Scottish) and 34th were committed to battle.

On 18 July, Ludendorff was in Mons, planning Operation Hagen. Mangin's counter-offensive wrecked his plans. Accepting the inevitable, the Marne bridgehead was evacuated, and the Germans fell back on other parts of the front. By 6 August, the battle was over. Foch, his judgement vindicated, richly deserved his promotion to Marshal of France, announced that day. Operation Hagen never took place. The strategic initiative had passed decisively from the Germans to the Allies.

BELOW: A group of Allied soldiers, July 1918. The French soldiers have their eyes bandaged, probably as a result of the gas.

OPPOSITE BELOW RIGHT: Highland troops, who played an important role at the Second Marne, escort German prisoners to the rear. Increasing numbers of Germans surrendered as 1918 progressed.

ABOVE: A French-built Renault FT-17 tank. The Renault was used by American as well as French units, and saw much action in 1918.

ABOVE: The 15 July 1918 marked the first day of the last German offensive of the war. Here, French stretcher-bearers bring wounded to a field hospital during the Second Battle of the Marne.

4 JULY–11 AUGUST 1918

HAMEL AND AMIENS

THE BLACK DAY OF THE GERMAN ARMY

The spring offensives left the German army exhausted, stuck at the end of tenuous supply lines, unable to make any further headway and vulnerable to attack. Just how vulnerable was revealed by a limited action that took place in early July at Le Hamel near Villers-Bretonneux.

Monash's Australian Corps, reinforced by American troops, captured all of its objectives in just 90 minutes. An updated version of the bite-and-hold operations used in 1917, this small-scale action was of enormous significance because it provided a model of a carefully prepared, tightly controlled, set-piece battle. Tellingly, Monash later described his methods as being akin to a conductor working from a musical score. A pamphlet on the lessons of 4 July was quickly produced and disseminated to the rest of the BEF.

Le Hamel proved to be a dress rehearsal for a battle fought on a far larger scale which has a good claim to be the turning point of the war on the Western Front. It was carried out by British Fourth Army, commanded by Rawlinson, in combination with General Debeney's French First Army. For this operation "Rawly" controlled British III Corps and both the Australian and Canadian Corps, two of the most powerful and effective formations in the Allied order of battle. Preparations for the battle were meticulous. Perhaps the most impressive piece of staff work was to bring the Canadians down, in great secrecy, from the northern part of the Western Front. The Canadians Corps was fresh, having taken little part in the spring battles, and in comparison to the British and Australians was very strong in numbers. A map captured during the battle showed that the Germans were totally unaware of the presence of the Canadian Corps in the Amiens area. In sharp contrast to the Battle of the Somme launched just a few miles to the north on 1 July 1916, at the Battle of Amiens the Allies achieved complete surprise.

OPPOSITE: US and Australian troops dug in at Hamel, 4 July 1918. Pershing initially opposed US involvement in the battle.

ABOVE: British artillery, like these 60 pounders, achieved dominance over its German counterparts during the Battle of Amiens and made a crucial contribution to victory.

LEFT: Badge of 10th Battalion, Canadian Expeditionary Force.

The attack began at 04:20 on 8 August 1918. Thanks to the advanced gunnery techniques that had been developed by this stage of the war, 2,000 Allied guns were able to fire without any preliminary bombardment – another crucial element in the maintenance of surprise. The

JOHN MONASH (1865–1931)

Lieutenant-General Monash had an unusual background for a Great War commander. Of German-Jewish origin, before the war he was a civil engineer and member of the part-time Australian militia. After service on Gallipoli, he took command of 3rd Australian Division in 1916 and then the Australian Corps in June 1918. A brilliant organizer, he had a methodical approach to combat. Despite sharing Haig's views on the importance of discipline, Monash became an Australian national hero, and deservedly gained a reputation as one of the finest Allied generals of the war.

number of guns and shells that were needed had been carefully calculated, and unlike in previous years, the BEF had a superfluity of both: 700 field guns fired 350,000 shells. The counter-battery work of the heavy guns was highly effective, with most of the German guns neutralized, their crews either killed or driven off. A total of 580 tanks were used, including 72 "Whippet" light tanks and supply tanks. Infantry moved in close support of the armour, and 800 aircraft flew overhead to bomb and strafe the Germans. The plan called for reserve forces to follow on the heels of the initial waves. This was to allow them to pass through the assault troops once the first objective had been captured, and so maintain the momentum of the attack.

British III Corps, attacking over the difficult terrain of the Chipilly spur in the north of the battlefield, had the toughest job. Its problems were exacerbated by the fact that, thanks to a preliminary German attack, it had to recapture part of its old front line before it could make the attack proper. Even so, it made a substantial advance. In the centre, the Canadians and Australians, advancing over more favourable ground, pushed forward as much as 13 km (8 miles). On the southern flank, French First Army also made progress. In total, Allied casualties came to 9,000. German losses amounted to some 27,000 plus 400 guns. It was the most dramatic victory of the war up to that date. Ludendorff called it the "black day of the German Army". Amiens was also significant for its aftermath. On 11 August, with the Allies finding it increasingly difficult to get forward, the battle was halted and guns and troops moved northwards to begin a new offensive. In contrast to 1916 and 1917, the BEF now possessed the guns and logistics to allow the point of attack to be switched quickly from sector to sector. This was to be a key factor in the defeat of the German army over the coming months.

BELOW: German prisoners head for the rear past a British tank and advancing infantry.

OPPOSITE RIGHT: The War Diary of the 2nd Australian Infantry Division covering 8 August 1918.

WAR DIARY or **INTELLIGENCE SUMMARY.** (*Erase heading not required.*)

GENERAL STAFF, SECOND AUSTRALIAN DIVISION.

Army Form C. 2118.

Instructions regarding War Diaries and Intelligence Summaries are contained in F. S. Regs., Part II. and the Staff Manual respectively. Title pages will be prepared in manuscript.

Vol. XXV. Page 5.

Place	Date	Hour	Summary of Events and Information	Remarks and references to Appendices
	1918.	a.m.		
GLISY.	Aug.	6.20	Identification wire from D.I.O. - 41st Div. identified - repeated to Corps.	
	8.	6.30	Right Bde. report prisoners say our forces in MARCELCAVE.- probably Canadians.	
			Right Bde. report prisoners now 1 Off. and 74 O.Rs. - heavy ground mist - everything O.K.	
			Left Bde. report prisoners now 1 Off. and 28 O.Rs. of 152 I.R. - out of touch with left Bn. - everything satisfactory. - heavy fog.	
		6.35	Situation reported to Corps.	
		7.5.	Identification wire from D.I.O. - 117th Div. identified, arrived during night from OSTEND - Repeated Corps.	
		7.9.	2nd Canadian Div. reported outskirts MARCELCAVE. - some trouble JAFFA TRENCH.	
		7.20	Right Bde. report timed 7 a.m. Left Bn. on 1st objective - 140 prisoners to-date. - enemy artillery practically nil - mist clearing. 5th Aust. Div. moving forward.	
		7.30	Left Bde. report WARFUSEE being cleared up and prisoners coming in - casualties slight. Reorganisation in P.22.d., 28.b. and d. proceeding.	
		7.45	Right Bde. report prisoners state 2 Reserve Bns. and M.G. Coy. in Q.23. and 29. - Corps advised.	
		8.0.	Situation reported to Corps - total prisoners now 300.	
		8.10	Left Bde. report 7.40 a.m. WARFUSEE rushed by 17th Bn. and troops now on both sides of village and through it. Our Artillery and Tanks moving forward.s	
		8.15	Above repeated to Corps.	
		8.20	Right Bde. Right Bn. report having reached GREEN line - Corps advised.	
		8.25	Command of Battle front handed over to G.O.C., 5th Aust. Div. Corps and flank Divs. advised.	
			H.Q. of 6th A.I.Bde. moved to DOLL'S House - east edge VILLERS BRETONNEUX.	
			Centre Bn. Right Bde. report digging in 200 yards west GREEN line owing short shooting. 5th Aust. Div. passing through them.	
		8.45	Wire from D.I.O. giving identifications and general intelligence - repeated Corps and flank divs.	
		9.0.	1st and 3rd Can. Divs. reported on GREEN line.	
		9.3.	Right Bde. reports all Bns. on objective and digging in - Centre Bn. being withdrawn and reorganised - consolidation in depth proceeding - repeated to Corps.	
		9.5.	Prisoners of War counted by A.P.M. to 8.30 total 651	
		9.25	Left Bde. report all on GREEN line. Artillery now going through.	
		9.30	Congratulatory message from Div. Commander to G.Os.C., 5th and 7th A.I.Bdes.	
		9.48	Left Bde. report timed 9 a.m. armoured cars, tanks and cavalry have passed through.	
		9.50	6th A.I.Bde. report 20 officers and 800 O.Rs. now passed through collecting stations - reported to Corps.	
		9.55	Wire from D.I.O. giving further identifications repeated to Corps.	5

D. D. & L., London, E.C. (Altered) Wt. W2958/M2291 750,000 5/17 Sch. 52 Forms/C2118/14

WAR DIARY or **INTELLIGENCE SUMMARY.** (*Erase heading not required.*)

GENERAL STAFF, OF SECOND AUSTRALIAN DIVISION.

Army Form C. 2118.

Instructions regarding War Diaries and Intelligence Summaries are contained in F. S. Regs., Part II. and the Staff Manual respectively. Title pages will be prepared in manuscript.

Vol. XXV. Page 4.

Place	Date	Hour	Summary of Events and Information	Remarks and references to Appendices
	1918.	p.m.		
GLISY.	Aug. 6.		During night 5th and 7th A.I.Bdes. moved forward to close assembly areas without incident.	
		a.m.		
	7.	5.0.	Morning Situation: Situation quiet. Scattered shelling of whole area. Some gas at intervals on O.22. M.Gs. normal	
			Fine sunny morning.	
		p.m.	Advice from Corps that to-day is "Y" day - units advised.	
		2.30	G.S.O.III. synchronised watches with Artillery and Brigades.	
		5.5.	Evening report. Scattered shelling of O.29. with 77s. and 10.5 cm. between 10 a.m. and 12 noon Wagon movement in W.8. at 5.5. a.m. engaged by artillery. M.W. active on P.25.d. and P.26.c. silenced . E.A. nil.	
			Fine evening; sunny and warm.	
		7.15	Supply Tank Park at O.29. central set on fire by shelling. 13 tanks destroyed and 3 saved.	
		8.0.	G.S.O.III. and Capt. BAZELEY left for liaison duty with flank Divs.	
		8.0.	5th A.I.Bde. Battle H.Q. closed at GLISY and opened at O.28.c.8.5.	
		11.30	All units warned against unauthorised tapping in on telephone lines.	
			2nd Aust. Div. Intelligence Summary issued No. 195.	App.
			2nd Aust. Div. Order of Battle issued.	App.
		a.m.		
	8.	1.30	Sector quiet for past two hours.	
		3.30	Heavy shelling astride railway line - counter battery action requested.	
		4.0.	Hostile shelling reported to have ceased - no damage done.	
		4.30	Artillery bombardment opened - heavy ground mist developing at GLISY.	
		4.35	Right Bde. report barrage opened on time and excellent. No retaliation.	
		4.40	Left Bde. report barrage opened on time - one tank out of action.	
		4.45	Above message repeated Corps.	
			During next half hour Bdes. reported verbally that things apparently going well and enemy retaliation still continues feeble.	
		5.26	Right Bde. report prisoner from JAFFA TRENCH 18th I.R. says no attack expected.	
		5.40	Right Bde. report centre Bn. all O.K. at 5 a.m. - 6 prisoners 18th I.R.	
		5.50	F.O.O. of 27th F.A.R. taken by Left Bn. of Right Bde.	
			Left Bde. report at 5.35 a.m. that Right Coy., Right Bn. on objective - Corps advised.	
		6.5.	1st Canadian Div. reported through HANGARD WOOD and 3rd Div. through ACCROCHE WOOD.	
		6.9.	Right Bde. report all going well - visibility bad - 75 to 80 prisoners.	4

D. D. & L., London, E.C. (Altered) Wt. W2958/M2291 750,000 5/17 Sch. 52 Forms/C2118/14

SPECIALISTS

SIGNALLERS, POLICE, TUNNELLERS AND MEDICS

At the beginning of the First World War, armies were fairly simple bodies consisting of infantry, cavalry, artillery, supply troops, engineers and a limited number of specialists such as signallers and staff officers.

By November 1918, in response to the challenges posed by warfare on the Western Front, armies had become vastly more complex and sophisticated organizations. Units appeared on orders of battle that had been unknown before the war, concerned with new weapons such as tanks, flame-throwers and gas, while some branches of armies expanded enormously. Typical was the British Corps of Military Police, which grew from 500 men in August 1914 to 13,300 in 1918, having acquired important operational roles in addition to the enforcement of discipline. Much the same happened to the French military police. The German equivalent, the Feldgendarmerie, also expanded, with five cavalry units being assigned to policing duties to handle the increasing indiscipline in the German army in 1918.

The arrival of new weapons in the front line meant that increasing numbers of troops became specialists. In 1914, most French infantry were armed with a rifle and bayonet. By early 1917, the platoon had evolved to consist of four rifle sections, each of 12 men with two grenade launchers; two bombing sections of eight men; and a light machine-gun section armed with one gun. The platoon of 1918 was different again, with four light machine-gun sections and only two of riflemen. The British and German armies saw broadly similar changes. There was a tendency to form new weapons into separate organizations. In the German army, Minenwerfer (short range mortar) units were formed at the end of 1914. Later, independent units were attached to armies. As the light Lewis machine gun became increasingly available, the British withdrew heavier weapons from its battalions and formed them into Machine Gun Companies attached to brigades. In October 1915, the Machine Gun Corps was formed.

OPPOSITE: Left to right: British, French and US military policemen at Amiens, 13 May 1918.

BELOW LEFT: Men of 3rd Australian Tunnelling Company labouring beneath the ground at Hulluch, January 1918.

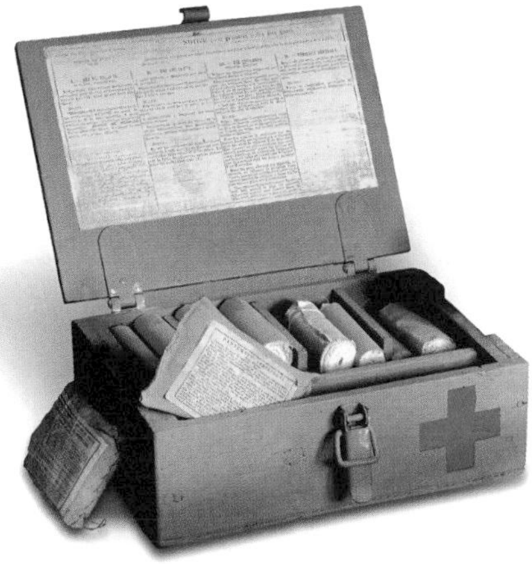

LEFT : Medical supplies, such as this French first aid box containing an assortment of bandages, were essential for the upkeep of the health and morale of frontline troops.

BELOW: British signallers at work on the Western Front.

SIGNALLERS

Advances in battlefield communications technology symbolize the birth of modern war on the Western Front. The visual signalling using flags in use at the beginning of the war was generally ineffective and dangerous, while many decorations were won by signallers crawling out into No Man's Land to repair broken telephone wires. By the end of the war, portable radio sets had been developed, and each British tank brigade at Cambrai in 1917 (see pages 100–01) had three tanks equipped with wireless and one for laying telephone cable.

TRENCH WEAPONS

A variety of specialized weapons were developed for trench fighting. At the beginning of the war there was a high degree of improvization that produced fearsome clubs, sharpened entrenching tools, grenades manufactured from jam tins and spring-operated grenade throwers. Later on weapons became much more sophisticated. The British Mills Bomb (grenade) and Stokes mortar, both invented during the war, were among the most effective weapons developed for trench fighting. Some 75 million Mills Bombs were produced during the war.

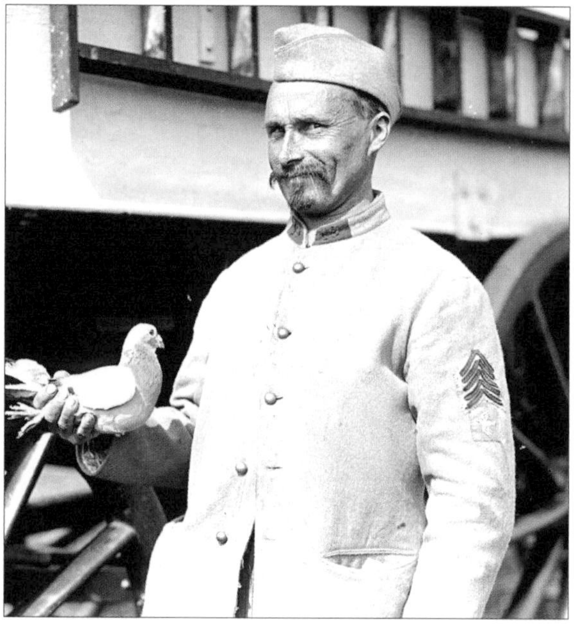

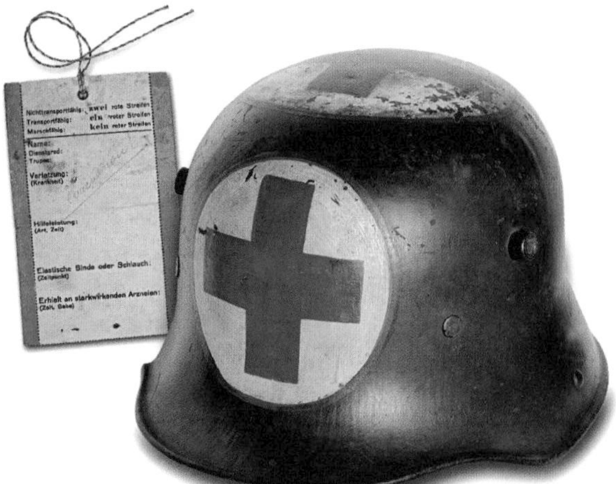

The demands of trench warfare brought about the formation of specialist units of miners and tunnellers. An informal group of German units had evolved to handle mining from the beginning of trench warfare, and in April 1916 Pioneer Mining Companies were formed. In February 1915, the British created similar units under the auspices of the Royal Engineers. Mining companies were also formed in French divisions. Some infantry came to specialize in patrolling and trench raiding. The Germans formed units of elite storm troops, although the British shied away from this development.

The shortcomings of the French medical service were exposed by the battles of 1914. It was equipped with insufficient and poorly designed ambulances. There were five properly equipped hospital trains, with 30 standard trains pressed into service. Brancardiers (stretcher-bearers) often had little medical training. The subsequent years saw huge improvements in the quality of French military medical care. The German medical service was 7,500 strong on the outbreak of war, and grew steadily in size. The German division of 1914 had a medical company of stretcher-bearers and a dressing station, but at the end of 1916 another was added to the establishment in addition to independent companies. Similarly, under the leadership of Sir Alfred Keogh, the strength of the British Royal Army Medical Corps grew from about 10,000 to some 170,000 during the war.

TOP: A British fatigue party fuse Stokes mortar bombs, October 1917.

ABOVE LEFT: A member of the French Carrier Pigeon Service plus bird, June 1918.

LEFT: A German helmet that belonged to Alphonse Bauer, first aid officer of the 75th Infantry Regiment. Left: Casualties were given wound labels once they entered the medical system. This one is German.

OPPOSITE ABOVE: Training diagrams of gas and anti-gas equipment. As warfare grew more sophisticated and complex, a number of specialist training programmes were introduced.

OPPOSITE BELOW: A fine study of a French horse-drawn ambulance of the 52nd Infantry Division, taken in July 1915 at Sacy (Marne).

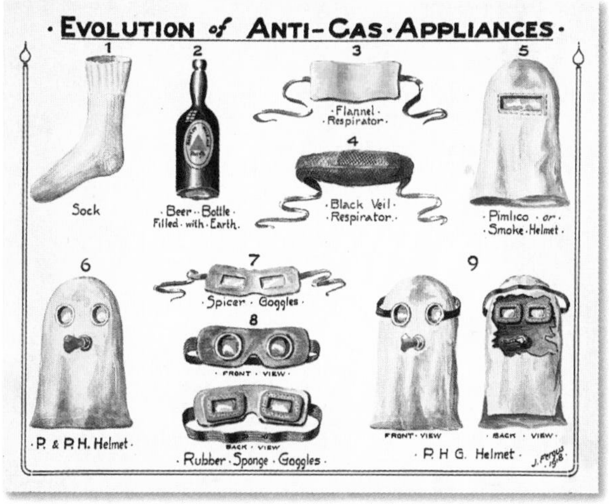

The increasing sophistication of artillery tactics depended to a large degree on specialists. Ernest Gold, a brilliant British meteorologist, was a pioneer in the field of providing information on atmospheric conditions, his staff of three eventually expanding to 120. All armies used highly skilled sound rangers and flash spotters, who used acoustic methods and visual observation to determine the whereabouts of enemy guns. Reconnaissance aircraft "spotted" the fall of shot for the artillery, radioing back data that allowed gunners to adjust the range.

Battlefield communications were primitive at the beginning of the war, but the semaphore flags, homing pigeons and field telephones were increasingly supplemented by wireless (radio) as the war went on. This was reflected in the growth of communication specialists – the German signal service increased from 6,300 to 190,000 men during the course of the war. The 50 wireless sets used by the French army in 1914 had grown in number to 30,000 by 1918.

Many other specialist troops, such as logisticians, staff officers and veterinarians, could also be mentioned as essential parts of the armies of the Western Front. The backbone continued to be the infantryman, but increasingly the Tommy, Poilu and Landser (the ordinary German soldier) was supported by a bewildering array of arms and services.

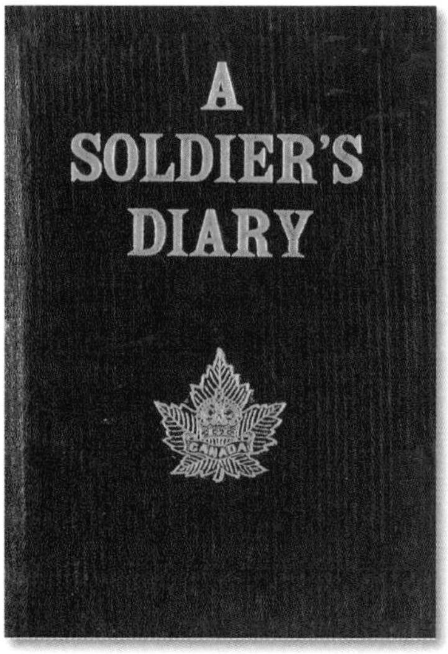

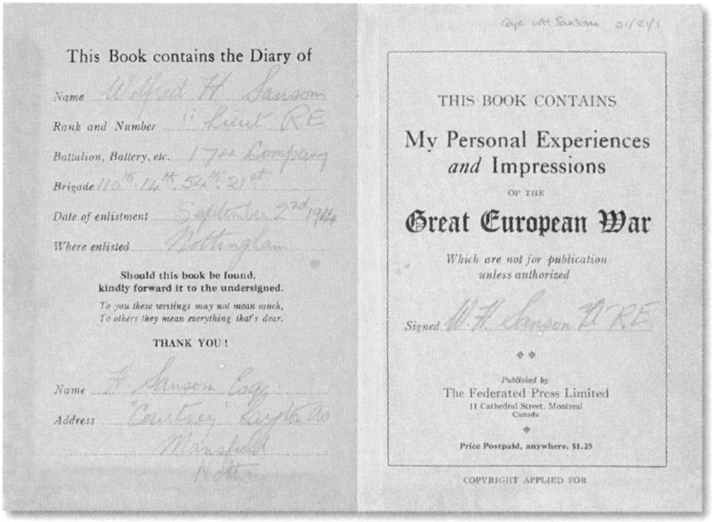
This Book contains the Diary of

Name Wilfred H Sansom
Rank and Number 2nd Lieut RE
Battalion, Battery, etc. 17th Company
Brigade 110th, 14th, 54th, 21st
Date of enlistment September 2nd 1914
Where enlisted Nottingham

Should this book be found, kindly forward it to the undersigned.

To you these writings may not mean much,
To others they mean everything that's dear.

THANK YOU!

Name F Sansom Esq
Address "Courtney" Leighton Rd
Mansfield
Notts

THIS BOOK CONTAINS
My Personal Experiences *and* Impressions
OF THE
Great European War

Which are not for publication unless authorized

Signed W H Sansom 2/Lt RE

Published by
The Federated Press Limited
11 Cathedral Street, Montreal
Canada

Price Postpaid, anywhere, $1.25

COPYRIGHT APPLIED FOR

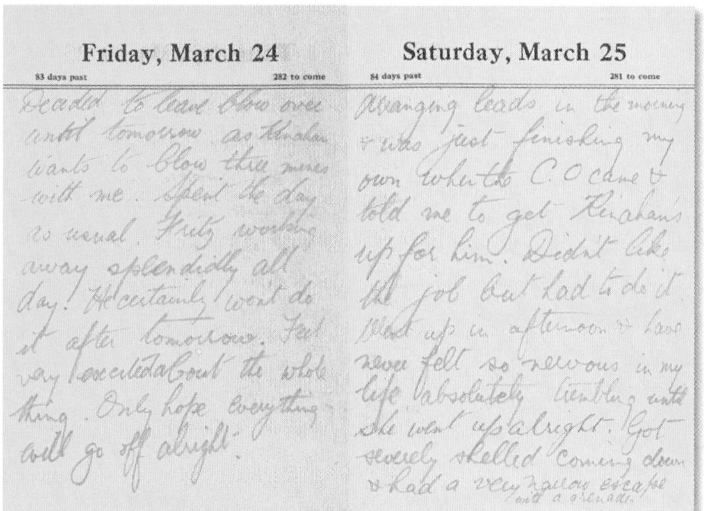
Friday, March 24
83 days past — 282 to come

Decided to leave blow over until tomorrow as Kinahan wants to blow three mines with me. Spent the day as usual. Fritz working away splendidly all day! He certainly won't do it after tomorrow. Feel very excited about the whole thing. Only hope everything will go off alright.

Saturday, March 25
84 days past — 281 to come

Arranging leads in the morning & was just finishing my own when the C.O came & told me to get Kinahan's up for him. Didn't like the job but had to do it. Went up in afternoon & have never felt so nervous in my life absolutely trembling until she went up alright. Got severely shelled coming down & had a very narrow escape with a grenade.

ABOVE AND OPPOSITE:
Extracts from the 1916 personal diary of Lieutenant W H Sansom, a British sapper officer.

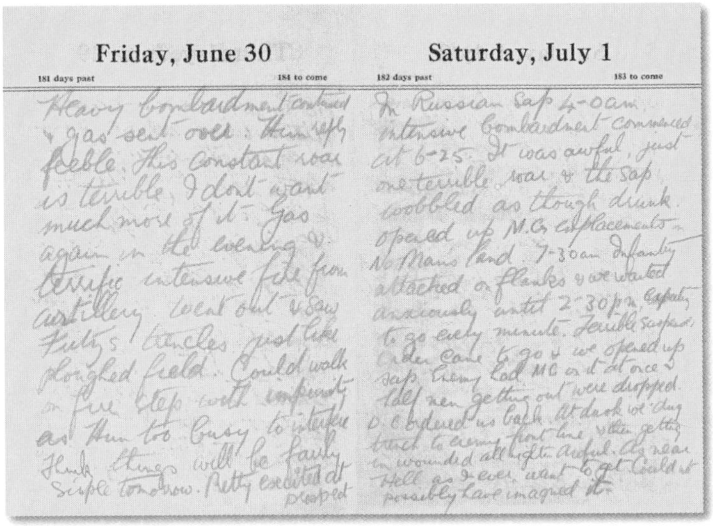

Friday, June 30

181 days past — 184 to come

Heavy bombardment continued & gas sent over. Hun reply feeble. This constant roar is terrible. I don't want much more of it. Gas again in the evening & terrific intensive fire from artillery. Went out & saw Fritz's trenches just like ploughed field. Could walk on fire step with impunity as Hun too busy to interfere. Think things will be fairly simple tomorrow. Pretty excited at prospect

Saturday, July 1

182 days past — 183 to come

In Russian sap 4-0am. Intensive bombardment commenced at 6-25. It was awful, just one terrible roar & the sap wobbled as though drunk. Opened up M.G. emplacements in No Mans land. 7-30am Infantry attacked on flanks & we waited anxiously until 2-30pm. Expecting to go every minute. Terrible suspense. Order came to go & we opened up sap. Enemy had MG on it at once & 1st men getting out were dropped. O.C. ordered us back. At dark we dug trench to enemy front line & then getting in wounded all night. Awful. As near Hell as I ever want to get. Could not possibly have imagined it.

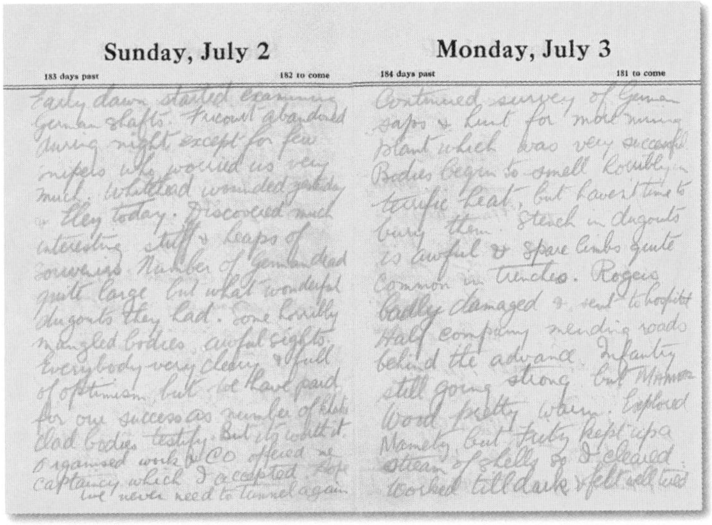

Sunday, July 2

183 days past — 182 to come

Early dawn started examining German shafts. Fricourt abandoned during night except for few snipers who worried us very much. Whitehead wounded yesterday & Riley today. Discovered much interesting stuff & heaps of souvenirs. Number of German dead quite large but what wonderful dugouts they had. Some horribly mangled bodies, awful sights. Everybody very cheery & full of optimism but we have paid for our success as number of khaki dead bodies testify. But it's worth it. Organised work & CO offered me captaincy which I accepted. Hope we never need to tunnel again

Monday, July 3

184 days past — 181 to come

Continued survey of German saps & hunt for more mining plant which was very successful. Bodies begin to smell horribly in terrific heat, but haven't time to bury them. Stench in dugouts is awful & spare limbs quite common in trenches. Rogers badly damaged & sent to hospital. Half company mending roads behind the advance. Infantry still going strong but Mametz Wood pretty warm. Explored Mametz but Fritz kept up a stream of shells so I cleared. Worked till dark & felt well tired

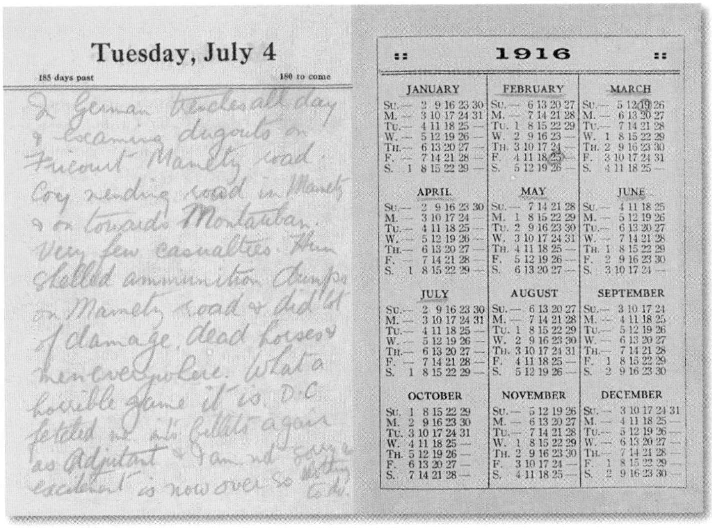

Tuesday, July 4

185 days past — 180 to come

In German trenches all day & examining dugouts on Fricourt Mametz road. Coy mending road in Mametz & on towards Montauban. Very few casualties. Hun shelled ammunition dumps on Mametz road & did lot of damage, dead horses & men everywhere. What a horrible game it is. O.C fetched me into billets again as Adjutant & I am not sorry excitement is now over so nothing to do.

:: 1916 ::

	JANUARY	FEBRUARY	MARCH
SU.	— 2 9 16 23 30	— 6 13 20 27	— 5 12 19 26
M.	— 3 10 17 24 31	— 7 14 21 28	— 6 13 20 27
TU.	— 4 11 18 25 —	1 8 15 22 29	— 7 14 21 28
W.	— 5 12 19 26 —	2 9 16 23 —	1 8 15 22 29
TH.	— 6 13 20 27 —	3 10 17 24 —	2 9 16 23 30
F.	— 7 14 21 28 —	4 11 18 25 —	3 10 17 24 31
S.	1 8 15 22 29 —	5 12 19 26 —	4 11 18 25 —

	APRIL	MAY	JUNE
SU.	— 2 9 16 23 30	— 7 14 21 28	— 4 11 18 25
M.	— 3 10 17 24 —	1 8 15 22 29	— 5 12 19 26
TU.	— 4 11 18 25 —	2 9 16 23 30	— 6 13 20 27
W.	— 5 12 19 26 —	3 10 17 24 31	— 7 14 21 28
TH.	— 6 13 20 27 —	4 11 18 25 —	1 8 15 22 29
F.	— 7 14 21 28 —	5 12 19 26 —	2 9 16 23 30
S.	1 8 15 22 29 —	6 13 20 27 —	3 10 17 24 —

	JULY	AUGUST	SEPTEMBER
SU.	— 2 9 16 23 30	— 6 13 20 27	— 3 10 17 24
M.	— 3 10 17 24 31	— 7 14 21 28	— 4 11 18 25
TU.	— 4 11 18 25 —	1 8 15 22 29	— 5 12 19 26
W.	— 5 12 19 26 —	2 9 16 23 30	— 6 13 20 27
TH.	— 6 13 20 27 —	3 10 17 24 31	— 7 14 21 28
F.	— 7 14 21 28 —	4 11 18 25 —	1 8 15 22 29
S.	1 8 15 22 29 —	5 12 19 26 —	2 9 16 23 30

	OCTOBER	NOVEMBER	DECEMBER
SU.	1 8 15 22 29	— 5 12 19 26	— 3 10 17 24 31
M.	2 9 16 23 30	— 6 13 20 27	— 4 11 18 25 —
TU.	3 10 17 24 31	— 7 14 21 28	— 5 12 19 26 —
W.	4 11 18 25 —	1 8 15 22 29	— 6 13 20 27 —
TH.	5 12 19 26 —	2 9 16 23 30	— 7 14 21 28 —
F.	6 13 20 27 —	3 10 17 24 —	1 8 15 22 29 —
S.	7 14 21 28 —	4 11 18 25 —	2 9 16 23 30 —

22 AUGUST–22 SEPTEMBER 1918

ALLIES ON THE ADVANCE

THE DRIVE TO THE HINDENBURG LINE

Coming so quickly after the failure of the German offensive on the Marne and the Allied counter-offensive, Amiens came as a tremendous blow to German morale at the top and bottom of the army.

Victory was now clearly impossible, but the German High Command believed that if a stubborn retreat could inflict heavy losses on the Allies, the Germans might end the war on moderate terms. They were wrong; the strategic initiative had passed to the Allies, and under Foch's strategic direction, they made the most of it.

The key to their success lay in fighting a series of limited operations, breaking off the battle when the attack began to lose momentum. A fresh attack (or attacks) would then be mounted on a different part of the front. The defenders were thus placed at full stretch, unable to initiate, constantly struggling to fend off defeat. The Allied infantry did not advance too far away from the safety of their artillery support, or outrun their lines of supply. This was very different from the German approach in the spring offensives, and also a distinct improvement on some of their own fumbling efforts earlier in the war.

The next phase of the Allied offensive began in the third week of August. In the previous week or so, reinforcements – including guns – were moved north from the forces at Amiens to Byng's British Third Army around the Somme area. It is noteworthy how quickly this could now be done, in comparison to the problems of moving troops and guns from Messines to Ypres in June–July of 1917. The Canadian Corps moved up to join First Army to the north of Arras. Beginning on 20 August, Fayolle's French Army Group struck heavy blows against the southern face of the German-held Montdidier-Amiens salient. French Tenth Army, under the ever aggressive Mangin, pushed the Germans back some 13 km (8 miles) between the rivers Oise and Aisne.

British Third Army attacked on 21 August over the all-too-familiar battlefield of the 1916 Somme offensive. On the following day, Rawlinson's Fourth Army came into action on Byng's right flank, and on 26 August part of Horne's First Army attacked on Third Army's left, extending the battlefront to some 65 km (40 miles). This too was a battle in an area well known to British veterans, around Arras. On the Somme, 18th (Eastern) Division had the bizarre experience of capturing Trônes Wood for the second time, having first attacked and taken this objective in July 1916. Now, there were very different conditions on the battlefield. With superiority in the air, in artillery support and logistics, using sophisticated all-arms tactics, with experienced and confident staff officers and commanders, and up against a visibly weakening enemy, the BEF was achieving the success that had eluded it.

OPPOSITE: The advance to victory: New Zealand and British infantry, Mark V tanks and captured guns following following the capture of Grevillers, 25 August 1918.

ABOVE: An aerial reconnaissance photograph of the Hindenburg Line taken from 2,438 m (8,000 ft). Note trenches, mine craters and shellholes.

BELOW: Albert in ruins. This key town was recaptured by the BEF during the Hundred Days.

ALBERT RECAPTURED

The small town of Albert was, for the BEF, the gateway to the Somme. The most famous landmark was the gilded statue of the Virgin and Child on the basilica, which was hit by a shell and leaned out over the streets. Superstitions soon attached to the Golden Virgin, including that the war would only end when the statue fell. Albert was captured by the Germans on 26 March 1918 and was retaken by the British 18th Division on 22–23 August 1918. The statue actually fell in April 1918.

The strain proved too great for the Germans to bear and on the night of 26–27 August they retreated to the Hindenburg Line. In doing so they gave up the ground they had captured in the German Spring Offensive. For the Germans, the news grew ever worse. French First and Third Armies on the right of the BEF attacked on 27–29 August and captured the key town of Noyon. By 1 September, the Australians held both Mont St-Quentin and the city of Péronne, putting paid to any hope the Germans had of holding the line of the River Somme. On First Army's front on 2 September, the Canadians smashed through the formidable Drocourt-Quéant Switch Line near Arras and triggered another German withdrawal. Fayolle's French Army Group capitalized on the BEF's successes by carrying out operations against the retreating Germans.

South of Ypres, the Germans were forced out of another piece of territory captured at a huge cost in lives in the spring. The withdrawals to the Hindenburg Line left the German troops defending the salient captured during the Battle of the Lys uncomfortably exposed. British Fifth Army, now commanded by Birdwood, had commenced operations on 23 August, keeping up the pressure on the Germans. By 6 September, accepting the inevitable, the defenders on the Lys, too, fell back.

The BEF followed the retreating Germans, fighting the battles of Havrincourt and Epéhy between 12 and 26 September as divisions sought to reach good positions from which to attack the main German positions on the Hindenburg Line itself. The achievements since Amiens were real, but they were costly. The BEF had pushed forward some 40 km (25 miles) along a front of 65 km (40 miles) at a cost of 180,000 casualties. And perhaps the worst was still to come. Their next objective was the Hindenburg Line.

HAIG IN THE HUNDRED DAYS

Opinion is divided about how much credit Douglas Haig can claim for the British Empire's victories in 1918. Some see him as an "accidental victor", who was largely irrelevant to the BEF's successes in 1918, the important decisions being taken by Foch and by Haig's subordinates at army and corps level. A fairer view is that Haig played a crucial role in improving the BEF between the Somme and the Battle of Amiens, and in the Hundred Days steered his generals to victory and guided and advised Foch.

ABOVE: Under the cover a creeping barrage and smoke, Australian infantry advance towards German Hindenburg Line positions on 18 September 1918.

RIGHT: Field Marshal Sir Douglas Haig reviews Canadian troops on 31 August 1918, prior to their succesful assault on the Drocourt-Quéant switch Line.

OPPOSITE: During the Battle of Albert Captain B H Geary, 1st East Surreys, is brought in by German prisoners after being wounded. He had won the VC in 1915.

12 SEPTEMBER–11 NOVEMBER 1918

THE AMERICAN OFFENSIVES

SAINT-MIHIEL AND MEUSE-ARGONNE

The arrival of the American Expeditionary Force (AEF) in France brought a powerful accretion of strength to the Allies. American divisions were roughly double the size of comparable British and French formations, and the numbers of "Doughboys" (as the ordinary US soldier was nicknamed) seemed limitless.

Having gained control of American divisions in order to train them and to give them combat experience, the British and French were reluctant to give them up. Throughout 1918, Pershing, the AEF commander, strove to create an American operational command fully independent of his Allies. US First Army became operational on 29 August 1918. The battlefield debut of the new force was to be an offensive to reduce the Saint-Mihiel salient.

However, the rapid tempo of events elsewhere on the Western Front placed this plan in jeopardy. The success of the BEF convinced Foch that Haig's concept of large-scale concentric offensives should be adopted. Rather than attacking Saint-Mihiel, Pershing should attack northwestwards through the Argonne forest towards Sedan and Mézières. This would threaten major railways that were critical to German lines of supply. Foch believed that this attack could be decisive. The clash of two different plans resulted in an uneasy compromise. The Americans would attack Saint-Mihiel, but would then redeploy to attack in the Meuse-Argonne area.

The Saint-Mihiel offensive began on 12 September 1918. The French II Colonial Corps, under the command of General Blondlat, was deployed alongside three American Corps. Although the defensive position was strong, the Allies achieved surprise, and the Germans were in the process of evacuating this bulge in the Allied line as the attack went in. The result was less a formal assault than the following up of a withdrawing force. Poor American staff work led to disorder among the advancing troops. Nonetheless, the operation was a success, with Saint-Mihiel being captured by French troops on 13 September. With 16,000 prisoners and 450 guns falling into American hands, Saint-Mihiel gave a timely boost to US morale. Curiously, at one stage two future American generals of the Second World War met during the battle, when Lieutenant Colonel George S. Patton of the Tank Corps encountered Brigadier General Douglas MacArthur of 42nd (Rainbow) Division.

Some Americans believed that an opportunity had been missed by not capitalizing on St-Mihiel, but the "Doughboys" headed for a new battlefield in the Argonne. To move an army 95 km (60 miles) on three minor roads, get it into position and launch an attack in less than two weeks was a huge logistic challenge. Late on 25 September, the artillery bombardment commenced. The first phase of Foch's Grand Offensive was on an appropriately grand scale. Two French Armies, the Second (Hirschner) and Fourth (Gouraud) plus I, III and V US Corps commanded by Hunter Liggett, Robert L Bullard and George H Cameron respectively, were supported by 700 tanks and 400 guns. At 05:30 on 26 September, the tanks and infantry attacked. On the first day the French and Americans advanced about 5 km (3 miles). It was a hard, grinding slog. The Germans had the advantage of deep belts of defences – trenches, barbed wire, strong-points, machine-gun posts – based on no less than four separate positions. Up against the inexperienced Americans, the defenders caused heavy casualties even as the advance continued. Three regiments of black American troops served alongside the French. They treated the African-Americans much like their own colonial divisions, and the black troops did well, although like their white American counterparts, they lost heavily in the process.

Pershing had insisted on training for open warfare and treating the rifle-armed infantryman as the most important part of the tactical jigsaw. He disdained the hard-won lessons of the French and British armies, and the AEF paid the price in heavy casualties and slow progress. This was an army reminiscent of the British on the Somme in 1916, still learning how to fight a modern battle. Co-operation between the artillery and infantry was often poor and the Americans faced considerable logistical difficulties compounded by bad weather. Three days after the initial attack, with the battered infantry in poor shape, the offensive had clearly run out of steam. "Those Americans will lose us our chance of a big victory before winter," complained Georges Clemenceau, the French Premier. His criticism was unjust: although the Franco-American battle was not as successful as the other phases of Foch's offensive, it contributed to the overall effort by tying down German troops and grinding away their strength. Foch's comment was fairer: the Americans "are learning now, rapidly".

OPPOSITE: A US 14-inch railway mounted gun fires during the Argonne offensive, 1918.

ABOVE: In a town captured by the Americans near St Mihiel, US troops give a new name to a street named after Hindenburg – "Wilson USA!"

26 SEPTEMBER–2 OCTOBER 1918

THE GRAND OFFENSIVE

BREAKING THE HINDENBURG LINE

One critical difference between the "Hundred Days" (August–November 1918) and earlier Allied offensives was the role of co-ordinator played by Ferdinand Foch as Allied Generalissimo. By ensuring that the efforts of the Allied armies meshed into an overall plan, he avoided the situation that had occurred during the Somme in 1916, when the British and French had often appeared to be fighting separate battles side by side rather than a truly combined offensive.

Foch's relationship with Douglas Haig, who commanded the principal Allied strike force, was crucial. They did not always see eye to eye, but the partnership proved highly effective. This was demonstrated by the plan for the Grand Offensive launched at the end of September 1918. While Pétain was pessimistic, judging that the fighting would continue into 1919, Haig believed that a decisive victory was possible by the end of the year. He successfully urged Foch to extend the original scope of the attack.

Foch's motto was *"Tout le monde à la bataille!"*("Everybody into battle!"). He unleashed a series of blows up and down the German positions over a four-day period. First to act were to be the Franco-American forces that attacked on 26 September, in the Meuse-Argonne area (see pages 120–21). Next in the sequence came two British Armies, Horne's First and Byng's Third, kicking off their offensive towards Cambrai on 27 September. This was to be followed on the 28 September by a major attack at Ypres by French, Belgian and British divisions under King Albert of the Belgians, who had the French General Jean-Marie Degoutte as his chief-of-staff. The climactic push would be made on 29 September by Rawlinson's British Fourth and Debeney's French First Armies. For the first time, Foch was able to wield the full force of Allied combat power on the Western Front.

As we have seen, Foch expected much of the Meuse-Argonne offensive, but the results were a little disappointing. The attack on the following day was much more significant. British First Army, with Currie's Canadian Corps in the lead, tackled the formidable defences of the Canal du Nord (the canal connecting the Oise River and the canal Dunkirk-Scheldt). Under the cover of a barrage described by the infantry as "very good", the Canadians assaulted on a narrow front and then spread out like the fingers of a hand. Third Army also penetrated the German defences, although not as deeply as the Canadians, and by the end of the day Byng and Horne had between them advanced 10 km (6 miles) on a frontage of 19 km (12 miles). The 27 September attack was, as one historian has commented, "Currie's operational masterpiece".

Such were the changed conditions of battle that around Ypres on 28 September, King Albert's Army Group attacked right across the old Passchendaele battlefield and broke out of the Salient altogether. Plumer's British Second Army advanced up to 10 km (6 miles), a distance that would have been unthinkable 12 months earlier, and on the next day it recaptured Messines Ridge. After an advance of about 14 km (9 miles), logistic chaos brought the French and Belgian forces to a halt; food was dropped to forward troops by air, probably the first time in history this had been done. At last the deadlock in Flanders was at an end.

The most difficult task in the Grand Offensive, carrying the Hindenburg Line in the St Quentin sector, had been assigned to Rawlinson's Fourth Army. It was faced with the problem of

OPPOSITE: Against the background of a damaged bridge, a British 18 pounder gun team moves up during the Battle of the Canal du Nord, 27 September 1918.

LEFT: Badge of the North Staffordshire Regiment, featuring the Staffordshire knot.

BELOW: King George V crosses Riqueval Bridge. The capture of the bridge was a crucial element in 46th Division's victory on 29 September 1918.

46TH DIVISION

The 46th (North Midland) Division was a Territorial formation comprised of battalions of regiments recruited from central England. Its achievement on 29 September 1918, under the command of Major-General G. F. Boyd, is testimony both to the high standards of even an average British division by that stage of the war and the impressive support of the BEF's artillery. Captain A. H. Charlton, a pre-war farmer, led the party that seized the Riqueval Bridge, the only bridge in that sector across the St Quentin Canal. This was perhaps the pinnacle of the achievements of the British citizen army in the war.

OPPOSITE: Brigadier General J. C. Campbell VC addresses his victorious 137 Brigade, 46th Division, from the newly captured Riqueval bridge.

ABOVE: Mark V tanks of 8th Tank battalion and men of 5th Australian Division with German Prisoners of War, September 1918. The tanks are carrying "Cribs", designed to help them cross the Hindenburg Line defences.

BELOW: German troops resignedly marching into captivity at the hands of the French at Vauxaillon, Department of the Aisne, September 1918.

crossing a wide strip of defences, including the St Quentin Canal, which was up to 11 m (35 ft) wide and 15–20 m (50–60 ft) deep. The best going was at Bellicourt, where the canal ran through a tunnel, but it was very heavily defended. Preceded by a two-day bombardment, the Australian Corps (reinforced by two American divisions) attacked here but, faced with stiff opposition, it made slow progress. The US 27th and 30th Divisions fought bravely but revealed their inexperience and tactical naivety. The major break-though came a little further south at Bellenglise on the front of Lieutenant General Sir Walter Braithwaite's British IX Corps. Here, a surprise bombardment was followed by 46th (North Midland) Division attacking straight across the canal. No fewer than 216 heavy guns were concentrated on an attack frontage of only 2,750 m (3,000 yds). The infantry crossed the canal using lifebelts from Channel steamers, or hopped across the rubble blown into the watercourse, or simply used a bridge captured in the early stages of the battle. By nightfall, these Staffordshire Territorials could boast, in the proud words of their divisional history of "Breaking the Hindenburg Line".

4 OCTOBER–11 NOVEMBER 1918

THE FINAL BATTLES

VICTORY IN SIGHT

With the breaking of the Hindenburg Line, the German Army's last realistic hope of halting the Allies vanished. At a meeting of the High Command on 1 October 1918, Ludendorff stated that Germany faced "an unavoidable and conclusive defeat". Events moved rapidly; in Berlin, the Chancellor resigned and was replaced on 3 October by Prince Max of Baden.

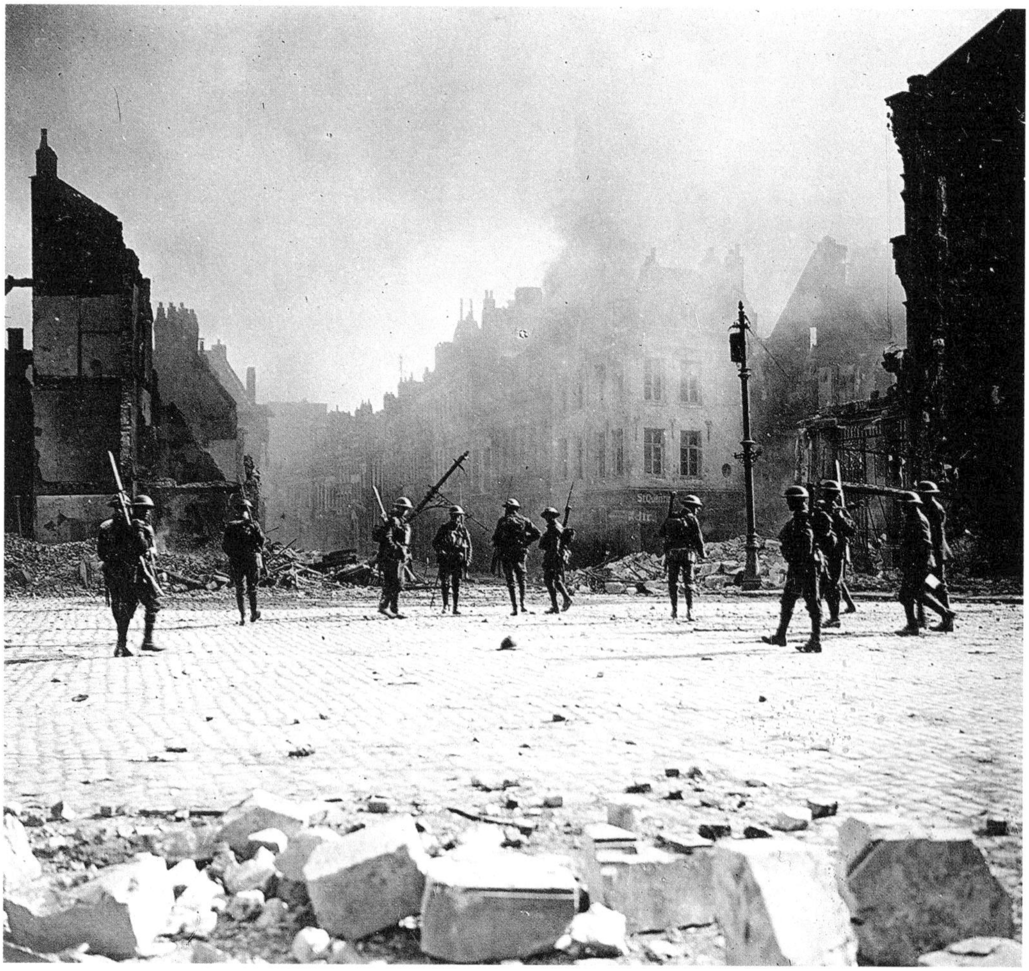

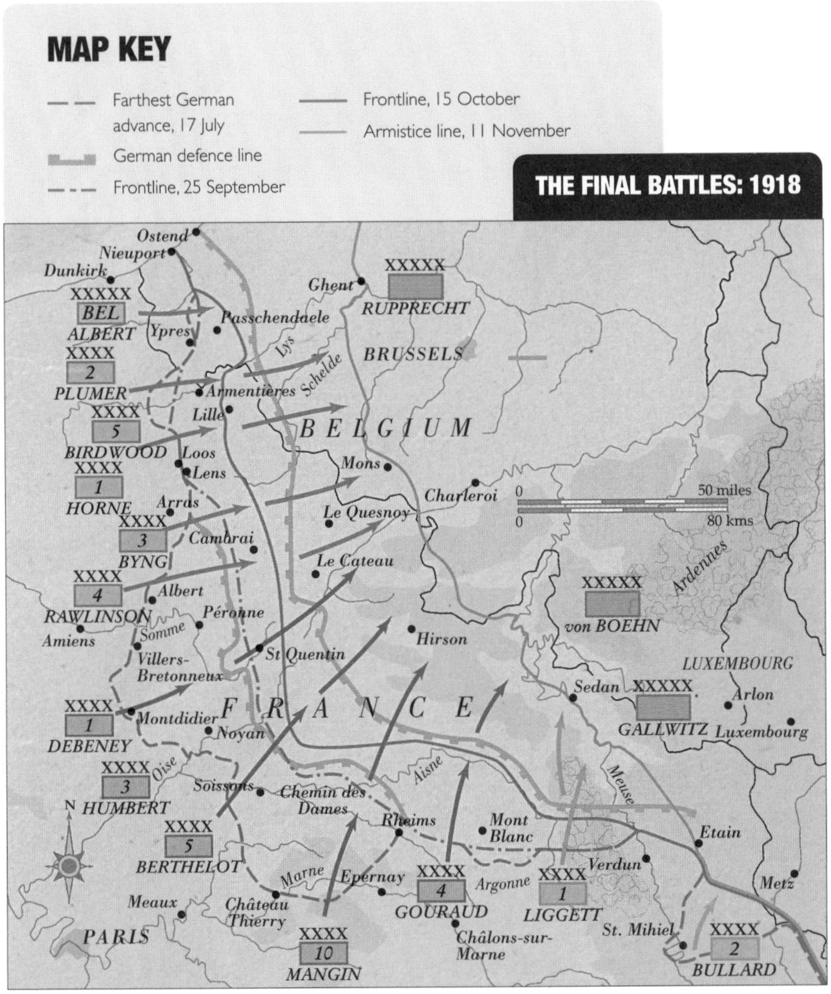

OPPOSITE: Cambrai was liberated by the Canadians in October 1918. In this picture the buildings of the city are still burning.

He was a man of liberal views who presented a very different public face of the German government. Ludendorff had cynically suggested that opposition politicians should be given responsibility in government, blaming them – utterly unfairly – for the defeat: "They should make the peace that must now be made. They made their bed, now they must lie in it!"

Meanwhile, the relentless Allied pressure continued on the Western Front. French First Army took St Quentin on 2 October, and progress was made early in the month by Fifth and Tenth Armies in the Soissons area, and Gourard's Fourth Army on the flank of the Americans. Foch, however, was displeased with the slow rate of advance compared to the British. The Allied Generalissimo was ungenerous to his own countrymen. Having born the main burden of the fighting on the Western Front for so much of the war, the French Army was almost played out.

The BEF was in better shape. By this stage its divisions consisted of a mixture of wary veterans and young conscripts, and as the ordinary officers and soldiers began to realize that the end of the war was at last in sight, there was a perceptible rise in morale. Fourth Army cleared the Beaurevoir Line to the rear of the main Hindenburg positions on 4 October. The Germans were forced to abandon Cambrai on 8–9 October, regrouping on the River Selle. First, Third and Fourth Armies followed up, while in the Lens area, Fifth Army (Birdwood) was able to push forward about 16 km (10 miles) as the defenders retreated. Having untangled their logistic knot, King Albert's Army Group began to advance in Flanders on 14 October, with the ever-reliable Plumer's British Second Army in the lead. Six days later, Albert's troops reached the River Lys, where there was another operational pause, before the Army Group advanced again on 28 October.

To the south, the French and Americans continued the Meuse-Argonne offensive. They pushed forward, but at heavy cost, and Clemenceau and Foch grew angry and frustrated at Pershing's handling of the battle. In late October, the Americans reorganized and on 1 November the US First and French Fourth Armies attacked and made substantial progress. By that stage, British Fourth Army, which included two American divisions, had

PRESIDENT WILSON AND THE "FOURTEEN POINTS"

Woodrow Wilson was elected US president in 1912 and re-elected for a second four-year term in 1916. He proposed his "Fourteen Points" in January 1918. These included an end to secret diplomacy, self-determination for nations and a post-war League of Nations to keep the peace. These idealistic principles for ending the war and organizing international relations were unrealistic (and opposed by Britain and France) but gave Wilson huge moral authority at the Paris Peace Conference. However, the 1919 Treaty of Versailles only partially reflected the Fourteen Points. Isolationist opposition prevented the USA from joining his cherished League of Nations.

already defeated the Germans in the Battle of the Selle (17–25 October), which resulted in the return of the BEF to Le Cateau (see pages 12–13) for the first time since August 1914. In October, the BEF advanced about 32 km (20 miles) and suffered 120,000 casualties.

The Germans desperately sought a way out of the war before they were overtaken by military catastrophe. Prince Max appealed to the US President, Woodrow Wilson, on 4 October to end the war on the basis of the Fourteen Points, and this was followed by the transformation – at least in theory – of Germany into a constitutional monarchy. General Wilhelm Groener replaced Ludendorff in late October. While some elements of the German Army continued to fight effectively, if unavailingly, others in effect went on strike, and ominous signs of revolution appeared on the home front. Part of the German Navy mutinied on 29 October when ordered to sea. Gradually Germany's allies – Austria-Hungary, Turkey and Bulgaria – collapsed in defeat as the Allies advanced in Italy, the Middle East and the Balkans.

Foch launched another major offensive on 4 November. Haig's First, Third and Fourth Armies won a major victory on the line of the Sambre and French First Army captured Guise, while in the Argonne, the Germans finally conceded defeat and withdrew. French Fourth Army and the Americans pursued, US forces reaching outskirts of the key city of Sedan on the Meuse by 7 November. Across the entire front the Allies moved forward. In a throwback to an older form of war, the New Zealanders captured Le Quesnoy, a walled town, using scaling ladders. With his armies beaten, and Germany sliding into revolution, the Kaiser abdicated on 9 November, the same day as Prince Max resigned in favour of a moderate Social Democrat. Two days later, at 11 a.m., an armistice between Germany and the Allies came into effect. The war was over and the Allies were victorious.

ABOVE RIGHT: The Allied representatives (Foch is second from the right) stand in front of the railway carriage on 11 November 1918 in which the Armistice had been signed moments before.

TOP: Woodrow Wilson, the President of the United States, speaking from a podium in 1917.

BELOW: A New Zealand "lemon squeezer" hat.

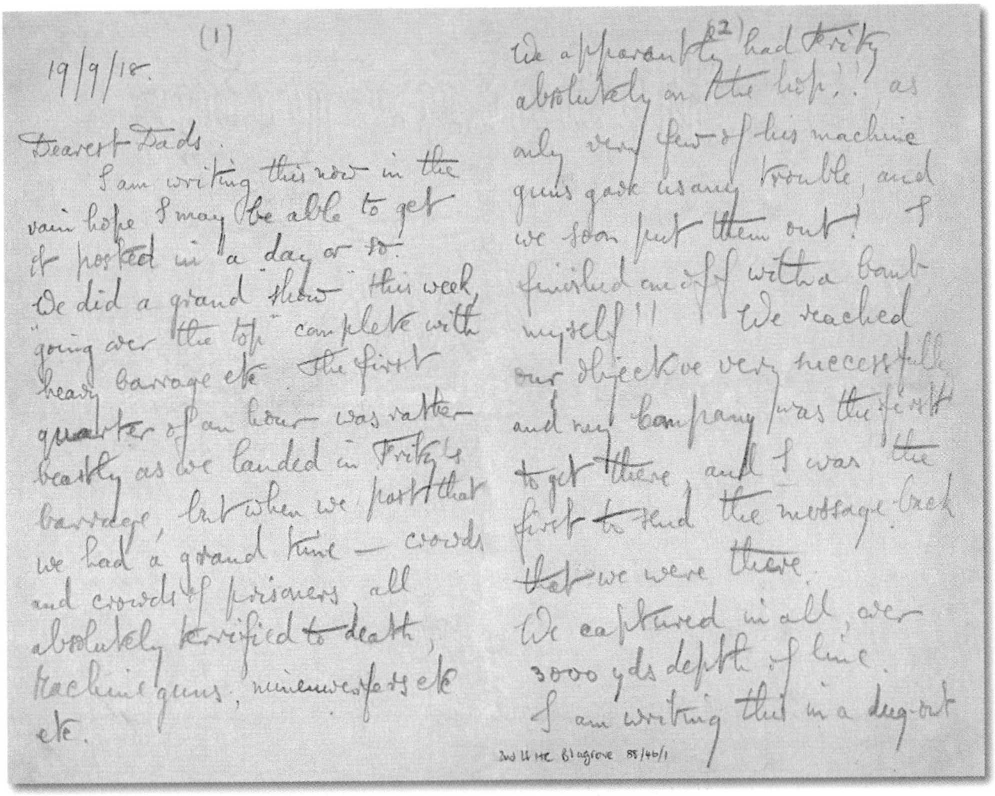

(1)

19/9/18.

Dearest Dads.

I am writing this now in the vain hope I may be able to get it posted in a day or so. We did a grand "show" this week, "going over the top" complete with heavy barrage etc. The first quarter of an hour was rather beastly as we landed in Fritz's barrage, but when we past that we had a grand time — crowds and crowds of prisoners all absolutely terrified to death, machine guns, minenwerfers etc etc.

(2)

We apparently had Fritz absolutely on the hop!! as only very few of his machine guns gave us any trouble, and we soon put them out! I finished one off with a bomb myself!! We reached our objective very successfully and my Company was the first to get there, and I was the first to send the message back that we were there. We captured in all, over 3000 yds depth of line. I am writing this in a dug-out

2nd Lt HC Blagrove 88/46/1

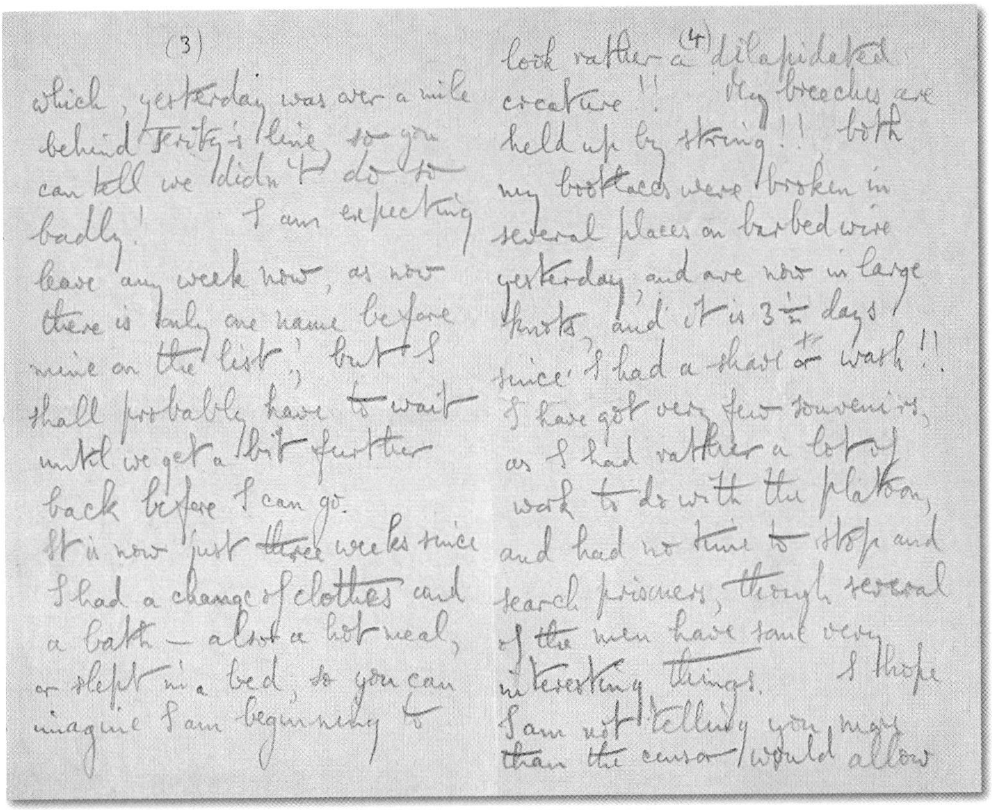

(3)

which, yesterday was over a mile behind Fritz's line so you can tell we didn't do so badly! I am expecting leave any week now, as now there is only one name before mine on the list; but I shall probably have to wait until we get a bit further back before I can go. It is now just three weeks since I had a change of clothes and a bath — also a hot meal, or slept in a bed, so you can imagine I am beginning to

(4)

look rather a dilapidated creature!! My breeches are held up by string!! both my bootlaces were broken in several places on barbed wire yesterday, and are now in large knots, and it is 3½ days since I had a shave or wash!! I have got very few souvenirs, as I had rather a lot of work to do with the platoon, and had no time to stop and search prisoners, though several of the men have some very interesting things. I hope I am not telling you more than the censor would allow

LEFT: In this letter, a British soldier describes the BEF's final battles from September 1918.

AFTERMATH AND LEGACY

THE SHADOW OF THE WAR

Conflict and turmoil continued across Europe for months after the Armistice. A rumbling guerrilla war in Ireland led in 1921 to independence from Britain for all but Ulster. Revolutionary violence took place in various parts of Germany, while the Austro-Hungarian and Ottoman Empires fell apart. In Russia, there was an increasingly brutal civil war underway as various White (anti-Communist) groups, supported by British, French and American forces, sought to reverse the result of the Bolshevik coup of November 1917.

The Russian Civil War was to end in 1922 with the victory of Lenin's Bolsheviks. An attempt to export the revolution by armed force to eastern and central Europe was thwarted, however, by the victory of the Poles against the Russians in the Battle of Warsaw in 1920.

Formally, the war with Germany was ended on 28 June 1919, with the signing of the Treaty of Versailles. This stripped Germany of various territories, forced it to pay reparations of £6,600 million, restricted the size of its armed forces and obliged it to admit responsibility for the outbreak of the war. The Treaty was denounced as a harsh peace that left Germany thirsting for revenge and led inevitably to the Second World War. In reality, the terms were not as savage as those imposed by Germany on defeated Russia at Brest-Litovsk in 1918. Given the scale of the war, German's culpability for its outbreak, and the bitterness in France and Britain in 1919, the terms were not unduly harsh. The main problem was a failure by the victorious Allies to enforce the Treaty. Versailles soon lost moral authority in the eyes of many in Britain, and steps were taken to revise the settlement in Germany's favour even before Hitler came to power in 1933. The feeling that Germany had been badly treated influenced public opinion in Britain and fed into the policy of appeasement in the 1930s. The Great Depression, which began in 1929 and helped to destroy the German Weimar Republic and contributed to the rise of the Nazi regime, was at least as important a factor as Versailles in the origins of the Second World War. The new states created in Eastern and Central Europe such as Poland and Romania tended to move towards authoritarian rule, although in Czechoslovakia democracy survived until destroyed by Hitler in 1939.

Although Britain's Empire reached its greatest size after the war, British power had been damaged. No longer would the dominions (Canada, Australia, New Zealand and South Africa) automatically support Britain, and economic weakness was to undermine the British military. Similarly, France's position in Europe was weaker in 1919 than it had been in 1914. It no longer had an alliance with Russia, and understandings with the newly emerged states on Germany's eastern flank such as Poland were a poor substitute. Britain and the USA, meanwhile, proved fickle friends. The wartime alliance rapidly unravelled, and when in 1923 the French did try to enforce the terms of Versailles by occupying the Ruhr, London and Washington did not support them. The USA retreated into isolation, its people disillusioned by the experience of breaching its long-held tradition of distancing itself from European power politics.

After 1918, the French abandoned the costly cult of the offensive, and instead adopted a defensive mentality epitomized by the construction of the Maginot Line, an updated version of the Verdun defences of 1916, along the French-German border. The German Blitzkrieg of 1940 apparently showed the folly of this idea, but for the most part the military methods so painfully developed during 1914–18 proved to be the foundations of modern warfare, improved upon but not substantially changed in the Second World War and subsequent conflicts.

After the Armistice, people across Europe struggled to come to terms with the vast loss of life. There were 1 million from the British Empire dead; 1,400,000 French; 1,800,000 Germans and 115,000 Americans. In addition there were those badly wounded in body, mind or both; over three-quarters of a million in France alone. People in the victor states began to question the belief that war was a sensible or moral way of settling international disputes. Instead, pacifism grew in influence, alongside – in Britain and the USA at least – the erroneous idea that the war had been "futile". Everywhere the attitude was "never again". Germany was the exception to this. Western Front veteran Hitler channelled the thirst for revenge, the belief that the German army had not been defeated in 1918, but rather had been betrayed, and in 1939 once again took the German nation – and hence Europe, and eventually the world – to war.

OPPOSITE: French tanks at the Arc de Triomphe on the first post-war Bastille Day parade, 14 July 1919.

BELOW LEFT: At a cemetry in Abbeville members of the Women's Army Auxiliary Corps tend to the graves of British soldiers in 1918.

ADOLF HITLER (1889–1945)

The First World War was the formative event in the life of Adolf Hitler. Although an Austrian citizen, he volunteered for the German Army in 1914. Hitler rose to the rank of Lance Corporal and served on the Western Front until 1918, part of that time opposite the British in the Fromelles sector. He had a dangerous job as a runner, delivering messages, and was wounded and gassed. Part of Hitler's post-war appeal to the electorate as a politician was that he had fought in the war as an ordinary soldier.

INDEX

Page numbers in bold type refer to maps.

TRANSLATIONS

Page 56 Raynal's Pigeon Message

We are still holding on, but we are coming under attack from gas and dangerous fumes.
We urgently need to disengage — send me an immediate visual communication via Souville, which isn't responding to my calls.
This is my last pigeon
Raynal

Page 57 Petain's On Les Aura Order

2nd ARMY
Major State
Office 3

To the Q.G.A., 10 April 1916

ORDER

The 9th of April is a glorious day for our armies. The furious assaults of the Crown Prince's soldiers were overcome everywhere. Foot soldiers, artillery, sappers and aviators of the 2nd Army rivalled for heroism. Honour to all!

The Germans will doubtless attack again. Everyone must work and ensure that the same success as yesterday is achieved. Take courage. We'll get them.

[signature]

Page 80 bottom Petain's Mutinies Telegram

GRAND QUARTER GENERAL
of the North and North-East
STAFF HEADQUARTERS

No. 2433/M at 10am
and 2434/M at 10am

CODED TELEGRAM
General Commandant in Chief
[list of names]

CODED TELEGRAM

FOR THE ARMY TEAMS AND ARMIES

During the recent incidents, it seems to me that the Commandant was not entirely doing his duty. Certain Officers hid the clues from their superiors about the bad spirit that reigned within their regiments. Others did not show the required initiative and energy in repression.

It is important that the Officers should be aware of the entire responsibility incumbent upon them in such cases. Inertia is equivalent to complicity. The General in Chief has decided to take all necessary sanctions against the pusillanimous. On the other hand, he will shield with

Page 80 top Petain's Letter to the Minister of War

26 June 1917

General Commandant in Chief
The Minister of War
Cabinet Paris

Confidential

I have the honour to inform you that General Nivelle, on returning from leave, has arrived at his general quarters in Senlis.
On the one hand, I do not have any special mission to give General Nivelle at present, and on the other hand I do not foresee any holiday for the commandant of the Group of armies or army in the near future.
In these conditions, I am obliged to provisionally remit General Nivelle to your disposal.

(Pétain)

Pages 38–39 Toudy's Gas Diary (extracts)

APRIL
6 and 7 : In first line in Steinstraet. We are working firmly to organise our trenches and shelters. The Germans are taking note of this activity and frequently bombard us.

22 : We are still at the post. At about 4pm strong canon fire was heard, and we see a big cloud in the direction of Steinstraet. Immediately Van Couvveulleighe received the order to proceed with the Company. But I am in charge of taking the command even though I am still ill and exempt from service by the doctor. It'll be hard for me, but this is war...I put myself at the head of the Company and we leave at gymnastic pace through fields as far as Segers farm. Our artillery fires well and the big black shells explode in all directions...I quickly give the latest information to the officers and take myself off again to Steinstraet with cries of « Forward!! ». All my men follow the example I give and we march without hesitating. A plane flies over us. Our movement is signalled to the German gunners, who fortunately fire too far. On arrival at Pétain farm, I take advantage of the ridge to make a movement to the right, to then avoid the fire barrage. I arrive without obstacles at Bernauds Plasts Breiz. What can we do, the road is swept by a machine gun and the German artillery. I examine the land and about a hundred metres to the right there is a field of turnips that have grown very high, maybe we could pass through without being seen. I engage myself in this with one section that I lead into a trench situated on the ridge, and this operation was a perfect success, so I immediately made the other sections follow. We still have about 200 metres to go before arriving at my combat placement. But how do we get out of here? The machine gun and rifle bullets are going over our heads by the thousand and the racket of the shells is frightful. But we've got to make it. Several of my men are already wounded. The German artillery is firing heavily on the site that I am about to occupy. However, there is a way to get there more or less in the shelter of the bullets by using a ditch that leads directly to the hill of Cizerne. I run quickly to the Company and tell the men to follow me. I settle in the ditch and the men follow me in single file, then we reach a communication trench behind the Mill of Cizerne... When I have given all my instructions we go forward in the open over a space of about 50 metres. The men immediately start digging. It took barely a quarter of an hour to construct a trench for the whole of the company. My company is on horseback on the road that leads from the Mill of Cizerne to the bridge of Steinstraet. There, we are subject to intense fire (artillery, machine guns etc.). The bombardment directed at my trenches is of extreme violence, it's enough to drive you crazy. This bombardment is uninterrupted. At about 8pm we are told that the whole Company of Captain Danhieux has been taken prisoner, that the Germans have passed the bridge and the canal between Steinstraet and C'sas, and that the French have withdrawn as far as Cizerne. I immediately send patrols to find out what was happening. In fact, the French trenches that were located immediately to the right of the company were unoccupied. I have the trenches occupied by a platoon of my company, which gave me a few hours after returning to liase with the French troops. All night, I fired uninterruptedly in the direction of Steinstraet in order to avoid the German advance by this road....Several of my officers and men were killed or wounded and I still have no orders.

Pages 44–45 Plans from Joffre

GRAND QUARTER GENERAL OF THE ARMIES OF THE EAST
TO THE GRAND QUARTER GENERAL,
23 September 1915
STAFF HEADQUARTERS
3rd Office

VERBAL NOTE for Colonel PENELON

I

The instructions given to the Commandants of the Group of Armies have the object of:
breaking the enemy front;
once this rupture is achieved, seeking a strategic operation as soon as possible, facilitated by the enveloping form of our front between the sea and the Argonne.

II

The Group of the Armies of the North, the operations of which are joined with the English offensive, is seeking the rupture of the enemy front in the region of ARRAS, on the general front of LA BASSEE – FICHEUX.
For the purposes of this attack, General Foch has at his disposal 17 Infantry Divisions, 2 Cavalry Divisions, about 700 parts of 75 and 380 heavy parts.
The English Cavalry (5 Divisions), must act in cooperation with the French Cavalry. The 1st English Army pronounces its major offensive in the direction of LOOS – HULLUCH, supported by 903 canon, including 269 of large calibre, with 9 Divisions, and two secondary offensives to the North of the Canal.
The 2nd English Army will do a demonstration with 2 Divisions to the East of YPRES.

The Group of Armies of the Centre will execute its offensive between the plain of MORONVILLERS and the ARGONNE, on the front of the 4th, 2nd and 3rd Armies, with 30 Infantry Divisions, 7 Cavalry Divisions, 1200 parts of 75 and about 850 heavy parts.

The further progression of these Armies will be facilitated by an attack of the 5th Army between the plain of CRAONNE and the Valley of the AISNE, which the General Commandant of the Group of Armies of the Centre will disengage when he considers it appropriate (after the entry into action of the 4th and 2nd Armies). Forces of the 5th Army dedicated to this action: 6 Infantry Divisions, about 250 canon of 75 and as many heavy parts.

The aviation has received the instruction to destroy the most important points of the railways that may be used for the transport of enemy reinforcements towards the zones of interest, by means of bombardment squadrons.

The Group of the East will keep itself ready to participate in the general offensive once the order has been given, by disengaging the overall action that it has prepared in WOEVRE.

III

If the Armies of the North and Centre achieve the rupture of the enemy front, their mission will be to push the right enemy in front of them without stopping, in an easterly and northerly direction, aiming at its communications.

Any search for lateral movement would play into the hands of the enemy, by giving its reserves sufficient time to occupy the successive lines that it will have prepared. The 1st British Army Grouping – the 10th Army, will aim at the front of Le QUESNOY – FRASNES-les-BUISSENAL.

The Armies of General Castelnau, the front of LE NOUVION-SEDAN.
The other British Armies and the 16th British Army will participate in the forward movement according to the circumstances.

The mission of the Cavalry will be:
To carry out a fierce pursuit on the broadest possible front;
To launch detachments in charge of proceeding with destruction on the adversary's communications in order to hinder the movements of its reserves and supplies.

Pages 94–95 Lange's War Diary (extracts)

Inside front:
12th war diary
covering the period from 20th. July 1917 up to and including 16th. November 1917.

Page 1:

The battle of Ypres.
10.11.17, 8:00 in the evening, departure from Roulers through Ostnieuwkerke to Westrosebeke. There we were accommodated in cellars. Staff in a small concrete shelter at the southern exit, in 10 to 15 cm of water.

Page 3

The III./14 batallion staff that we relieved was beaten down from its efforts, and did not hand over any position files. The position at the front remained unknown to us. Telephone connections were continually impossible. The regiment staff initially went through a tunnel to the commanders' hill, but Colonel Thierry gave the command at 12 at night to return to Bryke.

Page 4

The village was completely destroyed. In the evening, 2 men from 8th Company were killed directly by a shell and 8 wounded. Shortly before 8th Company arrived, one of their cellars was smashed to pieces, killing 37 men of 467 Regiment, mainly through the blast. – For the whole of the evening, the horror of the ruins of Westrosebeke stood out in the light of a burning house. On Sunday, 11th. November, the weather was fine; air battles could be observed at an early hour. The Germans maintained their superiority. Harassing fire. I went to the regiment on the commanders' hill. A shell landed close to me but I wasn't hurt.

Page 5

There Commander Thierry was talking about Asiago. To protect people from losses, 4 trains were removed and relocated to Ostnieuwkerke. Supervisor: Artificer Lieutenant Meyer. At 3:40 in the afternoon, we could see a plane drop a red flare, after which destructive fire started against the enemy. 6: 30 – 7:40 Heavy artillery shelling from Westrosebeke.

Page 6

Tuesday, 13th. November 6:00 Our own heavy artillery fire and then that of the enemy

Page 7

In the evening, the batallion was to become the battle battalion. All preparations were made, reconnaissance, forward units, patrols were instructed, also the leaders of the occupation forces in front of the battle line, then the countermand came at 4:15 in the afternoon. II Batallion was made subordinate to Regiment 114. I received the command to go with the company leaders to the 114 Regiment command post. There it was already getting dark – I heard that I/114 had suffered badly on stand-by and would have to be withdrawn. I was to replace the batallion but to remain further back so as not to be also shot in that area without cover around 114 Stand-by troop command. At the same time an operation took place by 1124, which will be spoken about later. I had to leave from Bryke before I went to 114, the battalion summoned back there

Page 8

but on arriving back in Bryke there were only 8th. Company and weakened sections of the other companies. What had happened? Before the batallion assembled, the enemy suddenly subjected Westrosebeke to the heaviest fire. Almost all of the cellars were struck, the people in them buried alive, the same for the 08 and 08/15 machine guns.

Inside back cover:

Losses
during the first action in the battle of Ypers from 10. – 17.11.17

	dead	wounded	missing
Staff:			
5th. Company:	6	4	2
6th. Company:	1	13	2
7th. Company:	3	7	3
8th. Company:	4	21	6
2nd. Machine gun company:	3	5	1
2nd. Mortar unit:	-	-	-
Total:	17	50	14

Officers: Lieutenant Elster 6th. Company head wound
Lieutenant Krenter 6th. Company
Bloody losses: 2 officers, 81 non-commissioned officers and men.

CREDITS

The publishers would like to thank the following sources for their kind permission to reproduce the pictures in this book.

Imperial War Museums photographs

The majority of the photographs reproduced in the book have been taken from the Photograph Archive at the Imperial War Museum. The Museum's reference numbers for each of the photographs are listed below, giving the page on which they appear in the book and any location indicator (t-top, b-bottom, l-left, r-right, c-centre).

1, 3: Q55371 (c), 6: Q91840, Q81831 (bl), 7: Q41435, 8: Q53446, 9: PST2735, Q81788 (tr), 10 (tl), Q67397 (tr), 11: Q81730 (tr), Q65860 (br), 12: Q45995, 13: Q53625 (bl), 14: Q70232 (t), 15: Q53422 (tl), Q81806 (tr), Q53271 (b), 16: Q53337, 17: Q70071 (t), Q28858 (br), 18: Q70457 (bl), Q80449 (br), 19: Q70054 (tr), Q60698 (b), 20: HU57678 (t), 22: Q23726 (bl), Q51511 (br), 24: Q57214, 25: Q55105, 26: Q57287 (c), Q54992 (br), 27: Q70075 (t), 30: Q69482, 31: Q49750 (br), 32: Q49241 (t), Q49217 (b), 33: Q53517 (l), 36: Q55085 (br), 37: Q114867 (b), 41: HU63277B (tl), 43: Q17390 (t), Q29001 (b), 46: Q485, 47: Q53286, 49: Q23740 (br), 52: Q23744, 54: Q58317 (br), 55: Q69619 (b), 58: Q2393, 59: Q24440, 60: Q3990, 61: Q4031 (br), 62: Q1142, 63: Q5817 (t), Q65442 (cr), 66: Q5572, 68: Q62793, 69: Q69073 (b), Q20343 (br inset), 70: Q50473 (t), Q114044 (br), 71: Q106217 (t), Q114805 (b), 72: Q1177, 74: Q6434, 76: CO1155 (b), 77: Q5127 (b), Q82969 (tr), 78: Q56400, 79: Q58154 (b), 80: (tr), Q5659 (bc), 82: Q5460, 83: Q23665 (tr), Q4649 (b), 84: E(AUS)4487 (tr), (br), 85: Q4649(b), 86: Q5723, 88: Q5773, 89: Q45320 (tr), Q5935 (b), 90: Q2909, 91: CO2120 (cr), 92: CO2265 (t), 98: Q10617, 99: Q8801, 100: CO1763, 102: CO1757 (tl), CO1761 (b), 108: Q71653 (tr), Q6311 (c), 109: Q11146 (tr), Q6432 (b), 110: Q47997, 111: Q10797 (t), Q48178 (br), 112: Q23904 (tr), Q57466 (bl), Q10290 (br), 114: Q6530, 116: Q6588 (t), Q11586 (cr), Q363 (br), 117: Q37344 (tr), Q6676 (b), 118: Q23896, 119: Q56140 (tr), 120: Q64213, 121: Q107381 (tr), CO2859 (b), 123: Q69317, 128: Q6864, 129: Q11120 (tl), Q8191 (b), 131: CO3007 (t), E(AUS)2350 (br), 132: CO2975, 134: Q11142, 135: E(AUS)1681 (bl), Q4131 (br), 136: Q6025 (tr); Q8877 (cl); 140: Q11262, 141: Q11204 (br), 142: E(AUS)3248 (t), 143: Q11216, 144: Q81616, 145: HU56409, 146: Q9374, 147: Q9743 (b), 148: Q9534, 149: Q9365 (t), Q9534 150: CO3373, 155: Q8467 (bl), NYP68037 (br)

Photographs from sources outside Imperial War Museums with the kind permission of:

AKG Images: 50, 51(bl), 80 (tr), 106, 152 (cr),

Australian War Memorial: 101 (br), 130

Corbis: 10 (tl), 20 (b), 75(br)/Hulton-Deutsch Collection: 119(tl).

Getty Images: 35(t), 35 (br), 48, 84(br), 87(t), 129(tr), 141 (tr) /Time & Life Pictures: 152 (tr).

Mary Evans Picture Library: 93 (br).

Photos12.com: 28(tr), 63 (br), 73/Ann Ronan Picture Library: 87(br)

Private Collection: 41 (br), 53 (br)

Topfoto.co.uk: /Print Collector/HIP: 36 (tr), 54 (tl), /Roger Viollet: 37 (t), 51 (tc), 103(br), 142(br)

Specially photographed items with the kind permission of:

Imperial War Museum: 18 tl (Exhibits and Firearms), 18 bc (Exhibits and Firearms), 25 cr (Exhibits and Firearms), 61 tr (Exhibits and Firearms), 75 cr and c (Exhibits and Firearms), 102 tr (Exhibits and Firearms), 107 (Exhibits and Firearms), 119 br Exhibits and Firearms), 131 cr (Exhibits and Firearms), 147 cr (Exhibits and Firearms).

In Flanders Fields: 22 br, 26 tc, 63 cl, 152 br.

Historial de la Grande Guerre, Château de Péronne; 31 cr, 33 bl, 109 tl, 115 tr, 136 bl

Musée du fort de la Pompelle à Reims: 11 cr, 14 bl, 21 br, 41 tr, 51 cr, 93 bl, 117 tr, 120 tr, 120 cl, 135 tr

Somme Trench Museum: 61 cl, 80 br, 85 tl, 121 tl.

Memorial de Verdun: 51 tl, 54 tr, 55 tr

Every effort has been made to acknowledge correctly and contact the source and/or copyright holder of each picture and Carlton Books Limited apologizes for any unintentional errors or omissions which will be corrected in future editions of this book.

Memorabilia printed on the page with the kind permission of:

Imperial War Museum (text in brackets indicates accession numbers and departments): 10 (PST 002765), 23 (Documents), 27 (99/83/1) (Documents), 56-57 (Documents), 64–65 (66/144/1), 96–97 (Documents), 65 enclosure 2 (69/53/1-17 & 69/53/18), 137 (Printed Books), 138–139 (01/21/1), 153 (88/46/1)

Australian War Memorial: 133 (AIF unit war diary, General Staff, HQ 2nd

Australian Division, August 1918, Australian War Memorial, AWM4 1/44/37).

German History Museum, Berlin: 113 (1988_93-4),

In Flanders Fields: 38–39, 47 enclosure 1, 94–95

Musée du fort de la Pompelle à Reims: 122.

Service historique de la Défense, Chateau de Vincennes: 44–45, 81, 104–05, 124.

Every effort has been made to trace copyright holders of the memorabilia items and the author and the Imperial War Museum would be grateful for any information which might help to trace those whose identities or addresses are not currently known.